Advance Praise for *Why Our Drug Laws Have Failed and What We Can Do About It*

"Judge Gray's thorough and scholarly work, based as it is on his personal experience, should help considerably to improve our impossible drug laws. [His] book drives a stake through the heart of the failed War on Drugs and gives us options to hope for in the battles to come."
— Walter Cronkite

"However harmful the ingestion of drugs are to their users, the attempt to prohibit drugs has made matters far worse, threatening our basic rights to life, liberty and property. That is Judge Gray's thesis in this important book and he cites overwhelming evidence to support it. His proposals to improve the situation do not go as far as I would like, but they are all feasible and in the right direction. If adopted, they would produce a major improvement."
— Milton Friedman

"The war on drugs cannot be a war on discussion of this problem. We can fight drug use and abuse and still explore viable options. Judge Gray illuminates options and in the process will promote necessary discussion of them."
— George P. Shultz

"It's all here! A stinging indictment of today's drug strategies and a rallying cry around new strategies for tomorrow."
— Gary E. Johnson, Governor of New Mexico

"It has been said that in public policy development we must distinguish between ideas that sound good and good ideas that are sound. In this book, Judge Gray provides sound ideas for a more effective national drug control policy. He recognizes that the War on Drugs needs new thinking for this new century."
— Kurt L. Schmoke, former Mayor of the City of Baltimore

"This book is a powerful indictment of our failed war on drugs. Jim Gray not only communicates the devastation wrought by a war he witnessed from the frontlines as a trial judge and federal prosecutor, but he displays in these pages the moral courage it takes to cry out that the emperor wears no clothes."
— Arianna Huffington, syndicated columnist
and author of *How to Overthrow the Government*

Why Our Drug Laws Have Failed and What We Can Do About It

A JUDICIAL INDICTMENT

OF THE WAR ON DRUGS

Why Our Drug Laws Have Failed and What We Can Do About It

A JUDICIAL INDICTMENT

OF THE WAR ON DRUGS

Judge James P. Gray

Temple University Press
PHILADELPHIA

Temple University Press, Philadelphia 19122
Copyright © 2001 by Temple University
All rights reserved
Published 2001
Printed in the United States of America

⊗ The paper used in this publication meets the requirements of the
American National Standard for Information Sciences—Permanence
of Paper for Printed Library Materials, ANSI Z39.48-1984.

Library of Congress Cataloging-in-Publication Data

Gray, James P., 1945–
  Why our drug laws have failed and what we can do about it :
a judicial indictment of the War on Drugs / [Judge] James P. Gray
    p. cm.
Includes bibliographical references and index.
ISBN 1-56639-859-2 (alk. paper) — ISBN 1-56639-860-6 (pbk. :
alk. paper)
  1. Drug abuse—Government policy—United States.
2. Narcotics, Control of—United States. I. Title.

HV5825 .G6954 2001
362.29'16'0973–dc21   0-047677

Friends tell friends the truth

This book is dedicated to

Rufus King, Esq.
Prof. Alfred Lindesmith
Dr. Milton Friedman
Edward M. Brecher
Justice Gerald LeDain
Dr. Herbert Berger
Mayor Kurt Schmoke
William F. Buckley, Jr.
Secretary of State George Shultz
Richard Dennis
Dr. Willis P. Butler
Judge Robert W. Sweet
Chief Joseph D. McNamara
Prof. Ethan Nadelmann
Prof. Arnold S. Trebach
Kevin Zeese, Esq.

and all of the other pioneers who had
the audacity and courage years ago to
challenge our country's failed drug policy.

Contents

PART I

Introduction

On April 8, 1992, I did something quite unusual for a trial judge: I held a news conference in the plaza behind the courthouse in Santa Ana, California, and openly set forth my conclusions that our country's attempts through the criminal justice system to combat drug use and abuse, and all of the crime and misery that accompany them, were not working. In fact, I had concluded that drug reform was the most important issue facing this great country and that our so-called War on Drugs was our biggest failure. I had reached these conclusions after spending years as a federal prosecutor in Los Angeles, a criminal defense attorney in the navy, and a trial judge since 1983 in Orange County, California. I had seen firsthand that we were wasting unimaginable amounts of our tax dollars, increasing crime and despair, and severely and unnecessarily harming people's lives, particularly our children's, by our failed drug policy. In short, I had seen that our drug laws were a failure, and I simply could not keep quiet about it any longer. Some people listened; some agreed; some were outraged and wanted to punish me for my comments.

We have been following essentially the same Drug Prohibition policy for many decades, and it has given us the worst of all worlds. Today there are more drugs available in our communities, and at a lower price, than ever before. We have greatly expanded the number of prisons in the United States, but all of them are overflowing. As a direct result of the enormous amount of money available from illicit drug sales, the corruption of public officials and private individuals in our society has increased substantially. We have a much higher incidence of diseases, such as hepatitis and AIDS, caused by the use of dirty needles, than most industrialized countries in the world. The War on Drugs has resulted in the loss of more civil liberties protections than has any other phenomenon in our history. Instead of being shielded, our children are being recruited into a lifestyle of drug selling and drug usage by the current system. And revolutionaries and insurgents abroad are using money procured from the illegal sale of drugs to undermine legitimate governments all over the world. We could not have achieved worse results if we had tried. These are strong allegations, but the pages that follow will prove that all of them are true.

Our current Drug Prohibition policy is centered around the criminal justice system, in which we judges are required to play a significant role. There may be a few judges in this country who believe that our current drug policy is working, but they are surely a small minority. Most judges have strong views about how to improve our drug policies, and some of them are quite advanced. I have had many private conversations on this subject with other judges, who know that the war on drugs has failed, i.e., that "The Emperor has no clothes." But just like many politicians and law enforcement officers, judges are also concerned about undermining their effectiveness or exposing themselves to an electoral challenge by addressing this issue publicly.

There is also, however, a gratifyingly large number of judges and justices from all over the country who have agreed to be quoted publicly, or have already published their thoughts themselves. Some of these judicial officers are quoted in this book, but space limitations prevent me from quoting the many, many others. Many of the statements quoted in this book were derived from a letter that U.S. District Court Judge Robert W. Sweet of the Southern District of New York sent on July 30, 1998, to state and federal judges and justices around the country, requesting their responses to several articles about our nation's drug policy that he had enclosed.[1] Judge Sweet graciously provided me with a copy these responses, and I sought permission from the authors to publish some of them here. The vast majority agreed, many supplying

---

1. See Judge Robert W. Sweet, United States District Court for the Southern District of New York, "The War on Drugs Is Lost," *National Review*, February 12, 1996: 44–45.

additional statements that I was free to quote as well. Unless otherwise noted, the quoted remarks in the pages that follow were obtained in this fashion. It must also be stated that I and all of the judges quoted herein are speaking only as individuals, and that we do not speak for any of the various courts upon which we serve.

A clear and concise statement of the problem is given in "An Open Letter from Judges and Attorneys," sponsored by the Voluntary Committee of Lawyers, Inc. This letter was originally signed by eleven judges and appellate justices, and reads as follows:

> As judges and lawyers, we share with all Americans a deep concern about the threat that drugs pose to our children and our country. For more than twenty years, our nation's response to this threat has been a "war on drugs," enforced primarily through a criminal justice process which we administer and observe on a daily basis.
>
> Though we differ in political orientation and career experience, we unanimously observe that neither drugs nor drug abuse has been eliminated or appreciably reduced, despite massive spending on interdiction and harsh punishments. Attempts at enforcement have clogged the courts, filled the prisons with non-predatory offenders, corrupted officials at home and abroad, bred disrespect for the law in important communities, imperiled the liberties of the people, burdened the taxpayers, impeded public health efforts to stem the spread of HIV and other infectious diseases, and brought the nation no closer to abstinence. As Congress and state legislatures enact more punitive and costly drug control measures, we conclude with alarm that the war on drugs now causes more harm than drug abuse itself.
>
> Accordingly, we join with our colleagues in calling upon our profession, elected officials, the media and the public to initiate a truly open and honest evaluation of the efficacy and consequences of our drug control laws. Only a public debate guided by mutual respect can yield better drug laws in which fear, prejudice and punitive prohibitions yield to common sense, science, public health and human rights. As America must never "surrender" to drugs, neither must she surrender to inertia or fear that shuts off debate, suppresses critical analysis, dismisses alternatives to current policies, and vilifies those who express dissenting views.[2]

> Judge Morris S. Arnold, U.S. 8th Cir. Ct. of Appeals, Little Rock, Arkansas;
> Judge Myron H. Bright, U.S. 8th Cir. Ct. of Appeals, Fargo, North Dakota;
> Judge Nancy Gertner, U.S. District Court, Boston, Massachusetts;
> Judge Douglas W. Hillman, U.S. District Court, Grand Rapids, Michigan;

---

2. See <http//www.vcl.org> for a current list of signatories.

Justice William E. Hunt, Sr., Montana Supreme Court, Helena,
  Montana;
Judge Morris E. Lasker, U.S. District Court, New York City,
  New York;
Judge James C. Paine, U.S. District Court, West Palm Beach, Florida;
Judge J. Dickson Phillips, Jr., U.S. 4th Cir. Ct. of Appeals, St. Paul,
  Minnesota;
Judge R. A. (Jim) Randall, Minnesota Court of Appeals, St. Paul,
  Minnesota;
Judge Marvin H. Shoob, U.S. District Court, Atlanta, Georgia; and,
Judge Robert W. Sweet, U.S. District Court, New York City,
  New York.

This sensible but passionate plea for public debate on our failed drug
policies has also been raised by such distinguished public figures as Milton Friedman, a Nobel laureate in economics; George Shultz, secretary
of state under President Ronald Reagan; William F. Buckley, Jr., a
nationally syndicated columnist; Kurt Schmoke, mayor of Baltimore;
Joseph D. McNamara, former chief of police of both Kansas City and
San Jose; Gary Johnson, governor of New Mexico; and Arianna Huffington, another nationally syndicated columnist. Most of these are very
conservative people who see that we are inflicting unnecessary harm
upon ourselves by our current drug policy and have called out publicly
for reform. I received a standing ovation from both the Orange County
Chapter of the ACLU and the Young Republicans of Orange County
after giving essentially the same speech on our failed drug policies. This
is a nonpartisan issue that crosses all political boundaries.

The raw information for this book came from twenty years' worth
of newspaper and magazine clippings, from extensive reading in the
great number of books already published on the subject, and from the
government's own information—in addition, of course, to my own personal experience with the criminal justice system, including my active
involvement as a former "drug warrior."

I have learned over twenty years of experience that although the War
on Drugs makes for good politics, it makes for terrible government. The
War on Drugs is about lots of things, but only rarely is it really about
drugs. We pursue it not because it is effective, but because it is "fund-
able." I am convinced, however, that when the American people realize the huge and unnecessary costs, both human and financial, that we
are paying because of our failed drug prohibitionist policy, they will
demand its repeal.

I begin with three guarantees: (1) No one who reads this book and thinks objectively about the issues it raises will favor a continuation of our present drug policy—unless that person himself is making money or has some other vested interest in its perpetuation. Many people do have such vested interests, of course, including, most obviously, those who smuggle and sell large quantities of illicit drugs. But there are also people with careers and expertise in government-funded projects and drug law enforcement, and people who build and work in our country's jails and prisons, and people who build and supply burglar alarm equipment and other devices to protect us from increased crime. And there are many politicians who continue to get elected by "talking tough" about the War on Drugs. (2) Our country *will* someday change to a materially different drug policy. I do not know when, and I do not know to what; but there will definitely be a substantive change. (3) Within a few years of this change, we will look back in astonishment that we allowed our former policy to persist for so long, much as we look back now at slavery, or Jim Crow laws, or the days when women were prohibited from voting—and we will wish fervently that we had not waited so long to abandon these failed and destructive policies. But do not expect many of the people who make up our prison-industrial complex to lead the charge for reform. Asking these people if we should continue with the status quo is like asking a barber if you need a haircut. Expecting these people to work for change is like expecting cigarette manufacturers to help people quit smoking.

For a very short time back in 1978, I held the record as an Assistant U.S. Attorney for the largest drug prosecution in the Central District of California. This was a case involving seventy kilograms (about 154 pounds) of heroin that had been smuggled into the United States from Mexico, repackaged in Los Angeles, and sent on to Detroit for distribution. We were able to convict the rancher who grew the poppies and manufactured the heroin down in Mexico, as well as the prime mover of the operation, who was a very dangerous man, and two of his assistants.[3] That was and is a large amount of drugs. However, to my knowledge, the record now in the central district is eighteen *tons* of cocaine, which was seized from one location in Sylmar.

---

3. Narda Zacchino, "Mexican Citizen Convicted in Dope Case," *Los Angeles Times*, June 17, 1978, Part I: 16.

The fact that these amounts are now so large should not be a surprise. In October 1999, Colombian and U.S. agents arrested a cocaine-smuggling ring in Colombia accused of smuggling around *thirty tons* of cocaine *each month* into the United States and Europe.[4] There is no question that law enforcement is doing a better job today than ever before—we now see larger seizures of drugs, larger forfeitures of assets, more arrests and convictions of drug offenders, and longer prison sentences than ever before. But this does not mean that we are in fact better off than we were back when I was a prosecutor.

So what exactly is the current drug policy in the United States of America? Over the past several decades, our government has attempted to combat the critical problem of drug use and abuse with a program of massive prisons, demonization of drug users, and prohibition of debate about our options. This policy approaches drug use and abuse as a moral issue: "Drugs are evil, and if you take them, you are evil, and we will punish you." But decades of failed attempts to make this policy work have shown that we cannot effectively take a medical problem and treat it as a character issue. Unfortunately, because we tend to see issues of drug usage in moral terms, many people actively resist opening their eyes to the severe damage this policy is visiting upon us, and fail to consider viable alternatives.

Part II addresses the damage we have inflicted on ourselves through our current drug policy. There is abundant and graphic evidence, both historical and immediate, that our present policy has violated the credo of the medical profession, "First do no harm." It will also be shown clearly that there are inherent limits to what can effectively be done in a free society to keep people from selling small amounts of drugs for large amounts of money. In short, the drug policy our government has pursued for decades has worked directly against the people of this country, and actually strengthens the things that it attempts to destroy.

Most people agree that our War on Drugs is not working, but most people are simply not aware that we have viable options. Former Secretary of State George Shultz voices this fact succinctly when he says, "I have a zero tolerance attitude, but I am still searching for the best

---

4. Karl Penhaul, "Cocaine Ring Busted by U.S., Colombia," *Orange County Register,* October 14, 1999: News 21; Eric Lichtblau, "Huge Cocaine Ring Smashed," *San Francisco Chronicle,* October 14, 1999: A14. As a further symptom of the depth of the problem, note that the arrest of this major drug ring rated coverage only on pages 21 and 14 of these newspapers.

way of implementing it." Regrettably, however, a common tactic of the drug prohibitionists is to lump all of the possible alternatives together and label them all the "legalization of drugs." They exploit this idea of legalization, a concept that understandably frightens people, and equate it with surrendering in the "War on Drugs" and giving up our children to the menace of drug addiction. This strategy enables them to refuse to discuss or even acknowledge other possible approaches. We have only one realistic course, they disingenuously argue, which is to step up our efforts in the current "Zero Tolerance" War on Drugs.

In truth, however, there are numbers of distinct and very workable options to the extremes of zero tolerance on the one hand and drug legalization on the other. Some of those options, which will be discussed in some depth in Part III, are programs to "de-profitize" these drugs, such as *drug decriminalization*, which basically means that although the drugs remain illegal, as long as people stay within very clear guidelines the police will leave them alone; *regulated distribution*, which is the strictly controlled and regulated sale to adults of designated drugs, similar to the way alcohol is sold in some states; and *legalization of drugs*, which basically leaves the distribution of these drugs to the marketplace with all of its protections under the *civil* justice system, and uses the *criminal* justice system to govern people's behavior. Additional options are different types of *drug treatment*, such as *rehabilitation* programs, both voluntary and involuntary, public and private; and *medicalization*, which fundamentally puts drug-addicted people under the control of a medical doctor and her staff, using programs of drug treatment, needle exchange (which exchanges a dirty needle for a clean one without charge), drug maintenance (which allows prescriptions for the subject's drug of choice to be filled at a local pharmacy or medical clinic so that the subject neither gets a "high" nor goes through withdrawal but is maintained at an equilibrium level), and drug substitution (which substitutes one drug, such as methadone, for the subject's drug of choice). Many countries in Western Europe are not as concerned as we are with puritan morality and are taking a much more practical approach to their drug problems by utilizing combinations of these alternative approaches—with successful results!

Another option, of course, is an even more strictly administered War on Drugs, or "Zero Tolerance"—"only this time we will really get tough!" Unfortunately, we have been getting tougher and tougher for the last several decades, and literally every time we have done so it has made our problems worse. Finally we will examine the option of *federalism*, the rationale for the repeal of Prohibition in 1933 (which I will refer to as "Alcohol Prohibition" to distinguish it from "Drug Prohibition"), which allowed each individual state to pursue its own policy and limited the federal government to helping each state enforce its laws. This approach was contemplated by the Tenth Amendment to the U.S. Constitution and many of the Federalist Papers. Some states chose to stay "dry," others allowed alcohol to be sold in government package stores under a program of regulated distribution, and still others allowed the sale of alcohol to adults by licensed private vendors.

Finally, whatever option or combination of options we eventually pursue, it must include a major educational component. The need for education about drugs and drug abuse is almost universally agreed upon, even by those who would maintain our current War on Drugs.

Throughout this book you will be presented with the perspectives of state and federal judges from all over the United States. They will provide you with their insights, feelings, and conclusions about how poorly our present system has been doing, with examples from their experiences, and with recommendations for reform. And of course my own insights, gained from my experience as a former federal prosecutor and current trial judge, are also sprinkled throughout the book.

Part IV looks more closely at what we can do about this situation. Each one of us, as inhabitants, citizens, and voters in this country, can effect a change away from our failed drug policy. For many years as a trial judge I had a clerk who kept a hand-written sign on her desk that read, "If it's to be, it's up to me." She was right, of course. Ultimately we are responsible for the failure of our current drug policy, but at the same time no one is in a better position to change it. The Appendix contains a resolution that those who wish to may sign, and also presents some additional supporting information, including a brief summary of many governmental commission studies and other public inquiries that have taken place in the United States, Canada, and England over the last hundred years. Each study has concluded that while a new policy may, at least in the short run, result in some increased drug use, we must move away from the incarceration of people for using drugs and treat this matter as a medical and social problem. The beginning of the end for the Alcohol Prohibition was the publication of the findings of the Wickersham Commission—which basically made the same recommendations as have the commissions on Drug Prohibition—and there is every reason to believe that our current prohibition on drugs may be reformed in the same way.

Before launching too deeply into the subject matter itself, I want to present nine threshold points so that we can begin this discussion with a common understanding:

1. We are all on the same side of this issue, i.e., we all desire to reduce drug use and abuse and all of the crime and misery that accompany them. Our disagreements center on which drug policy option can best accomplish that goal.
2. Whatever drug policy we utilize should encourage more individual responsibility and accountability in our society, not less.
3. Without a doubt, heroin, cocaine, methamphetamines, and so on are dangerous and sometimes addictive drugs. But so also are alcohol and tobacco dangerous and sometimes addictive drugs, and virtually everyone agrees that we would only compound their harm by (again) making them illegal.
4. Just because some people discuss various options about how best to combat drug use and abuse, or even believe that we should employ a different option, does not mean that those people condone drug use or abuse.
5. Education in the area of drug policy is critically important, and it has definitely had some positive results; but education will continue to be used effectively no matter what drug policy option(s) we choose to employ.
6. Law enforcement has been doing a magnificent job in attempting to enforce our current drug laws. The problem is with the drug laws themselves, not the police, the courts, or the rest of the criminal justice system. Blaming law enforcement for the failure of Drug Prohibition is no more appropriate than blaming Elliott Ness for the failure of Alcohol Prohibition.
7. We have never been a drug-free society and we never will be. Recognizing this fact, and recognizing the fact that these harmful drugs are here to stay, we should try to employ an approach that will most effectively reduce the deaths, disease, crime, and misery caused by their presence in our communities.
8. No matter what option we employ, there will always be an important role for the criminal justice system. Our present system is fairly effective in holding people accountable for their actions after drinking

alcohol, even though it is not illegal for adults to use this dangerous and sometimes addictive drug. There is no reason why the justice system cannot play a similar role with these other drugs.
9. Drug policy is a complex and multifaceted issue that does not lend
itself to little sound bites and slogans. But if we must adopt a slogan, we should use something like: "If you want to keep gettin' what
you're gettin', keep doin' what you're doin'."

So what should we do now? First, we should approach this issue as
managers, not as moralists. This means that we must look for ways to
bring these dangerous drugs back under our laws. At first glance, that
seems like a strange mandate: bring these drugs back under our laws?
But the more one focuses on our current system, the more one under-
stands that today the only "laws" addressing the actual use, sale, and
quality of these drugs are those enforced by the illegal drug sellers. In
truth, to a large degree we have experienced a literal collapse of the rule
of law in this area. The more we are able to bring these dangerous
drugs back under the law, the fewer collateral problems we will have.

Investigating our options, or even choosing to pursue a different
option, does not mean that we condone drug use or abuse. But we must
also recognize that, while the use of drugs often has some harmful consequences, Drug Prohibition has its own unique harmful consequences
as well. For example, when drug dealers shoot police officers, witnesses,
innocent bystanders, or even each other, that is a "drug prohibition"
problem rather than a "drug" problem. Similarly, when drug users are
forced to steal or prostitute themselves in order to get money to buy
artificially expensive illicit drugs from the criminal underworld, that is
a Drug Prohibition problem more than it is a drug problem. So too is
the diversion of billions of dollars from the prosecution of violent street
crime and fraud to the prosecution of hundreds of thousands of nonviolent drug sellers and millions of drug users a distinct problem of
Drug Prohibition.[5] For those who are interested in balance-of-payment
deficit issues, illicit drug sales are responsible for a larger drain of cash
than anything else in our economy except oil. The image I see is a
never-ending line of people pushing wheelbarrows full of fifty-dollar
bills out of our country with cash generated from the sale of illicit drugs.

---

5. See Ethan A. Nadelmann, "The Problem Is Prohibition," *Los Angeles Times*, February
7, 1996, Orange County ed.: B11.

This is uniquely a problem of Drug Prohibition, not a problem of the drugs themselves.

Since pursuit of the same failed policy has no reasonable hope of improving our position, we should study our options. Accordingly, the president and Congress should appoint one final, neutral blue-ribbon commission to study our options as fully and as publicly as possible. The members of the commission should include representatives from law enforcement, medical and drug treatment professionals, former addicts, members of the clergy, university scholars, and so on. It could be chaired by someone like General Colin Powell, former Surgeon General C. Everett Koop, or a person of similar stature and credibility.

This commission should examine how the U.S. government originally chose to employ the current approach. Professors Richard J. Bonnie and Charles H. Whitebread II published an extensive inquiry into the legal history of American marijuana prohibition in the October 1970 issue of the *Virginia Law Review*.[6] Their work includes many citations of the Congressional Record that show that public health and safety issues were not even considered by Congress in making this substance illegal. Instead, the motives appear to have been racism, fear, empire building, and ignorance.[7] The commission should examine and publish these facts.

The commission should also investigate successful approaches to drug regulation over the past decades, as well as failures. It should look at the approaches of other countries as well. And it should inquire into the causes of the upsurge in drug use, crime, and court and prison overcrowding in the United States, an upsurge that has not occurred on the same scale elsewhere.

We must remember that no matter which option we choose, it will not be perfect. While a large part of this book is devoted to a discussion of the problems inflicted upon us by our current policy, we must recognize that alternative policies will have problems as well. These drugs are dangerous and can be very harmful. Our goal must be to adopt a policy that most reduces the harms that can and will be caused

---

6. Richard J. Bonnie and Charles H. Whitebread II, "The Forbidden Fruit and the Tree of Knowledge: An Inquiry into the Legal History of American Marijuana Prohibition," *Virginia Law Review*, October 1970.

7. See also David F. Musto, *The American Disease: Origins of Narcotic Control* (New York: Oxford University Press, 3d ed., 1999), in which this author from the Yale School of Medicine came to similar conclusions.

by the presence of these drugs in our communities. We must, that is, adopt a more medical, public health-oriented approach to our national drug policy. Every major neutral study in the United States in the past hundred years has recommended that some form of drug decriminalization be adopted *because* of the dangers of these drugs, and because prison is the worst and least effective approach. In short, we must openly discuss this entire area, consider all of the evidence, and adopt programs that will work. I suggest that any such program will have large helpings of the following four ingredients:

1. *Education*—Virtually every social problem besetting our society can be mitigated by a strong program of education, and this is certainly true with regard to drug abuse;
2. *Prevention and Treatment*—Programs of preventive maintenance and repair are effective for our automobiles, our airplanes, and our own bodies, and they work in the area of drug abuse as well;
3. *Positive Incentives*—Set up a system that encourages people to do what is socially acceptable, instead of the system we have today, which presents such strong financial incentives to sell drugs and otherwise to violate the law; and,
4. *Individual Responsibility*—Hold all of our people personally accountable for their *actions* through the criminal justice system. If someone burglarizes a house to get money for a new stereo or for drugs, that is a crime and it must be prosecuted. Similarly, if someone drives a motor vehicle under the influence of alcohol, cocaine, or marijuana, he or she must be held accountable. By contrast, if people go home after work and take a mind-altering drug, whether it be alcohol, marijuana, or anything else, without harming anyone but themselves, we should try to educate them away from this conduct and make drug treatment available if they need it. But prosecuting and incarcerating them for this activity is counterproductive.

All of our options in the area of combating drug abuse include a strong segment involving the education of our people about the harmful effects of these dangerous, mind-altering, and sometimes addictive drugs. Beyond that similarity, each option has its own features and, necessarily, each has its own particular strengths and weaknesses. The only real enemy to change is the decades of rhetoric that prohibit an open and honest discussion of our options and equate these discussions with the condoning of drug use and abuse.

In June 1995, the Discovery Channel broadcast "The Cronkite Report—The Drug Dilemma: War or Peace?" At the end of this hour-long broadcast, Walter Cronkite made the following statement:

> Just about every American was shocked when Robert McNamara, one of the master architects of the Vietnam war, acknowledged that not only did he believe the war wrong, terribly wrong, but that he thought so at the very time he was helping to wage it. That's a mistake we must not make in this tenth year of America's all-out war on drugs. It's surely time for this nation to stop flying blind, stop accepting the assurances of politicians and other officials that if only we keep doing what we're doing, add a little more cash, break down a few more doors, lock up a few more [people], then we would see the light at the end of the tunnel. Victory would be ours. . . .
>
> It seems to this reporter that the time has come for President Clinton to do what President Hoover did when [alcohol] prohibition was tearing the nation apart: appoint a bipartisan commission of distinguished citizens, . . . a blue ribbon panel to reappraise our drug policy right down to its very core with a commission with full investigative authority and the prestige and power to override bureaucratic concerns and political considerations. Such a commission could help us focus our thinking, escape the clichés of the drug war in favor of scientific fact, more rationally analyze the real scope of the problem, answer the questions that bedevil us, and present a comprehensive drug policy for the future. We cannot go into tomorrow with the same formulas that are failing today. We must not blindly add to the body count and the terrible cost of the war on drugs only to learn from another Robert McNamara thirty years from now that what we've been doing is wrong, terribly wrong.

Without question, our present drug policy materially affects everyone in our country, abusers and non-abusers alike. The evidence of its failures is all around us. Pick up today's newspaper. The odds are good that there will be at least one account of a tragedy that was caused solely by our current drug policy. The papers are full of stories of an innocent bystander or a police officer being injured or killed during a shootout with drug dealers; of overdoses caused by the unknown strength or purity of a drug; of the corruption of people in this country and others because of the enormous profits to be made by the selling of illicit drugs; and of the cutting back of hours or outright closing of a county library because of increased spending for prisons and the other necessities of the War on Drugs. The only people whose positions have improved since this country implemented its current policy are those who have made money by selling drugs as well as those who have made money either by attempting to enforce the drug laws or by attempting to reduce the crime that has been generated by drug sales.

In 1988, Congress adopted a resolution that declared its intention that the United States be "drug free" by the year 1995. Obviously that goal was hopelessly naïve. By February 1994, President Clinton more realistically adopted a national drug control strategy of "Reclaiming Our Communities from Drugs and Violence." But even this more modest goal has not been realized. Actor Carroll O'Connor, after observing this nation's drug policy for years, and after losing his son Hugh to drugs, put the case succinctly:

> It's time to admit that our approach to the drug problem has failed. After more than a decade of the "war on drugs," too many lives are still being shattered. We spend billions to enforce laws that return small benefit. The hard drug market is strictly illegal, and the drugs are everywhere easily obtainable. We run from the drug problem and hide behind verbiage that demands no special action and no new expense: "Work on education! Education is the sole remedy! People must learn to refrain; they have to do it by themselves!" Meanwhile, nothing changes. Why should it? Nothing has been done.
>
> Is legalizing drugs an answer? I don't advocate legalization, but people who yelp that legalization would "open the floodgates" haven't noticed, or perhaps won't admit, that the floodgates were pushed open years ago. Addiction is created by a number of conditions, but availability of drugs is not one of them.[8]

Surprisingly enough, all of the multifaceted and complex issues surrounding illegal drugs can be distilled into two fundamental questions. First, understanding that no matter what we do in a free society, these drugs are here to stay, do we want to address this situation as managers or as moralists? And second, if we choose to be managers, and we understand that any other drug policy option that would take at least some of the profit out of these drugs and bring them back under the law would result in significant benefits to society, would those benefits outweigh the increased drug use that might—or might not—result from that different policy?

As a trial judge and former federal prosecutor, I have seen firsthand the devastation brought upon the people of this country both by the presence of dangerous drugs in our communities and by our failed policy of Drug Prohibition. For me—and for fellow judges who are quoted in these pages, the evidence is in, and now is the time to act upon it. My own view is that we should readopt the concept of federalism,

---

8. Carroll O'Connor, "Let's Get Real," *Parade Magazine*, July 16, 1995: 8.

described above, and allow each state to adopt the policy or policies that it concludes will best meet its needs. We should likewise revise our treaties so that all other countries will be able once again to address their domestic drug problems in the manner they deem most effective. It is clear after all these many years that our federal government does not have the right answers. It is time for other, more local governments to retake command.

Dick Cavett was once quoted as saying, "It's a rare person who wants to hear what he does not want to hear." To that comment I offer a corollary: "Friends tell friends the truth." The real problem in this area actually is not the drugs themselves. The real problem is that our citizens and our leaders simply will not look at the evidence, even though it is all around us. Our present policy is exacerbating the problems and will not stand up to scrutiny. What we really need to do is to open the subject to rigorous public debate. This is our best and perhaps our only hope for moving forward to a better strategy, and to adopting programs that will actually work. The advocates of the status quo stand firmly against any full or open discussion of federal drug policy, but what we really need to do is explore our options realistically, and tell each other the truth.

PART II

Our Drug Laws Have Failed

1

Past and Present

The results of our country's Zero Tolerance Drug Prohibition policy are multifaceted, overlapping, and overwhelmingly negative. We will see from an historical perspective that Drug Prohibition had its beginnings way back in 1913 and has become accepted in our everyday lives. Its failings have for the most part been unquestioned. Throughout the twentieth century, recreational drug usage has waxed and waned, but hard-line drug usage has remained proportionally about the same.

The common theme throughout this country's history of Drug Prohibition is that the federal government has been increasingly active, but both federal and state governments have continually passed tougher and tougher laws. With each upping of the ante, however, the situation has become worse. To the old saying that enforcing prohibition *always* leads to violence, corruption, and crime, it can be added, at least in this instance, that it has also resulted in the creation of an enormous bureaucracy—a prison-industrial complex—and it has thrived. This bureaucracy has been funded by unimaginable amounts of money and has become jealous of its power and scornful of people who ask questions about it.

An Historical Perspective

I sit there on the bench and send these small dealers, who are black, off to prison for years and years and years. And they look at you almost uncomprehendingly. They don't even know why we're mad at them.[1]
Presiding Judge James Ford, Superior Court, Sacramento, California

The first laws addressing any of the currently illicit substances were passed during colonial times, and they required the various townships to grow a certain amount of cannabis sativa, or hemp, based on the size of their populations.[2] Hemp is the stalk of the marijuana plant, but it has no psychotropic properties whatsoever. The stalk consists of threadlike fibers and bits of "hurd" or pulp, and during colonial times it was put to a wide variety of uses. For example, the sails on the U.S.S. Constitution (*Old Ironsides*) were made from hemp. Several drafts of the Declaration of Independence were printed on parchment made from the same natural substance. Hemp was also widely used in the making of rope, textiles, and gunny sacks, and was even used as money from 1631 until the early 1800s. George Washington, Thomas Jefferson, and a large number of famous planters in the colonial period all grew large crops of hemp, and Benjamin Franklin was one of the most active hemp paper merchants.[3]

The first prohibitionist laws in our country were passed during the last years of the nineteenth century. These were state and local ordinances that limited commerce in cocaine, marijuana, and opium, and were fundamentally racist laws aimed at perceived threats to white women from drug usage by black, Mexican, and Chinese men, respectively.[4] In 1875, for example, the city of San Francisco, claiming that

---

1. Michael G. Wagner, Jim Mayer, and Faizah Alim, "Drug War Results in Endless Cycle," *Los Angeles Daily Journal*, December 24, 1990: 18.

2. See Chris Conrad, *Hemp, Lifeline to the Future* (Los Angeles: Creative Xpressions Publications, 1993) 23–27.

3. For a summary of the extensive role of hemp both industrially and medically in the history of mankind, see Conrad, *supra*, at 6–37; Rowan Robinson, *The Great Book of Hemp* (Rochester, Vt., Park Street Press, 1996) 102–23; Edward M. Brecher and the Editors of Consumer Reports, *Licit and Illicit Drugs: The Consumers Union Report on Narcotics, Stimulants, Depressants, Inhalants, Hallucinogens, and Marijuana—including Caffeine, Nicotine, and Alcohol* (Boston: Little, Brown, 1972) 397–409; Jack Herer, *The Emperor Wears No Clothes* (Van Nuys, Calif.: Hemp Publishing, 1990); and Chris Conrad, *Hemp for Health: The Medicinal and Nutritional Uses of Cannabis Sativa* (Rochester, Vt., Healing Arts Press, 1997) 1–63.

4. Brecher and the Editors of Consumer Reports, *supra*, at 42–46; Steven B. Duke and Albert C. Gross, *America's Longest War: Rethinking Our Tragic Crusade against Drugs* (New York: G. P. Putnam's Sons, 1993) 82–83; and David F. Musto, "Opium, Cocaine, and Marijuana in American History," *Scientific American*, July 1991, 40, 42.

Chinese men drugged by opium were bent upon drawing white women into moral depravity, passed an ordinance prohibiting the smoking of opium in smoking houses or "dens."[5] Otherwise no laws addressed any currently illicit substance until 1906, when *the most effective law dealing with psychotropic substances in United States history was passed.* This was the federal Pure Food and Drug Act.

Narcotics addiction during the nineteenth century was primarily accidental. The first main cause of addiction was the liberal usage of morphine and opium as painkillers by mostly northern military hospitals during the Civil War. The hospitals in the South mostly used whiskey because they were not as well financed as those in the North. However, due to the wide availability of and ignorance about these drugs in the North, many war veterans who began using narcotics for legitimate medical reasons often became addicted. In fact, drug addiction during this period was often referred to as the "soldiers' disease."

The second cause of accidental narcotics addiction was the widespread use and availability of patent medicines, otherwise known as elixirs or "snake oils." These substances were advertised as a "cure for whatever ails you" and, since they were often loaded with large doses of cocaine or morphine, they usually made the user temporarily feel a whole lot better. As a result many people, including a large number of middle-class agrarian housewives, became addicted to narcotics. Cocaine was also an ingredient in the soft drink Coca-Cola from 1886 until 1900, and Bayer Pharmaceutical Products introduced heroin in 1898 and sold it over the counter for a year before marketing aspirin.[6]

The Pure Food and Drug Act of 1906 led directly to the demise of the patent medicine industry, not by prohibiting these substances, but simply by requiring that all medications contain accurate labeling of their contents. Subsequent amendments to the act required the labels to contain accurate information about the strength of the drugs and to state that federal purity standards had been met. This act, combined with various governmental educational efforts encouraging people not to use any medications containing narcotics, resulted in a prompt, substantial, and permanent decline in the sales of these products.[7]

---

5. Brecher and the Editors of Consumer Reports, *supra.*

6. Musto, "Opium, Cocaine, and Marijuana," *supra* at 40, 44.

7. Brecher and the Editors of Consumer Reports, *supra*, at 47. See also Bonnie and Whitebread, *supra*, at 981–85, and David F. Musto, *The American Disease: Origins of Narcotic Control* (New York: Oxford University Press, 3d. ed., 1999), at 22–23.

Unfortunately for those already addicted, and even though the problems created by drug abuse were not considered to be particularly serious at that time,[8] the benefits of the Pure Food and Drug Act were virtually eradicated by the passage of the Harrison Narcotic Act in 1914. This was a measure requiring registration, payment of an intentionally inflated tax, and filling out of intentionally cumbersome order forms before anyone could import, sell, or give away opium, cocaine, or any of their derivatives. The Harrison Act, along with the U.S. Supreme Court decision in *Webb v. United States*,[9] which held that it was illegal for doctors to dispense prescription drugs to alleviate the symptoms of narcotics withdrawal, inaugurated the Drug Prohibition era in which we still live. As a result, people, including those who were already accidentally addicted to these drugs, were forced to turn to the criminal black market in order to obtain these substances.

Soon only adulterated, unlabeled, and contaminated drugs were available to the public, and at prices that were many times higher than what they had been before. As the editors of *Consumer Reports* concluded, this "withdrawal of the protection of the food-and-drug laws from the users of illicit drugs ... has been one of the significant factors in reducing addicts to their present miserable status, and in making drug use so damaging today."[10] Thus our country was launched into wide-scale criminal activity, both by sellers, in order to make inflated underground profits, and by users, in order to obtain the money to buy the now higher-priced drugs. Clinics that had worked effectively with addicted people were closed; clinical experiments and research dealing with narcotics addition were abandoned; and public fear and misinformation increasingly demonized all people who used any of these now illicit drugs.[11] As far back as 1953, Rufus King, chairman of the American Bar Association's committee on narcotics, succinctly summarized the results of our country's drug policy since the passage of the Harrison Act, when he said:

> So long as society will not traffic with [the true addict] on any terms, he must remain the abject servitor of his vicious nemesis, the peddler. The addict

---

8. See Arnold S. Trebach and James A. Inciardi, *Legalize It?* (Washington D.C.: American University Press, 1993) 41–74.

9. 249 U.S. 96 (1919).

10. Brecher and the Editors of Consumer Reports, *supra*, at 47.

11. Bonnie and Whitebread, *supra*, 986–90.

will commit crimes—mostly petty offenses like shoplifting and prostitution—to get the price the peddler asks. He *will* peddle dope and make new addicts if those are his master's terms. Drugs are a commodity of trifling intrinsic value. All the billions our society has spent enforcing criminal measures against the addict have had the sole practical result of protecting the peddler's market, artificially inflating his prices, and keeping his profits fantastically high. No other nation hounds its addicts as we do, and no other nation faces anything remotely resembling our problem.[12]

In the meantime, pressure had mounted for the prohibition of another dangerous and sometimes addicting drug: alcohol. With the passage of the Eighteenth Amendment, Alcohol Prohibition went into effect nationwide on January 16, 1920. From that time until the repeal of Alcohol Prohibition with the passage of the Twenty-First Amendment in 1933, the United States saw a material increase in death from poisoned liquor, crime, violence, and corruption. It also saw a higher consumption per capita of stronger beverages like whiskey than of weaker beverages like beer, in accordance with a cardinal rule of prohibition: there is always more money to be made in pushing the more concentrated substances. In many cities there were actually more "speakeasies" during Alcohol Prohibition than there previously had been saloons.

Not surprisingly, federal funding for law enforcement efforts was increased from $2.2 million in 1920 to $12 million in 1929, and the federal prison population increased between 1920 and 1932 from 3,000 to 12,000, with two-thirds of inmates incarcerated for alcohol and other drug offenses. Interestingly enough, the federal murder rate, which had been rising steadily throughout Alcohol Prohibition, decreased for eleven consecutive years after its repeal.[13]

The prohibition of marijuana in the United States was also deeply rooted in racial prejudice. A wave of poor immigrants from Mexico and Central America during the 1920s was accompanied by stories of violent rampages by Spanish-speaking aliens crazed by marijuana, the "killer weed."[14] The other motivating factor behind marijuana prohibition appears to have been the substitution in the public mind of the

---

12. Rufus King, "The Narcotics Bureau and the Harrison Act," *Yale Law Journal* 62 (1953) 748–49.

13. David Boaz, "Lessons from the Failure of Prohibition," *Los Angeles Daily Journal*, December 28, 1993: 6.

14. Bonnie and Whitebread, *supra*, at 1012–16.

effects of drugs they knew about, like morphine and cocaine, for the effects of marijuana, since the actual properties of marijuana were generally unknown.[15]

The United States Bureau of Narcotics, under the direction of its commissioner, Harry J. Anslinger, took an active role in spreading this fear and misinformation, with an eye toward convincing both the state and federal governments to pass laws of marijuana prohibition. The movie *Reefer Madness*, for example, was produced in 1936 with the close collaboration of the Bureau of Narcotics, which was the direct predecessor of the Drug Enforcement Administration. This movie tells the story of how "one puff of pot can lead clean-cut teenagers down the road to insanity, criminality, and death." Although *Reefer Madness* was intended to educate the public about the "horrors of narcotics," it is now seen as unintentionally quite funny, except in the historical context. Similarly Commissioner Anslinger himself submitted an article entitled "Marijuana: Assassin of Youth" to *American Magazine*, which published the article in July 1937. This article told the lurid tale of a quiet young man who had become a "marijuana addict" and then proceeded to kill his entire family of five with an ax while "pitifully crazed" on marijuana.[16] Similar highly questionable articles, "culled from the files of the U.S. Bureau of Narcotics," were published frequently.[17]

As a result of these tactics, many states passed marijuana prohibition statutes; and in some cases, the tactics were so successful that the prohibitionist statutes actually mis-designated marijuana as a narcotic. Since little was known about the substance and no scientific studies had been conducted, since there was a fear that marijuana use would spread even to whites as a substitute for opiates and alcohol, and since wild stories

---

15. Ibid. at 1016–22.

16. *American Magazine* 124 (July 1937) 19, 150.

17. See, for example, M. W. Childs, "A Drug Menace at the University of Kansas—How a Number of Students Became Addicts of the Strangely Intoxicating Marijuana Weed," *St. Louis Post-Dispatch* (Sunday Magazine), April 8, 1934: 272–73, which reads, "the physical attack of marijuana upon the body is rapid and devastating. In the initial stages the skin turns a peculiar yellow color, the lips become discolored, dried and cracked. Soon the mouth is affected, the gums are inflamed and softened. Then the teeth are loosened and eventually, if the habit is persisted in, they fall out. Like all other drugs, marijuana also has a serious effect on the moral character of the individual, destroying his will power and reducing his stamina.

"[People in traveling jazz bands] take a few puffs off a marijuana cigarette if they are tired. . . . It gives them a lift and they can go on playing even though they may be virtually paralyzed from the waist down, which is one of the effects that marijuana may have."

in newspapers and magazines made it easy to prohibit a substance that was associated only with politically powerless ethnic minorities and the lower classes, legislators had no difficulty passing these "non-controversial" prohibitionist laws.[18]

Soon Commissioner Anslinger and other prohibitionists were able to convince the United States Congress to pass the Marijuana Tax Act of 1937, which was modeled after the Harrison Narcotic Act. This law did not actually ban the substance, however. In fact, it specifically recognized marijuana's medical utility and provided for medical doctors and others to prescribe it, druggists to dispense it, and others to grow, import, and manufacture it, as long as each of those parties paid a small licensing fee. It was only the non-medicinal and unlicensed possession or sale of marijuana that was prohibited. But that was enough. The cumbersome bureaucratic process, coupled with the stigma and the exorbitant tax of $100 per ounce for unlicensed transactions with marijuana, were sufficient to result in the substance being taken off the commercial market.

The legislative hearings leading up to the passage of the Marijuana Tax Act of 1937 lasted only three days and took up only 124 pages of transcript—including material that was not actually discussed but only read into the record.[19] And there was no medical testimony at all that favored the bill. In fact, the only medical witness that appeared at the hearing was a doctor who recommended that the bill be defeated. This doctor testified that marijuana was a recognized medication, was distributed by many reputable pharmaceutical firms, and was currently on sale at many of the nation's pharmacies. In addition, an editorial in the *Journal of the American Medical Association* strongly urged Congress to defeat the bill. Nevertheless, it passed the House without even a roll call vote, and with only two pages of "debate."

After the Senate summarily passed the bill as well, with only minor changes, it was returned to the House. On that occasion, the only question asked on the floor was whether the American Medical Association supported the bill. The response by Rep. Fred M. Vinson (who later would sit as a justice on the United States Supreme Court), was that

---

18. Brecher and Editors of Consumer Reports, *supra*, at 413-21; Bonnie and Whitebread, *supra*, at 1010–22; and Rufus King, *The Drug Hang-Up: America's Fifty-Year Folly* (Springfield, Ill.: Charles C. Thomas, 1972), 69–77.

19. Bonnie and Whitebread, *supra*, at 1053–55.

the bill had the full support of the AMA, even though the only medical witness before the committee had directly opposed it. And so the bill became law.[20]

As subsequent events have proved, one distinct, direct, and lasting effect of the laws to suppress the use of marijuana was that they led to the establishment of organizations in countries like Colombia to process and distribute cocaine in this country. The reason for this was simple: it was much easier to conceal and transport cocaine than marijuana, and much more lucrative, pound for pound.[21]

The United States government radically changed its prohibitionist position on marijuana during World War II, when our supplies of hemp from the Philippines and jute from India were cut off by the Japanese. This resulted in our armed forces running seriously short of raw materials for rope and course cloth. In response, the U.S. Department of Agriculture produced a fourteen-minute film in 1942 entitled "Hemp for Victory." This film began by acknowledging that hemp had been grown in ancient Greece and China for thousands of years, and that the word for "canvas" in ancient Arabic was the same word as "cannabis," or hemp. It went on to explain that our old cannistoga wagons had been covered with cloth made from hemp and that it had taken about sixty tons of rope made from hemp to outfit *Old Ironsides*. As the audience heard strains of "My Old Kentucky Home" in the background, the narrator exhorted patriotic farmers to plant hemp so that we could increase the number of acres planted from 14,000 in 1942 to 300,000 in 1943. The war effort demanded it. And then, to the sounds of "Anchors Aweigh" and with pictures of American flags waving proudly in the breeze, the narrator intoned: "Hemp for light-duty fire hoses," for "thread for shoes for millions of American soldiers," for "parachute webbing for our paratroopers," for supplying the "34,000 feet of rope for each of our United States Navy ships," and for "countless uses on ship and shore." "Hemp for mooring our ships!" "Hemp for tow lines!" "Hemp for Victory!"

After the war hemp reverted to being a prohibited substance "without any practical usages of any kind."

---

20. See Bonnie and Whitebread, *supra*, at 1053–62; and Brecher and the Editors of Consumer Reports, *supra*, at 415–18.

21. For a thorough discussion of this area, see Mike Gray (no relation), *Drug Crazy—How We Got Into This Mess and How We Can Get Out* (New York: Random House, 1998).

In the decades thereafter, U.S. presidents and Congress have continually reaped political benefits by passing a flood of "get tough" laws, which lump all illegal substances together regardless of their properties or their effects on the user. When these laws have failed to produce the desired results, Congress has responded by continually passing even more stringent ones. The Boggs Act of 1951 and the Narcotic Control Act of 1956, for example, imposed ever more strict sentencing requirements for all illicit drug offenses. In 1961, the U.S. government somehow convinced many other countries to ratify a treaty entitled the Single Convention of Narcotic Drugs, which said in effect that there was only one way to attack the drug menace, and that was *our* way. Richard M. Nixon, the first U.S. president formally to declare the nation's "War on Drugs," expanded the federal government's involvement, both by attempting to disrupt the importation of illicit drugs and by increasing our efforts to interdict them at our borders. The Comprehensive Drug Abuse Prevention and Control Act of 1970 consolidated prior anti-drug legislation and established schedules of illicit drugs. The Comprehensive Crime Control Act of 1984 increased bail amounts and lengths of sentences for drug offenders, and stepped up federal authority to forfeit assets and investigate money laundering.

The Anti-Drug Abuse Act of 1986 further increased federal drug penalties and instituted mandatory minimum sentences for simple possession of drugs, the doubling of penalties for anyone who knowingly involved juveniles in any drug activity, and mandatory life sentences for "principals" convicted of conducting a continuing criminal enterprise. The 1986 act also made it a federal offense to distribute drugs within 1,000 feet of a school and required the president to evaluate annually the performance of drug-producing and drug-transit countries and to certify those that were "cooperating" as anti-drug allies. Decertified countries were to lose foreign aid, face possible trade sanctions, and suffer U.S. opposition to loans from international financial institutions— unless such countries were granted waivers by the president in the interest of U.S. security.

The Anti-Drug Abuse Act of 1988 further expanded federal offenses to include the distribution of drugs within one hundred feet of playgrounds, parks, youth centers, swimming pools, and video arcades. The Crime Bill of 1994 provided for capital punishment for some types of drug selling, and instituted "criminal enterprise" statutes that called for mandatory sentences of from twenty years to life. The 1998 Higher

Education Act disqualified young people from receiving federal aid for college if they had ever been convicted of marijuana possession, even though no such disqualification applies to convictions for offenses like robbery, rape, or manslaughter. All of this "get tough" legislation still forms the basis of our nation's drug policy today.

Two fundamental factors have been driving this failed policy for all of these years. The first is our political system, which rewards (elects) politicians who posture as being "tough on drugs," and the second is the "runaway freight train" of federal spending. Politicians get elected and reelected by continuing to "talk tough," and entire state and federal agencies, as well as legions of private enterprises, are addicted to the enormous amounts of drug war funding. As of fiscal year 1999, the Office of National Drug Control Policy, *by itself*, was overseeing a federal drug control budget of $17.8 *billion* (in nine separate appropriations bills), plus an additional $1 billion for the National Youth Anti-Drug Media Campaign, $143.5 million for the Drug-Free Communities Program, and $184 million for the High-Intensity Drug Trafficking Area Program. That budget was increased again to $19.2 *billion* for fiscal year 2000.[22] To put this incredible amount of money into some kind of perspective, in the year 2000, United Airlines agreed to purchase US Airways for a total of $4.3 billion. This means that our Drug Czar would be able to purchase four major airlines *each year* on his office's budget alone, with substantial money left over. And of course that does not even begin to take into account all the additional state and federal budgets for a myriad of other programs.[23] It is up to us as caring citizens, taxpayers, and voters to make the government move forward to a more rational, workable, and, as good fortune would have it, vastly less expensive national drug policy.

Emergence of the Prison-Industrial Complex

One result of the attempt to control drug use with heavy penalties is, of course, an increase in the price of drugs, which assures an increase in crime both random and organized. Viewed in this context, the war on drugs, besides being laughably inept and already visibly lost, is in fact the driving force behind serious crime.

---

22. See the biography of Barry R. McCaffrey, director of the Office of National Drug Control Policy online at <www.whitehousedrugpolicy.gov/about/bio_full.htm>

23. For a detailed history of the War on Drugs since 1968, see Dan Baum, *Smoke and Mirrors—The War on Drugs and the Politics of Failure* (New York: Little, Brown, 1996), which demonstrates government spending that far exceeds the wildest waste, fraud, or abuse accusations of Rush Limbaugh or Ross Perot.

From shoplifting to prostitution, through burglary and armed robbery on up the scale to murder, the great majority of serious crimes in California are drug-related; that is to say, caused not by the perpetrator's ingestion of drugs, but by his or her need to obtain the large amounts of money necessary to purchase drugs on the street for personal use.[24]

Justice William A. Newsom, California Court of Appeal, San Francisco, California

Between 1973 and 1983, the number of state and federal prisoners in the United States doubled to about 660,800; and then that number more than doubled again by 1993 to 1,408,685.[25] By June 30, 1996, the number of men and women incarcerated in the United States in both the state and federal systems was 1,630,940, and by the end of 1998 the number was 1.8 million. Although in recent years crime has been decreasing, drug arrests and convictions and the numbers of people incarcerated in the United States have continued to rise. As a result, in 1991, considering both the federal and the state correctional systems, 445 out of every 100,000 of the U.S. population was locked up. By way of contrast, during that same year both Canada and China had 111 incarcerated per 100,000, and Japan had only 42 per 100,000. By 1996, the United States had increased its incarceration rate to 615 for every 100,000 residents, and by 1998 this number continued to climb to a staggering 668 inmates for every 100,000 residents. That gave the United States a higher rate of incarceration than any other country in the world except Russia, which reported a rate of 685.[26]

So even though crime in the United States has recently been decreasing, drug arrests have been climbing steadily. While the number of violent offenders in prison has doubled since 1980, *the number of drug prisoners has increased sevenfold.* There are *six times* more people behind bars in this country than in all twelve of the countries that make up the European Union combined, *even though they have 100 million more citizens.* More people are behind bars for drug offenses in the United States— about 400,000—than are incarcerated in England, France, Germany,

24. W. A. Newsom, "Prohibition Never Works," *San Francisco Bay Guardian*, October 5, 1994: 14, 16.

25. "Report and Recommendations of the Drug Policy Task Force," New York County Lawyers' Association (October 1996): 5, note 7.

26. Fox Butterfield, "Number of Inmates Reaches Record 1.8 Million," *New York Times,* March 15, 1999: A12; Associated Press, "Study Sees Slowing of Surge in U.S. Prison Population," *Los Angeles Times,* January 20, 1997, Orange County ed.: A 16. Also see M. Mauer, "Americans Behind Bars: One Year Later," The Sentencing Project (1992); and Associated Press, "Prison Population at Record 1.8 Million," *Orange County Register,* March 15, 1999: News 11.

and Japan for *all crimes combined.* The state of California alone has more people incarcerated than do France, Great Britain, Germany, Japan, Singapore, and the Netherlands combined, even though California has only about one-tenth of their combined populations. In fact, the United States, with less than five percent of the world's population, has one-quarter of the world's prisoners.[27] Statistics like this have caused even people like our nation's Drug Czar, General Barry R. McCaffrey, to say that "We have a failed social policy and it has to be re-evaluated. Otherwise, we're going to bankrupt ourselves. Because we can't incarcerate our way out of this problem."[28]

But we *have* been trying to incarcerate our way out of the drug problem, and along the way we have seriously harmed tens of thousands of people and their families.[29] As of 1991, according to the FBI's own statistics, more than 1 million arrests were already being made each year for drug offenses alone,[30] and as of September 1998, 58 percent of all federal prisoners were serving time for drug offenses. As of 1999, the California Department of Corrections estimated that 80 percent of its 162,000 inmates probably were substance abusers, and 37 percent were in custody expressly for drug offenses.[31] FBI statistics also show that the total number of arrests for marijuana offenses was higher in 1997 than in any other year in U.S. history. In that year, state and local law enforcement agencies reported 695,201 marijuana arrests, *of which 87 percent were for possession only.* Simple arithmetic yields the staggering statistic that someone is arrested for a marijuana offense somewhere in the United States every forty-five seconds! That number is almost as high as the number of total arrests for all murders, rapes, robberies, and aggravated assaults combined (717,720).[32]

---

27. Vincent Schiraldi and Jason Ziedenberg, "Incarceration of All Offenders Is Not the Right Answer," *Los Angeles Daily Journal,* January 21, 2000: 6; Gregg Easterbrook, "Run-On Sentencing," *New Republic,* April 26 and May 3, 1999: 57, 60.

28. Fox Butterfield, *supra,* at 20.

29. See Mikki Norris, Chris Conrad, and Virginia Resner, *Shattered Lives: Portraits from America's Drug War* (El Cerrito, Calif.: Creative Xpressions, 1998).

30. Lester Grinspoon and James B. Bakalar, "The War on Drugs—A Peace Proposal," *New England Journal of Medicine* 330 (1994): 357.

31. Editorial, " 'Smart on Crime' Is Better," *Los Angeles Times,* May 29, 2000, Orange County ed.: B12.

32. FBI's Uniform Crime Reports Division's Annual Report: "Crime in the United States," released November 22, 1998; *Dallas Morning News,* November 23, 1998; U.S. Department of Justice, "Federal Criminal Case Processing, 1998," September 1999: 14. As of September 30, 1998, 62,948 out of a total of 107,912 federal prisoners were incarcerated for drug offenses.

Let us focus, then, on the simple realities of what we are facing. According to the National Household Survey, about 18 million Americans used marijuana at least once during the year 1997, and more than 71 million have used marijuana at some time in their lives. During that same year, the United States had about 1.7 million people behind bars under badly overcrowded conditions. Since it is immediately obvious that we cannot put 18 million people in jail, even if we were to agree that this was a good idea, why are we following this course? Yet people who did nothing but smoke some marijuana are sent to state prison every day to serve years of time. How can that happen?

The answer is that lots of people are on parole, with conditions that they not possess or use any illegal drugs. But since marijuana stays in the body such that it can be detected by urinalysis testing for up to twenty-eight days, the parolee who has smoked marijuana often gets caught, one way or another. If he reports for testing, he will be found to be in violation, and if he fails to report, he is in violation for that as well. This makes an easy "stat" for probation and parole officers. But for this our taxpayers are wasting hundreds of millions of dollars each year, and many people are unnecessarily wasting their lives.

There have been a great many unintended consequences of this policy that most people do not seem to have considered. For example, by making these drugs illegal, we have forced users to associate with criminals and the criminal culture. As a result, we have made lifetime prisoners out of a nonviolent underclass of drug-using and addicted people. An additional consequence is that our system has arrested, imprisoned, and eliminated from the market the stupid, unorganized, and less violent drug traffickers and smugglers, thus leaving this phenomenally lucrative market open to offenders who are smarter, better organized, and more violent. These unintended results have led people like Bankruptcy Judge Paul Mannes of the U.S. District Court in Greenbelt, Maryland, to conclude: "I am convinced that the present drug policy is impotent and a dreadful waste of human resources and tax dollars."

In order to understand the country's criminal justice system, one must be aware that the federal courts are designed to handle large, complicated, and serious cases, while the various state systems are generally equipped to handle higher volumes of less complicated "street crimes." When translated to the War on Drugs, the federal system is supposed to prosecute large cases involving the interstate activities of "drug kingpins." But this is not what has been happening. Even though the number of people convicted in federal court has been steadily increasing for years, the average federal sentence for drug offenders has shrunk from an average of eighteen years in 1992 to only seven years in 1998. Independent researchers at Syracuse University concluded from their examination of these statistics that, instead of targeting the large and dangerous drug traffickers, federal law enforcement agencies have increasingly been focusing on higher numbers of lower-level marijuana crimes.[33]

The average prison term for drug offenders in state prisons, however, has increased—up 22 percent since 1986. But in the same period, average prison terms in state prisons for *violent offenders* have actually *decreased* by 30 percent.[34] For example, under the Rockefeller drug laws in New York, a man named Lawrence V. Cipolione, Jr. was serving a sentence of fifteen years to life for selling 2.34 ounces of cocaine to an undercover officer. Meanwhile, in the same prison, Amy Fisher was to be released after serving only four years and ten months for shooting a woman in the head, and Robert Chambers was serving a five-year sentence for a Central Park strangling. Under these circumstances, even the New York State Commissioner of Corrections was quoted as saying that "The people doing the big time in the system really aren't the people you want doing the big time."[35] So even though crime has gone down, by March 1999 one out of every 150 people in the United States was either in prison or in jail, and a high percentage of those were convicted of drug crimes.[36] According to these statistics, an American born in 1999 has about one chance in twenty of spending some part of his or her life in a correctional facility. For black Americans, the chance increases to about one in four.[37]

---

33. Eric Lichtblau and Josh Meyer, "Sentences Shorter in Federal Drug Cases," *Los Angeles Times*, March 13, 2000, Orange County ed.: B9.

34. Editorial, "A System Sentencing Itself to Despair," *Los Angeles Times*, April 25, 1993, Orange County ed.: M4.

35. Francis X. Clines, "Drug Law Catching Few Kingpins," *New York Times*, March 23, 1993.

36. A prison is run by the state and is reserved for felons serving a sentence of more than one year for a particular offense. A jail is run by local authorities and is used to hold criminal defendants before trial and for those who are sentenced to a year or less for an offense.

37. Timothy Egan, "Crime Off—but Prisons Swelling," *Orange County Register*, March 7, 1999: News 27, 29.

Regardless of what anyone might think about our current approach, sometimes the results mandated by our drug laws are transparently crazy, as is demonstrated by this anecdote from Judge Clay M. Smith, a member of my court in Orange County, California:

> The defendant was, as I recall, 20 years old. He had been stopped by police in a routine traffic stop. The officer became suspicious that the defendant was engaged in criminal activity, and ultimately the investigation reached a point of probable cause for a search of the defendant's vehicle. A narcotic-detection dog was called to the scene and used to inspect the vehicle. The dog alerted near the left front quarter panel of the car, and the officers found a baggie of marijuana. The marijuana in the baggie was subsequently determined to weigh slightly less than 28.5 grams, just less than an ounce. The weight of the dope was vitally significant because the maximum penalty for transportation of less than one ounce of marijuana is a misdemeanor conviction and a fine of $100.00. [Citation omitted.] If the weight had been more than one ounce, the offense would be chargeable as a felony and punishable by state prison time. [Citation omitted.]
>
> The defendant was transported to the Orange County Jail for booking. A body search was subsequently conducted and another baggie was discovered concealed in the defendant's rectum. Within the baggie was a very small quantity of marijuana which was found to weigh a few grams. The two quantities of marijuana were added together and determined to weigh just a tad—literally about a gram—more than one ounce. *Imagine the consequences! That extra smidgen of dope increased the defendant's exposure from a $100.00 fine to life in prison* [under the Three Strikes Law].[38] (Emphasis added.)

Of course, those rates of incarceration usually do not apply to people of means. Almost universally, when celebrities or people who have money get arrested for drug usage, they do not feel the effect of these laws. Celebrities such as Oliver Stone, Paul McCartney, and Lawrence Taylor have been arrested for drug possession, but none suffered more than a fine and probation.[39]

But for the rest of society, incarceration has become big business. From the time of statehood until the year 1984, California built a total of thirteen state prisons. Since 1984, however, its taxpayers have financed and built no fewer than twenty additional prisons by the end of 1999, for a total of thirty-three. This has made prison construction

---

38. Judge Clay M. Smith, "The Chains of Enslavement," *Orange County Lawyer*, August 1999: 25–27.

39. James P. Pinkerton, "A War for Some, a Lark for Others," *Los Angeles Times*, January 20, 2000, Orange County ed.: B15.

California's leading "public works" program. During that same period of time, however, California built only one new university.[40]

This prison construction has, of course, been necessary under the circumstances because the prison population in California has been growing by an incredible 1,000 inmates *per month*.[41] With such growth, the California Department of Corrections itself oversaw 162,000 inmates and 39,000 employees in 1999, and had a budget of $4.6 billion.[42] And even with these staggering numbers, prisons in California were at 193 percent occupancy in 1999.[43] In a very real sense, our governments have actually sponsored a "Prison-Industrial Complex," and have literally become "addicted" to all of the funding that has come along with it.

Because of these efforts to build, finance, and staff enough prisons to handle our drug offenders, our governments are going broke. In October 1999, with great fanfare and at the cost of millions of dollars, the sheriff of Orange County, California, announced an expansion of one jail by 384 beds. A neutral study released earlier in the year, however, said that the county needed 2,532 more jail beds *immediately* in order to ease overcrowding and end the early release of inmates, and further that the county will need an additional 4,600 more beds by the year 2010 just to stay even.[44]

Disturbingly, there are even further financial problems because California for a long time was unable to pay the $15 million it owed Orange County for its housing of state parolees. By law, the state must reimburse each of its counties $59 per day for each parolee the county holds. Each year, the state budgeted $22 million for this purpose; but the obligations were more than twice that amount. One administrator with the California Department of Corrections said in despair, "The counties keep billing us and we just got further and further in the hole

---

40. Gregg Easterbrook, *supra*.

41. John Roemer, "Taking Three Strikes Outside the Walls," *California Lawyer*, October 1996: 40, 41.

42. Editorial, "Let Light through Prison Walls," *Los Angeles Times*, September 1, 1999, Orange County ed.: B8.

43. Editorial, "Danger in Prison Overcrowding," *Los Angeles Times*, October 14, 1999, Orange County ed.: B14.

44. Daniel Yi, "Jail Makes Room for More," *Los Angeles Times*, October 23, 1999, Orange County ed.: A1, B1, 5; Tony Saavedra, "2,500 New Jail Beds Needed Now, Study Says," *Orange County Register*, March 17, 1999: News 1.

each year."[45] So the state's inability to pay its debts to the counties for the incarceration of prisoners has been a financial fact of life under our present drug policy.

As a direct result of increased drug prosecutions and convictions, virtually all of the jails and prisons throughout the country are severely overcrowded. Some states have tried to alleviate their prison over-crowding by sending some of their prisoners to prisons in other states— for a fee. For example, in January 1999, the state of Washington opened a new 1,936-bed prison, but it was already so overcrowded that they were forced to send another 250 of their inmates to Colorado, which will receive $51 per day per prisoner.[46] The situation was even worse in Hawaii when I was there a while ago. They had been forced to send several hundred of their prisoners to Texas under this same "rent-a-cell" program. Of course, the cost of transportation was much higher to Hawaii than it was to Washington, and that was in addition to the problems this program caused to the families who were trying to maintain visitation with the prisoners.

Another problem that is seriously aggravated by our current drug policy involves the mentally disabled. Since illegal drugs are readily available in our neighborhoods, these fragile people often attempt to "self-medicate" with the onset of their symptoms. As a result, they are brought into the criminal justice system either as a result of their purchase or use of illicit drugs. As a practical matter, this has resulted in our local jails becoming our nation's largest mental hospitals.[47] Not only is this an enormous misuse of scarce resources, it is also inflicting a great deal of unnecessary trauma on the mentally ill.

In short, no one is coming out ahead under this system except the people making money in the prison-industrial complex. Not only has this resulted in financial problems for our governments, but the entire criminal justice system has been losing credibility. Today, regardless of the bail that is set for many offenses, and regardless of what criminal sentences are imposed, offenders know that they will probably be released after a small fraction of time spent behind bars because of overcrowding.

---

45. Tony Saavedra, "State Jail Tab to Counties Rising Fast," *Orange County Register,* March 16, 1999: News 4.

46. David Ammons, "Jammed Washington Prisons Fly Inmates Out of State," *Los Angeles Daily Journal,* March 3, 1999: 5.

47. Fox Butterfield, "Prisons Replace Hospitals for the Nation's Mentally Ill," *New York Times,* March 5, 1998: A1, 26.

By 1996, the average offender in jail in Los Angeles County served only 25 percent of his or her sentence.[48] In a system of this kind, deterrence has little or no effect.

Another little-known result of prison overcrowding is that wardens throughout the country are routinely forced to grant an early release to violent offenders so that nonviolent *drug* offenders can serve their sentences in full. This is true because, for the most part, federal law requires that even nonviolent drug offenders must serve their entire sentences; however, there is no such law for bank robbers, kidnappers, or other violent offenders. This is a truly scandalous and unacceptable situation.

Prison overcrowding in the federal system is in large part caused by "mandatory minimum" sentencing laws, which require a judge to sentence a defendant by use of a set formula. Large numbers of federal judges disagree with these laws and often are quite vocal in their opposition. Senior Judge Myron H. Bright of the U.S. Court of Appeal wrote in 1995 about a drug sentence that was required to be imposed by a trial court in Cedar Rapids, Iowa:

> This case is the paradigm of what judges often see in the sentencing of drug law offenders. In this case, the sentences are excessively long, but required by the mandatory minimum sentencing provisions and the overlaying requirements of the federal sentencing guidelines.
>
> These unwise sentencing policies which put men and women in prison for years, not only ruin lives of prisoners and often their family members, but also drain the American taxpayers of funds which can be measured in billions of dollars. . . . This is the time to call a halt to the unnecessary and expensive cost of putting people in prison for a long time based on the mistaken notion that such an effort will win "The War on Drugs." If it is a war, society seems not to be winning, but losing. We must turn to other methods of deterring drug distribution and use. Long sentences do not work and . . . [actually] penalize society.[49]

The overcrowding situation became so desperate by 1996 that more than 1,000 suspected drug smugglers along our country's southwestern border were set free by federal law enforcement agencies and deported, even though they had been arrested with substantial quantities of nar-

---

48. Paul Feldman and Eric Lichtblau, "L.A. County Jail Inmates Serve 25% of Sentences," *Los Angeles Times*, May 20, 1996, Orange County ed.: A1, 10–11.

49. See *United States v. Hiveley* and *United States v. Henry*, 61 F.3d 1358, 1363 (8th Cir. 1995).

cotics and other illicit drugs. One had been arrested with 32 *pounds* of methamphetamines, another had 37,000 Quaalude tablets, and yet another had smuggled in 158 *pounds* of cocaine. Most of the marijuana arrests had been for quantities of 50 to 300 pounds. These people were released, and the charges dropped, because there was simply no room for them in the federal jails.[50]

After one of my talks on prison statistics at a local junior college, an accountant in the audience told me that he had penciled out the figures I gave on prison expansion. His arithmetic revealed that if the rate of imprisonment of the past twenty years were to continue, by the year 2020 literally *everyone* in California would be either in prison or running one. And California ranks only twelfth nationally in prison incarceration rates per capita, with a rate of 416 per 100,000 population. Texas is first at 653 per 100,000, Louisiana second at 568, and Oklahoma third at 561.[51] Further, it must be remembered that it costs taxpayers between $20,000 and $30,000 to keep just one inmate confined for a year. As of 1993, about one in every three state prisoners in the country was a drug offender, up from one in twenty-five in 1960.[52]

One must also remember that with the advent of "three strikes and you're out" legislation, which mandates sentences of twenty-five years to life for third felonies, many of these nonviolent drug offenders will grow old in prison. The average cost for a state inmate over the age of fifty-five increases to about $69,000 per year because of increased health costs. Health coverage for citizens not in jail, of course, is not mandated by the Constitution; but the taxpayers are obligated to provide adequate medical care for prisoners, whatever it costs.[53] As of the beginning of 1995, about 55,000 prisoners over fifty years of age were incarcerated

---

50. H. G. Reza, "Drug Runners Arrested at Border Often Go Free," *Los Angeles Times,* May 13, 1996, Washington ed.: B1; Ronald J. Ostrow and H. G. Reza, "Reno Stands By Border Drug Policy," *Los Angeles Times,* May 17, 1996, Washington ed.: B1; H. G. Reza, "Feinstein Plans Border Drug Crackdown," *Los Angeles Times,* May 16, 1996, Washington ed.: B1; *Los Angeles Times,* "Many Drug Suspects Go Free Along US Border," *Boston Sunday Globe,* May 12, 1996; Reuters, "Many Drug Smugglers Being Set Free by U.S.," *Rocky Mountain News,* May 13, 1996: 25A.

51. Kathy Walt, "Hard Line on Crime Has a Price," *Houston Chronicle,* December 5, 1996: 37A. The total numbers of prisoners nationwide is reached by adding those of the fifty states and the District of Columbia to those of the federal system.

52. Melinda Beck, "Kicking the Prison Habit," *Newsweek,* June 14, 1993: 32, 37.

53. Jennifer Reid Holman, "Prison Care: Our Penitentiaries Are Turning into Nursing Homes. Can We Afford It?" *Modern Maturity,* April 1997: 30–36.

nationwide; and even before the three-strikes legislation, some studies estimated that that number would increase to more than 125,000 by the year 2000.[54] And of the 2,750 felons already sentenced to twenty-five years to life through the end of 1996, 85 percent were sentenced for non-violent offenses. In fact, the statistics show that marijuana possession was *four times as likely* to lead to a third-strike conviction than murder, rape, and kidnapping combined.[55] The RAND Corporation estimates that if we continue with our current system and fully implement the three-strikes sentencing laws, the costs to California's criminal justice system alone will increase by an average of $5.5 billion *each year* for the next twenty-five years. This in itself will cost each California worker a tax increase of $300 per year for each of the next twenty-five years.[56]

Once built, at the cost of about $220 million, a prison must be staffed. Between 1980 and 1995, the California Correctional Peace Officers Association (CPOA) grew from 2,000 prison guard members to 24,000.[57] And it is expected that the 8 percent of the state general fund that paid in 1996 for the running of the prison system will grow over the next seven years to 18 percent, since it costs about $22.5 million per year to operate one prison alone. This has made the Department of Corrections the fastest growing governmental agency in the entire state of California.

Not surprisingly, with the growth and expansion of prisons has come increased political power. For example, after six years on the job the yearly salary of a California prison guard with a high school diploma was $45,000 in 1994. At the same time, the starting salary of a tenured University of California associate professor with a Ph.D. was $43,100.[58] In addition, in each election year throughout the decade of the 1990s, the California CPOA budgeted almost $1 million to be donated to sympathetic gubernatorial and legislative candidates, or against non-sympathizers. In the 1988 election it was the state's number-one donor to legislative races, with donations totaling $1.9 million. When the governor's and initiative campaigns were included, the total donations were

---

54. Ibid.

55. Editorial, *USA Today*, "Nonviolent Offenders Pay," *Los Angeles Daily Journal*, February 27, 1997: 6.

56. Holman, *supra* at 36.

57. Dan Morain, "Veto Steps Up Debate on Prison Spending," *Los Angeles Times*, August 7, 1995, Orange County ed.: A3, 16.

58. "Three Strikes . . . and You're In," *California Lawyer*, June 1995: 74–75.

$5.3 million. These contributions included a $100,000 donation to a group working for the passage of a tough three-strikes sentencing ballot measure.[59]

This power can be misperceived by the public. When California's governor used his line-item veto power to delete a requirement that the Department of Corrections report to the legislature all occasions on which it paid $100,000 or more in lawsuits, several critics linked that action with the CPOA's political contributions to the governor's recent campaign.[60] But it is the system set up by our country's drug laws, not individuals, that is fundamentally responsible for these abuses and potential abuses of power.

Other states have experienced the same type of prison growth. In New York the inmate population almost *tripled* between 1981 and 1991, and between 1983 and 1989 the number of inmates imprisoned annually for drug offenses increased by an astounding 500 percent. By 1990, half of all felony convictions in the state of New York and other large states were for drug and drug-related offenses. Alarmed by these developments, judicial leaders from the nation's nine most populous states held an executive symposium on April 21, 1989, in Philadelphia to assess the crisis and discuss possible options. A statement from the final report of this symposium outlined the problem:

> A drug epidemic is sweeping the nation. It's been termed "a disaster of historic dimension" requiring a national mobilization by all our institutions. Since major responsibilities for controlling drug offenses devolve upon the criminal justice system, the judiciary, as the fulcrum of that system, must perform its role with great competence if that effort is to succeed. However, campaigns to reduce drug supply and demand through vigorous enforcement of recently toughened drug laws have been mounted in many places without considering the impact of these actions on the courts and on prosecutors' offices, the defense bar, and corrections agencies. The effect of such policies can be highly counterproductive. When courts are swamped with cases, backlogs mount and delays increase. Particularly when prisons and jails are severely overcrowded and other meaningful sentencing alternatives are lacking, the effect of a massive increase in caseloads may be to undermine the credibility of a system whose resources are already severely strained.[61]

---

59. Ibid., 40–41 and 83–87; New York County Lawyers' Association, *supra*, at 5, note 7; and Jennifer Warren, "When He Speaks, They Listen," *Los Angeles Times*, August 21, 2000, Orange County ed., A1, 16.

60. Morain, *supra*.

61. Robert D. Lipscher, Administrative Office of the Courts, State of New Jersey, "The Judiciary Response to the Drug Crisis"—Final Report, July 7, 1989: 1.

This conference of judicial leaders recognized that drug cases include not only drug use, possession, and trafficking, but also criminal offenses "stimulated by drug use," such as burglaries, shoplifting, prostitution, forgeries, and other crimes perpetrated by drug users in order to get the money to purchase drugs. The judicial leaders concluded that the "general sense of the conference was that most trial courts are being overwhelmed by drug cases" and felt that the "heavy increases in drug cases now coming before the courts stem from concerted efforts by police to widen the criminal net and make enforcement more strict."

"The situation is desperate," the report continued. "The overload causes backlog, the backlog feeds delay, delay along with lack of jail and prison space imperils rights to timely consideration, undermines deterrence and breeds contempt for the law." The report then stated the obvious: "A weakened court system which doesn't have the muscle to deal effectively with accused offenders sends a message to the street that the system does not have the will nor the way to confront the drug problem. Once users and pushers know from their experience that swamped courts will treat criminal behavior lightly the court system loses credibility and the rule of law is threatened." This group of distinguished judges and court administrators concluded that " the courts face a profound emergency brought on by the efforts to control the use and sale of illegal drugs and concomitant criminal and juvenile behavior problems" and that the "courts are falling behind because they do not have the resources to deal with the volume of criminal and juvenile delinquency cases now coming before them."[62]

For justices of the supreme courts and administrative managers of the courts of the nine most populous states in the country publicly to present such dire conclusions was virtually unprecedented. This report must be seen as the revolutionary document that it is—a protest that the U.S. criminal justice system simply cannot handle effectively the number of cases thrust upon it by the War on Drugs. And without a radical change in policy, there is no hope at all that the situation will improve.

Since that conference, the situation has continued to deteriorate. All along the Mexican border, from Texas to San Diego, federal agents are continuing to arrest more and more people and seize ever larger quantities of illicit drugs in a futile attempt to reduce drug trafficking. But

---

62. Ibid., at 1–15.

it has become obvious that we cannot even stop the *people* coming illegally across the border—let alone the drugs, which are much easier to conceal than people. But even though the large numbers of arrests are not sufficient to stop record amounts of drugs from coming into the country, drugs that are "sending shock waves" through the system,[63] they are enough to have overwhelmed the criminal justice system along the border.

In Texas, the situation became so acute that the district attorneys in five of the eight counties along the border stated that they would refuse to take any more drug cases from the federal government after July 1, 2000.[64] The situation in the federal system is even worse. In San Diego, the federal trial courts declared a "judicial emergency" on October 30, 2000, due to the large increase in drug and alien-smuggling cases. This could result in the cessation of trials in all civil cases. Chief U.S. District Judge Marilyn L. Huff, reflecting on caseloads that have tripled between 1994 and 2000, said, "We've been working with bandaids, trying to adjust to this gigantic increase in volume." Judge Huff works in a twenty-five-year-old courthouse that each day averages nearly 400 inmates when it was built for only 95, and has a docket with more than 2,000 defendants awaiting attention while local detention facilities have a capacity of only 800. U.S. Marshals who try to control the large numbers of prisoners are often dangerously outnumbered and are frequently forced to escort as many as 80 prisoners with only two guards. In Tucson, one federal prosecutor was ordered to abandon her post when she found herself in a courtroom with 45 unrestrained prisoners and only two unarmed marshals. And, of course, with the increased volume of cases, prosecutors are forced into deals for shorter sentences for even heavy drug traffickers, while judges are forced to release many of these same people on their "personal bail," even though there is a high risk that they will not return for trial.[65]

---

63. Molly Moore of the *Washington Post*, "More Drugs Being Stopped at Border," *San Francisco Chronicle*, November 29, 1999: A1, 17.

64. Michelle Koidin, "DA's Bowing Out of Drug War," *Los Angeles Daily Journal*, May 8, 2000: 4.

65. Richard A. Serrano, "Border War on Crime Overwhelms Courtrooms," *Los Angeles Times*, April 30, 2000, Orange County ed.: A1, 12; Daniel A. Shaw, "Southwestern Federal Judges Lobby Members of Congress," *Los Angeles Daily Journal*, May 22, 2000: 1; Donatella Lorch, "Trail Spotting," *Newsweek*, March 6, 2000: 42; Claude Walbert, "Court Faces Civil-Case Moratorium," *Los Angeles Daily Journal*, November 1, 2000: 2.

There is no question that these drugs are harmful. But the biggest reason why this country continues on its present course is that for decades our leaders simply have not read the evidence. Long ago, the director of President Nixon's National Commission of Marijuana and Drug Abuse, Michael Sonnenreich, declared, "About four years ago we spent a total of $66 million for the entire federal effort in the drug abuse area.... This year we have spent $796 million, and the budget estimates that have been submitted indicate that we will exceed the $1 billion mark. When we do so, we become, for want of a better term, a drug abuse industrial complex."[66]

That was in 1973. In 2000 the federal budget for the War on Drugs came in at *$19.2 billion.*

The rationale for the enormous growth of this prison-industrial complex in our country is that to change it to any significant degree would send "the wrong message to our children." Well, maybe it is time to ask how many nonviolent drug offenders we must continue to incarcerate in order to send the "right" message?

Recently I had occasion to meet separately, one on one, with two sitting congressmen from southern California districts. Each one told me that of course he agreed with me that our nation's drug policy was not working, and then went on to say that the situation was actually worse than I knew. If I were in Washington, each one said, I would quickly find out that every federal agency we have is getting substantial extra funding for fighting the War on Drugs. Not just the obvious ones like the DEA, Bureau of Customs, each branch of our military services, and the State Department, but also more obscure ones like the Department of Land Management, the Bureau of Indian Affairs, and the Department of Agriculture. These congressmen told me very directly that all of our federal agencies are addicted to the funding provided by the War on Drugs, and they do not want to give up that money.

Of course state and local governments also devote enormous amounts of scarce resources to the prosecution of drug cases. Even as far back as 1992, almost 19,000 state and local police officers were engaged *full-time* in fighting drugs, and an additional 11,000 officers were involved in this activity at least part of the time.[67]

---

66. National Commission on Marihuana and Drug Abuse, *Marihuana: A Signal of Misunderstanding* (Washington, D.C., U.S. Government Printing Office, 1972). See Appendix B.
67. Drug Enforcement Report, May 8, 1992: 4.

The sentencing of nonviolent "three-strike" drug offenders has gotten so egregious that even a county prosecutor felt forced, as a matter of conscience, to write an op-ed piece in the *Los Angeles Times*, which said, in part:

> Our indifference to principles of fairness is reflected in California's three-strikes law. This law mandates life imprisonment for relatively insignificant offenses, including drug possession and minor thefts, if the defendant was previously convicted of two serious or violent felonies.
>
> By sending petty, drug-dependent offenders to prison for life, we do not stand well in comparison with other justice systems. Many European nations and Japan view addicts as redeemable human beings, an aspiration we have all but abandoned. While the middle class perceives addiction for its own family members as a medical condition that should be treated, the "war against drugs," combined with an all-inclusive three-strikes law, has made lifetime prisoners out of nonviolent underclass addicts.
>
> To be sure, other nations do not forgive thefts by addicts. But they do not punish them with the same ferocity that they reserve for violent members of society. The Europeans with whom I spoke found life imprisonment for drug possession and minor theft to be as unacceptable as we view convicting an innocent accused.[68]

The law enforcement net is even more effective in catching and incarcerating female drug offenders, to wit, the number of women in prison in the United States increased by 224 percent in the decade before 1993, and it has continued to climb. By the end of 1997, about 82,800 women nationwide were serving prison sentences, and between 1986 and 1996, the number of women incarcerated for drug offenses increased by 888 percent, compared to an increase of 129 percent for non-drug offenses.[69] In California, the number of women in the state prison system increased by 450 percent between 1980 and 1993, from 1,316 to 7,232. About 76 percent of these women were imprisoned for nonviolent offenses—mostly for drug possession, possession for sale, or drug-related crimes. Typically the women involved in the illicit drug trade are low-level lookouts or "mules" who transport drugs for short distances either as favors for their husbands or boyfriends or for a small fee.

---

68. Joseph Charney, Los Angeles Deputy District Attorney, "Courage of Our Convictions," *Los Angeles Daily Journal*, September 15, 1999: 6.

69. Daniel A. Shaw, "Women in Prison," *Los Angeles Daily Journal*, November 18, 1999: 4; Ann Donahue, "Female Prison Population Up," *Denver Post*, July 21, 1997: 1A, 13A.

What is seldom addressed, however, is that about 75 percent of all of these women prisoners are also the single parents of young children.[70] So what happens to the children when their mothers are arrested and incarcerated? By law, the mother has legally abandoned her children, so they must go into the child dependency court. Then, if the mother has no relatives or friends who are both able and willing to care for the children in their homes, the mother runs a large risk of having her children placed for adoption. Even setting aside the enormous human costs, the expense to the taxpayer of keeping one child in a group home can be $5,000 *per month*, above and beyond the costs of incarcerating the mother. For a mother with two children, this means that about $145,000 per year of taxpayer money is spent to keep a mother separated from her children.

Then there is the impact of our massive prison program on ethnic minorities. On September 1, 1992, the *Baltimore Evening Sun* shocked the country by reporting that on any given day "56 percent of Baltimore's black men between the ages of 18 and 35 were either in prison, on parole or probation, [or] being sought on arrest warrants or awaiting trial on an average day in 1991." The principal reason for this high rate of incarceration was the War on Drugs. In 1991, more than 11,000 of the approximately 13,000 people arrested for drug offenses in that city were black. For the same year, while only thirteen white juveniles were charged with drug sales, 1,304 black juveniles were charged with those offenses, up from only eighty-six in 1981.[71] Nationwide, 25 percent of black men in their twenties were in similar trouble with the law in 1990. That figure increased nationwide to 33 percent in 1995, or a total of about 827,440 young black men afoul of the law at some time during that year. The figure for Hispanic males was 12.3 percent, and for white males it was just under 7 percent.[72] In addition, this program of prosecution and incarceration has had the result of permanently

---

70. Religious News Service, "Remembering Mother's Day—Behind Bars," *Los Angeles Times*, May 7, 1994, Orange County ed.: B 11; Editorial, *Sacramento Bee*, "On Women—Too Many Moms Behind Bars," as quoted in *Los Angeles Daily Journal*, June 24, 1994: 6; Susan Howlett, "Women Behind Bars," *Los Angeles Times*, November 2, 1994, Orange County ed.: E1, 4.

71. Norris P. West, "Over Half of City's Young Black Men in Trouble," *Evening Sun*, September 1, 1992: 1A, 6A; Associated Press, "Baltimore Report Lambastes U.S. Drug War," *Washington Post*: 1.

72. Knight-Ridder Newspapers, "Study Details Black Incarceration," *Orange County Register*, October 5, 1995: 21.

disqualifying approximately 1.4 million black men from voting as a result of felony convictions. This is about 13 percent of the adult black males in our country.[73]

How has this happened? One of the reasons is that in many states, like Massachusetts, more than 84 percent of prisoners serving mandatory sentences for drug offenses are first-time offenders. Since most of those people are either blacks or Hispanics, and since the average mandatory minimum sentence for first-time drug offenders in Massachusetts is about five years, the drug laws result in hugely disproportionate numbers of minorities being incarcerated.[74]

Another more subtle impact this prison explosion has had, which I have seen a great deal from the bench, is that jail has lost its deterrent impact, especially for our youngsters. In fact, many of our young people think of jail as a rite of passage into manhood, since most of the people they know have served time. Even clothing fashions owe something to our criminal justice system. Take the example of the current youth fad of baggy clothes, which probably originated in our jails and prisons. Since administrators of these facilities want as few problems and as little bother as possible with inmates' clothing, it is much easier to give everyone oversized clothing, which all inmates can fit into, than to try and accommodate the different sizes of prisoners. So most jail-issue clothing is extra large. Young inmates became accustomed to baggy clothing and continue to wear it even after their release. Their peers on the outside start copying the look, and voilà, a new fashion trend. We can probably thank our nation's drug policy for the baggy, sloppy clothing favored by many young people today.

In 1994, the United States had as many drug offenders in prison as we had total prisoners for *all types of crimes* in 1970.[75] Based on calculations from federal government data, as of 1994 approximately one of every six federal prisoners—about 15,000 people—were incarcerated primarily for a marijuana offense.[76] For what purpose have we incarcerated such a huge number of our people for these drug offenses? Not to keep these drugs out of our communities. In fact, not only are we unable to keep these illicit substances out of our neighborhoods, we cannot

---

73. Tamar Lewin, "Crime Costs Many Black Men the Vote, Study Says," *New York Times*, October 23, 1998: A12.

74. Matthew Brelis, "A Big-Time Bust," *Boston Globe*, November 8, 1998: D1.

75. Eric Schlosser, "Marijuana and the Law," *Atlantic Monthly*, September, 1994: 84, 90.

76. Eric Schlosser, "Reefer Madness," *Atlantic Monthly*, August, 1994: 46.

even keep them out of our prisons.[77] Have we made drugs more difficult to obtain? No. Even though ever increasing amounts of tax monies are being spent on the eradication of various drugs both in our country and abroad, and even though virtually all of these efforts are increasingly successful, with more seizures, arrests, and convictions than ever, the price of illicit drugs like cocaine has declined considerably over the past decade. This, of course, means that the supply has *increased*.[78] What we in essence have attempted to do with our drug policy is to repeal the law of supply and demand. Not surprisingly, we have failed completely.[79]

---

77. Schlosser, "Marijuana and the Law," *supra*, at 92.

78. Kevin Jack Riley, *Snow Job? The War against International Cocaine Trafficking* (New Brunswick, N.J.: Transaction Publishers, 1996) 66–67. This RAND study traces source country cocaine-control policies and their effectiveness in reducing cocaine problems in the United States. Using many examples, Mr. Riley demonstrates that even though the United States spent more than $1 billion for eradication and crop substitution programs in the Andean countries from 1990 to 1994, market dynamics easily overcame these efforts, with the result that the supply and purity of cocaine in this country continued to increase and prices continued to fall.

79. For a thorough analysis of the effects of Drug Prohibition from an economic perspective, see Jeffrey A. Miron and Jeffrey Zwiebel, "The Economic Case against Drug Prohibition," *Journal of Economic Perspectives* 9, no. 4 (fall 1995): 175–92; and Riley, ibid.

2

Increased Harm to Communities

It is painfully obvious that our present approach to the drug scene is ineffective despite the billions of dollars that we have spent.
Judge Anthony A. Alaimo, United States District Court, Brunswick, Georgia

There once was a man on his deathbed who, at the very end of his life, called his wife to his side and said to her, "Dear, before I leave this earth, there is something that I really feel I have to tell you. For a number of years now, I have been having an affair with a particular woman who lives across the street. I do not mean to hurt your feelings, but I think you had a right to hear it, and hear it from me." The wife thought for a moment and then replied, "That's okay; I know. That's why I poisoned you."

In so many ways, we have been poisoning ourselves by the policy we have chosen to deal with the critical problem of drug use and abuse. As I have acknowledged, these drugs are certainly dangerous and harmful, but there are also separate and distinct harms that are directly caused by their prohibition. These additional harms might be tolerable if they actually stemmed the flow of drugs into our communities. But the opposite is true. Our drug laws have simply failed.

Communities Awash in Illicit Drugs

As a preface to my observations—which are purely my personal opinions—let me share two anecdotes.

I was formerly an Assistant United States Attorney in Dallas. In approximately 1971 an individual was arrested in Dallas in possession of approximately 20 pounds of cocaine. It was then the largest seizure of cocaine in this part of the country if not the entire United States. It was of such significance that the Attorney General, John N. Mitchell, *personally* monitored the investigation and prosecution of this case. Today, at least once a month seizures of this quantity of cocaine or more occur in Dallas.

I have served as a magistrate judge for more than 19 years. During that period I have issued hundreds of drug-offense search and arrest warrants. As a matter of personal curiosity I have asked the affiant DEA agents the question: "Are we winning the war on drugs?" To this date I have never received an affirmative response.

Magistrate Judge Wm. F. Sanderson, Jr., United States District Court, Dallas, Texas

A few years ago I received a letter from an elderly lady who first tried to assure me that she had never used any illicit drug but agreed that our laws were not working. She told me that she was an "activist" but that her issue was nuclear policy. For her opposition to nuclear policy she had been arrested on several occasions. She found it very discouraging to be in jail with women who were there for various drug-related offenses, because all they could talk about was their impatience to get out of custody so that they could go back to their drug-using lifestyle. All of the attempts by our drug laws to change the behavior of these women were simply a tremendous waste of time and money, she said, adding that she could not even take a shower in jail because there were so many women smoking marijuana in the shower stalls, and the guards did not even seem to care.

This is the reality we are facing. Under our current policy, drugs are everywhere. They have in fact become such a routine part of some people's lives that, for example, one woman in New Jersey came to court one day to enter a plea of "not guilty" to a prior drug possession charge. For some reason, the sheriff's deputy searched the woman while she was there, and found twenty-one bags of heroin and twenty-two bags of cocaine concealed in her wig and underwear.[1] Things like this probably happen frequently.

---

1. Associated Press, "Woman Hides Drugs in Wig," *Los Angeles Daily Journal*, July 21, 1999: 4.

Illicit drug use so permeates our country's prisons that General Barry McCaffrey, our nation's Drug Czar, said in February 1998 that "We've got 1.6 million men and women who are behind bars, and of that number—we just did a fairly widespread 1997 drug testing program—*some 9 percent tested positive for drugs behind bars*"[2] (emphasis added).

Even high security prisoners like Charles Manson are testing positive in prison for illicit drugs—in fact, Manson was transferred from one high security prison to another for being caught selling drugs to other inmates. But the money to be made by smuggling drugs into our prisons is simply more than many people can resist, and the arrests of prison guards for these offenses are unacceptably high. But given the amount of money to be made, the real surprise would be if large numbers of prison guards were *not* involved in this behavior.[3] Our laws are simply not deterring many people from a life of drug abuse and drug trafficking, and if we cannot even keep these drugs out of our prisons, how can we expect to keep them out of our communities?

The answer is that we cannot. Our current system is completely unable to keep illicit drugs out of our communities and away from our children. Even Joseph A. Califano, the former secretary of the U.S. Department of Health, Education and Welfare and the chairman of the Columbia University Center on Addiction and Substance Abuse was quoted as saying that "American children are telling us they are drenched in drugs." As shown in a recent nationwide survey by that same organization, "almost every American child—regardless of race, family structure or financial background—will be faced with the decision of whether to use illegal drugs before they graduate from high school." In addition, 58 percent of the eleventh and twelfth graders surveyed said that they had already been offered marijuana,[4] and a prior survey disclosed that 43 percent of all juvenile suspects booked into Juvenile Hall in California's Orange County had ingested some form of drug within three to five days of their arrest.[5] It is clear that any child of a mind to obtain illicit drugs can do so easily.

---

2. *New American*, February 16, 1998: 8.

3. See editorial, "Drugs in Prison," *Orange County Register*, January 13, 1999: Metro 6.

4. Andrea K. Walker, "Universal Drug Problem Haunts Children in U.S.," *Orange County Register*, July 18, 1995: A1.

5. Tony Saavedra, "Juvenile Hall Testing Finds Drugs in 43%," *Orange County Register*, March 27, 1993: B1.

Conduct your own informal survey. Ask your local high school or junior college students and they will tell you the same thing they tell me: that it is easier for our children and underage adults to get illicit drugs than it is for them to get alcohol. Certainly, as minors, they can get alcohol; but it takes some ingenuity and effort. But illicit drugs find our children without much effort on their behalf, because someone else has a profit motive to furnish them. When was the last time you heard of someone offering a student a free sample of alcohol on a high school campus? It does not happen because there is no illegal profit in it. But when was the last time our students were offered a free sample of marijuana, methamphetamines, or cocaine? It happens all the time, because of the money—the huge profits to be made by getting all of us and our children hooked on illicit drugs. We inflict this problem on ourselves by our current policy of Drug Prohibition.

The major reason, then, why our society is awash in illicit drugs is the unbelievable profits that can be realized in their being manufactured and sold. The drugs themselves are harmful, but what is really bringing us down is the money. It bears repeating that as long as the demand exists, it will be met. We have been and will always be totally unsuccessful in our attempts to repeal the law of supply and demand. We might as well attempt to repeal the law of gravity. The situation is similar to that of a man standing under a waterfall with a bucket: he can fill up lots of buckets, but he can do nothing to shut off the flow. Every time you see a report that a ton, or ten tons, or a hundred tons of cocaine have been seized by law enforcement officials, see it for what it is. It is not a victory but merely a symptom of the depth of the problem.

If you are not yet convinced, consider the following (unsolicited) column by U.S. Magistrate Judge Volney V. Brown, retired, published on September 10, 1996, in the *Orange County Register* in response to criticism I received after publishing an "Open Letter" to our nation's Drug Czar on August 12:

> In his open letter to the *Register* of Aug. 12, Superior Court Judge James Gray observed that drug law enforcement has been unable to stop the flow of street drugs....
>
> Well, I have fought the drug wars, and I am coming out of retirement to say that Judge Gray is right. What is wrong with drug law enforcement is that it has never worked, and it never will.
>
> In his first term, President Richard Nixon declared war on illicit drugs, particularly heroin, and sharply increased drug law enforcement. He directed Attorney General Richard Kleindeinst to create a new entity, patterned on

the Organized Crime Strike Forces, named Office for Drug Abuse Law Enforcement [ODALE]. . . .

ODALE greatly supplemented the efforts of existing federal, state, and local drug law enforcement agencies so that illicit drug sales could be ended once and for all. Because of my earlier experience as a federal prosecutor, I was recruited out of private law practice as ODALE regional director for California, Arizona, and Nevada. I established offices at San Francisco, Los Angeles, San Diego, and Phoenix (each headed by a tough drug prosecutor), with a combined staff of some 150 attorneys, drug agents, and support personnel.

We decided to test the effectiveness of simultaneously arresting every drug seller on the streets of an isolated city, and picked Phoenix for the exercise. Using more "buy money" than Arizona had ever seen before, we bought into each street dealer we could find, two or three times each. It turned out that Phoenix had 76 drug pushers. In the middle of a weeknight, with the help of state and local police, we arrested all 76 at the same time.

For a week it was impossible to buy drugs on the streets of Phoenix. The single local drug treatment program was swamped. Addicts who could not get treatment left town to score elsewhere. But on the eighth day, new street pushers began to appear in the city, and before a month had elapsed, it was business-as-usual. We had spent tens of thousands of federal tax dollars, and sent scores of pushers to prison, but there was no lasting effect on the availability or price of illicit drugs.

So, in San Diego, we tried another trick. We in ODALE learned that virtually all of the heroin there was being sold by a known gang. State and local police had been unable to bust the gang because the only really effective investigative tool—a court-ordered wire tap—was prohibited by California law.

Because our federal program was not inhibited by state law, our in-house lawyers applied for and obtained a federal wire tap order. After thousands of employee hours at a command center manned around the clock, we arrested all 39 members of the drug gang.

For a week it was impossible to buy heroin on the streets of San Diego. But on the eighth day new street pushers began to appear in the city, and before a month had elapsed it was business-as-usual.

We had spent hundreds of thousands of federal tax dollars, and we sent every one of the 39 pushers to federal prison, but there was no lasting effect on the availability of heroin or its price. In one respect we were worse off for our success. Before, we knew who was selling, but afterwards we had no idea.

The ODALE program did not survive the resignation of its presidential creator and patron. But in the 18 months permitted us, my 150 people identified, investigated, indicted, prosecuted, convicted and sent off to the penitentiary more than 1,100 drug dealers. We led all other ODALE regions. We were, as we remain, proud of ourselves.

But in the end, in our territory it was not more difficult or more expensive to obtain illegal drugs than it was in the beginning. We had failed to solve, or even affect, the "drug problem" with law enforcement. If we had been given 10 or 20 times the resources, we still would have failed.

I have learned from experience that there is no practical level of law enforcement that will prevent people from using the narcotics and dangerous drugs they wish to use. Judge Gray is right. We need to consider alternatives to the mindless repetition of useless and expensive drug law enforcement efforts.

I know because I have been there.[6]

If you are still not convinced, then read *Blow*, by Bruce Porter, or *The Cocaine Kids: The Inside Story of a Teenage Drug Ring*, by Terry Williams.[7] These books show graphically how our drug policy has made a mockery of the old saying "crime doesn't pay." In the sale of illicit drugs, crime pays very well indeed. Bruce Porter tells the true story of a "high-end" drug trafficker, a young man who dropped out of college and began smuggling marijuana by flying it from Mexico to the numerous dry lake beds of Southern California. When he was arrested, convicted, and sent to federal prison, this fellow described the result as the best thing that had ever happened to him. The reason: he made such good connections in this "school for scoundrels" that when he was released, he broke parole and hooked up with Carlos Lehder and Pablo Escobar of the Medillin Cartel in Colombia and began smuggling tons of cocaine into the United States. His first "shakedown" flight earned him $300,000, and soon he was clearing about $500,000 each week. Before he was arrested again, this drug smuggler had made about $100 million.

Terry Williams gives just as discouraging an account of drug sales at the low end of the drug-selling scale. He wrote his book after spending about two hours per day for three days a week from 1982 to 1986 with eight young cocaine dealers in the Bronx, Harlem, and Washington Heights areas of New York City. In the world of these young drug dealers, "Everybody has a girl. Everybody has cocaine. Everybody has a gun."[8] These young people got involved in this "business" as a result of the tough "Rockefeller drug laws," which required prison sentences for anyone over eighteen who was in possession of illicit drugs. In response dealers naturally started hiring juveniles to act as lookouts or runners in transporting the drugs. They soon found that not only were the youngsters trustworthy, they were also easy to frighten and control.

---

6. U.S. Magistrate Judge Volney V. Brown, Jr., retired, "A View from the Front Lines of the Drug War," *Orange County Register*, September 10, 1996: Metro 6.

7. Bruce Porter, *Blow* (New York: Harper Paperbacks, 1993), and Terry Williams, *The Cocaine Kids: The Inside Story of a Teenage Drug Ring* (Reading, Mass.: Addison-Wesley, 1989).

8. Williams, *supra*, at 1.

Over the years, the teenagers that Williams observed evolved into sophisticated drug distributors, both at the wholesale and retail level, which enabled them to make, as they called it, "crazy money" in a society in which they had very few alternatives. And who were their natural customers? Other young people—both as consumers and as people who could also be lured into making money at the same business. The individual lives of these youngsters became a wreck; but by the time they were arrested or died, their dirty business was continued through their recruits. We have here another demonstrable proof that the mixture of "get-tough" drug laws and the law of supply and demand are a destructive and in many cases lethal combination. These sobering stories, at both the high end and the low end of drug trafficking, are being repeated each day throughout this country and the world.

This corruption of our young people is brought about directly by our policy of Drug Prohibition. Every time the penalties for selling drugs are raised, adult drug traffickers have an extra incentive to recruit children for their drug transactions. Many young people are naively willing to take risks for a few hundred dollars, and juveniles are punished much less severely by the criminal justice system. To combat this situation, law enforcement in many jurisdictions has recruited juveniles to act as confidential informants in adult drug transactions. Tragically, some of these recruited juveniles have been killed by drug traffickers when their work for the police was discovered.[9]

This tragic result is being replicated in Mexico, where drug traffickers are recruiting children to smuggle drugs across our border. The number of children under sixteen arrested at the El Paso border rose from 63 in 1997 to 148 in 1999, and in the first seven months of 2000, 721 of these youngsters had been arrested along the Mexican border, up from 500 for the entire year of 1997. One of them was the fourteen-year-old daughter of an architect, who was promised $500 for smuggling 250 pounds of marijuana in a stranger's car. Some of the arrested drug smugglers were as young as nine.[10]

It is also ironic that law enforcement laboratories in several jurisdictions have actually produced crack cocaine for use in "sting" operations.

---

9. Stuart Pfeifer, "Slain Teen Informant's Family Sues Brea Police," *Orange County Register*, August 15, 1998; Matthew Heller, "Snitch Jr.," *California Lawyer*, April 2000, 44–48, 86.

10. Esther Schrader, "Smugglers' Youth Ends at Border," *Los Angeles Times*, August 9, 2000, Orange County ed., A1, 20.

Not only has our tax money been used to manufacture dangerous illicit drugs, but sometimes the police lost possession of the crack, and it ended up being sold and used on the streets.[11]

A further unintended consequence of our drug policy is that the potency of the illicit street drugs increases as a direct result of the drugs' illegal status. It is a cardinal rule of prohibition that illegal sellers will concentrate on the more potent substances, just as was the case with the prohibition of alcohol. Since the punitive risk was the same for selling whiskey or beer, bootleggers sold the stronger stuff because they could make a lot more money that way. We still see this today. Drug dealers either try to push people, including children, into harder drugs like methamphetamines or cocaine so that they can make more money, or, if the users prefer marijuana, the dealers try to sell them more potent varieties. For this reason the marijuana on the streets today is almost always much stronger than it was only ten years ago.

The same phenomenon can be seen in a slightly different context when college students attend football games. Whereas students normally drink more beer than hard liquor, prohibitions on alcohol at games convert the students into whiskey drinkers, since a flask of whiskey is easier to conceal than a six-pack of beer. Far from protecting or shielding our children from drugs and the destructive lifestyle they can bring, our country's drug policy is literally recruiting them to it. If we want to show our concern for the safety and future of our children, we will "Just Say No" to our nation's failed drug policy.

Sadly, it is a fact of life that if people really want a product, even a dangerous, self-destructive one, they will find a way to get it—and other people will find a way to supply them. Even if the government were somehow temporarily successful in making a popular drug unavailable, users would simply switch to something different. Junior high school students who have trouble finding marijuana or cocaine often inhale glue, paints, cleaning solvents, or even gasoline. Even though these are terribly dangerous substances that can cause brain damage or even death, society could never outlaw these products, nor would it try. The effective answer lies elsewhere: in education, treatment, access to the medical community, and individual responsibility.

---

11. "The War on Drugs—Are Our Rights on the Line?" *USA Today*, November 15, 1989: A1; Ken Ellingwood, "Police Abandon Drug-Making Sting Operation," *Los Angeles Times*, August 23, 1995, Orange County ed.: B1; Lee Romney and Kevin Johnson, "O.C. Making Drugs for Officers to Sell," *Los Angeles Times*, October 20, 1994, Orange County ed.: A1, 16.

We should not be surprised that our attempts to reduce the supply of illegal drugs have failed miserably. To begin with, we have been totally unsuccessful in our attempts to convince poor peasants around the world that *not* growing or producing their most profitable crop or product is good for them. U.S. government agents have gone all over the world with carrots and sticks, trying to persuade peasants not to grow these substances. We have tried crop substitution programs that offer money to people to switch crops. We have tried crop eradication programs in which U.S. agents with guns and helicopters have descended and uprooted, burned, and sprayed defoliants on peasants' crops, a strategy that has yielded only long-term environmental problems and an intense hatred of the United States.[12] Indeed, the scenario in Tom Clancy's thriller, *Clear and Present Danger*, in which the United States government covertly fields combat troops in Latin America to target drug lords and shoot down their airplanes as they smuggle drugs into the United States, is just one desperate but short step beyond our current policy—particularly considering United States involvement in the ongoing civil war in Colombia.[13]

But none of these efforts have accomplished anything—other than wasting our tax money. Even for peasants who do want to move away from their most profitable crop, the economic obstacles are simply too formidable. For example, when an Afghanistan refugee was interviewed in 1993 about the future plans of his people, he said realistically that with his country's small agricultural and industrial base in ruins, most of those returning home would turn to selling either drugs or guns. "Most will plant poppies. When I go back, I will too. What else can I do? I am a teacher, but there are no schools. No factories. No work. No irrigation. How can we eat?"[14] Since that time, thanks to economic realities and bumper poppy crops, Afghanistan has become one of the world's leaders in the production of opium, which is used to produce heroin, and is mainly sold in Pakistan, Iran, Central Asia, Russia, and most of Europe.[15]

This fact of life was brought home to Juan R. Torruella, Chief Judge of the U.S. Court of Appeals in San Juan, Puerto Rico, a few years ago.

---

12. See Kevin Jack Riley, *Snow Job? The War against International Cocaine Trafficking* (New Brunswick, N.J.: Transaction Publishers, 1996).

13. Tom Clancy, *Clear and Present Danger* (New York: Berkley Books, 1990).

14. Dirk Chase Eldredge, *Ending the War on Drugs, A Solution for America* (Bridgehampton, NY: Bridge Works Publishing, 1998), 158.

15. Jeffrey Bartholet and Steve LeVine, "The Holy Men of Heroin," *Newsweek*, December 6, 1999: 40–42.

He spoke of his experience in a lecture at Colby College in Waterville, Maine, on April 25, 1996:

> The fact of the matter is that my personal views on this subject have changed over my years on the bench, and they have changed dramatically. This has happened gradually, but if I were to pick a point in time when this process started, I could tell you it was towards the end of my district court tenure, and perhaps even more specifically, as a result of a trip that I took to El Salvador in the mid '80s, sponsored by the State Department, to speak to the Salvadoran judiciary and bar regarding the American legal system. . . .
>
> I was speaking to a bar group in one of the smaller cities. Somehow the discussion got around to issues related to drug enforcement. I expounded, I suspect somewhat long-windedly, my views to the effect that the United States needed the cooperation of Latin America in stopping the drug traffic by stricter enforcement, by stopping corruption, by eradicating the illegal crops, etc., etc. The audience was very polite, in fact one or two of those present may have actually clapped when I finished. A hand was then raised in the back of the room. The speaker identified himself as a lawyer, who said to me very deferentially, "Honorable Judge, we very much appreciate your presence and the advice you have given us, but don't you think the United States could help us in solving this problem?" I answered that as I understood the situation we were already sending considerable sums in aid, and that we had a lot of resources committed to the interdiction of drugs from Latin America and prosecution of violators. To which he responded, "Excuse me your Honor, that is not the help we are in need of. What we need is for your country to stop consuming these drugs. If your people were not buying drugs, we would not be growing and selling them. We would rather sell you coffee, or oranges, or bananas, if you would only stop buying and consuming drugs." At first glance this is a rather trite, and perhaps insignificant interchange, but it *hit* me like a sledgehammer between the eyes, and brought home what I had already suspected, that there might be something fundamentally wrong with our traditional approach to the drug problem in the United States.[16]

Judge Nancy Gertner of the U.S. District Court in Boston said the same thing in different words in a speech she gave on January 29, 1998:

> The reading that I've done suggests that, in fact, what we have done, the commentator said, is created price support for the drug industry. By attempting to restrict the supply, we have increased the profits and therefore created enormous incentives for people to continue this business no matter what. And in fact as one described it, if the cocaine industry had commissioned a consultant to design a mechanism to insure profitability, it couldn't have done

---

16. Chief Judge Juan R. Torruella, U.S. Court of Appeals for the First Circuit, "One Judge's Attempt at a Rational Discussion of the So-Called 'War on Drugs,'" unpublished manuscript of the Spotlight Lecture at Colby College, Waterville, Maine, April 25, 1996, at 3.

better than the war on drugs. There's just enough pressure to inflate prices but not enough to keep the product from the market. So this is enormously profitable. And another commentator described what he dubbed the Hydra Effect, which means drugs are so profitable and so cheap to produce that even if you begin to cut off the supply in one part of the world, it simply rears its head in another part of the world.[17]

Many other judges have made similar comments, but I will include just one more that was sent to me by Justice William E. Hunt of the Montana Supreme Court in Helena: "From the appeals I do see involving drugs, I can only conclude that the war is a failure because so many people are willing to risk so much to be able to sell the drugs. The people who come before our courts are often those who have been there before and received sentences that serve no purpose at all so far as deterring them from future sales."

So we are left with the economic reality that we could actually "bulldoze" places like Colombia, Peru, Bolivia, and many more countries as well if we wanted to, and it would not make more than a temporary difference in our domestic drug problem. Why? Because if the demand is here, the demand will be met—or, as one peasant farmer would put it, "If people will buy it, we will sell it." Even if these South American countries ceased to exist, the demand here would be met by other drug lords in Afghanistan, Thailand, Nigeria, Mexico, Caribbean countries like Haiti and Jamaica, or virtually any other developing country, or even from inside the United States itself. The artificially high profits caused by our policies of Drug Prohibition will ensure a continuing supply of illicit drugs to everyone who wants them. All a person is required to do to increase the value of $100 worth of cocaine in Colombia is to transport it to any city in the United States, where it would be worth between $5,000 and $10,000.[18] Police and military forces in a free society are helpless effectively to counteract economic forces of that magnitude.

In some ways this is just as well, because the biggest nightmare we could inflict upon ourselves would all of a sudden to be *successful* in closing off our borders to the importation of these substances. Why? Because if the demand is here, the demand will be met. The demand could and

---

17. Judge Nancy Gertner, U.S. District Court, Boston, Massachusetts, at a January 29, 1998, Voluntary Committee of Lawyers, Inc. forum in Boston, entitled "Is the Drug War Forever?" See <http://www.november.org>.

18. Eva Bertram and Kenneth Sharpe, "Surefire Way to Lose Drug War," *Chicago Tribune*, September 17, 1996: 13.

would be met by someone with a high school background in chemistry, who would manufacture synthetic or designer drugs in his kitchen, bathroom, or garage. Such people could make a lot of money this way—they already are. In one night's work in a makeshift lab, a person can make $2.5 million worth of methamphetamine, also known as "crank" or "speed," which is marketed as a bargain substitute drug for cocaine.[19] And where the ingredients used to manufacture methamphetamines, such as ammonia, are restricted in an attempt to limit their availability, the dealers simply steal them. With ammonia, this is often accomplished by breaking open the valves of commercial storage tanks and putting the toxic gas into propane tanks, which were never meant to be used for this purpose. All of this results in enormous increased dangers to the community at large of explosions and poisoning.

Why would this be such a major disaster? Because for all that substances like heroin and cocaine are dangerous, at least they are natural crops that have at least some quality control. Synthetic drugs like methamphetamines, PCP, "Cat," "Ice," and so on are even more harmful than the natural substances, and have almost no quality control whatsoever.

This is an enormously serious problem in the United States. In only the first half of 1999, the federal government reported that law enforcement authorities had already seized 238 methamphetamine or "speed" labs in Kansas, 242 in Iowa, and 223 in Missouri, and were expected to seize about 500 in the state of Washington before the end of the year. The nation's Drug Czar, General Barry McCaffrey, was quoted as saying that "We do not just have a national drug problem. What we really have is a series of local drug epidemics."[20] In truth, what is actually being said is that in the War on Drugs, victory is literally being defined as simply slowing down the pace of defeat.

Other countries, like Japan, also have a serious problem with methamphetamines. The roots of the problem in Japan go back to World War II, when this drug was often given to soldiers before they were sent into battle. When the war ended, the remaining stockpiles of the drug illegally found their way into civilian markets. Estimates are that about

---

19. Mark Arax and Tom Gorman, "The State's Illicit Farm Belt Export," *Los Angeles Times*, March 13, 1995, Orange County ed.: Al, 16–17.

20. Associated Press, "Drug War Now Many Local Battles," *San Francisco Chronicle*, December 16, 1999: A9.

2.2 million people in Japan now use about eighteen tons of "speed" each year. And since there is a demand for that drug in Japan, Asian countries like China, Thailand, and North Korea are hastening to satisfy it. Just as in the United States, in spite of increased efforts at interdiction, Japanese police estimate that they seize only about 10 percent of the drugs.[21] And, just like in the United States, Japan is awash in drugs.

Generally a bad batch of synthetic drugs is discovered only when a customer ingests some of it and has an adverse reaction, which is frequently serious and sometimes fatal. There is the story, for example, of a man from Goddard, Kansas, a high school dropout who manufactured an artificial form of heroin called fentanyl. This injectable drug was so strong that it could kill users before they even had time to withdraw the needles from their arms, and it was so lethal that in its pure form it could kill in dosages as small as three grains of salt. This man, who wanted to be known as a "drug wizard," was finally arrested by federal agents, but only after 126 drug users in New York and other cities on the eastern seaboard had turned up dead with traces of fentanyl in their blood.[22] Similar disasters occurred in Howard County, Maryland, where a potent synthetic narcotic killed 27 people before the people responsible could be found and arrested.[23]

But, for all of our efforts, we are really in no danger of closing off our borders and keeping the natural substances out. Anyone who has ever visited any of our large seaports, each of which handles tens of thousands of large shipping containers, realizes there is no practical way that the U.S. Customs Service or any other agency can inspect even a small percentage of all of the materials coming through these facilities, particularly with the recent implementation of the North American Free Trade Association (NAFTA). And that is not even taking into account all of the legal and illegal border crossing zones by air, land, and sea between our country and Mexico, as well as various legitimate mail and package services. These illicit drugs not only enter our country smuggled in legitimate and illegitimate shipments, or taped to

---

21. Mark Magnier, "Japanese on a Fast Track to Addiction," *Los Angeles Times*, March 25, 2000, Orange County ed.: A2.

22. John McCormick and Paul O'Donnell, "Drug Wizard of Wichita," *Newsweek*, June 21, 1993: 32.

23. Paul W. Valentine, "Ring Dealing in Deadly Drug Broken Up, Md. Officials Say," *Washington Post*, May 5, 1992: D9.

the bodies of people walking across the borders—some enter our country ingeniously hidden in cans of cling peaches or inside shipments of concrete pipes. We even had a seizure in southern California of some dog cages that were made out of fiberglass mixed with cocaine. Once the cages had entered the United States, the smugglers simply melted down the cages to extract the cocaine. If the demand is here, the demand will be met.

Other grounds for legitimate pessimism were discovered by government authorities at the end of 1999, when they finally realized that Colombia and other drug-producing nations had been harvesting a new high-yield variety of coca bush. As a result, "one senior law-enforcement official who asked not to be identified" acknowledged that the official estimates of cocaine production in Colombia alone have been about three times too low.[24] This made big headlines in the newspaper, and resulted in more pictures of General McCaffrey being published, but unfortunately this critical revelation has not had any apparent effect on U.S. drug policy.

To some degree, the cause of the use of illicit drugs by our children has to be the glamour that naturally attaches for some people *because* something is illegal. Although it is clear that our drug laws do have a deterrent effect for some people, it is equally clear that some of them, particularly our young people, use illicit drugs because this is an expression of rebellion or independence, or because of the extra glamour associated with "forbidden fruit." Also, of course, many of our young people join street gangs that sell drugs so that they too can be a "part of the action."

Back in my days as an Assistant U.S. Attorney in Los Angeles, our office prosecuted a recently retired, middle-level executive from a local public utilities company for attempting to smuggle several ounces of cocaine through the Los Angeles International Airport in his underwear. When he was about to come through customs, the man got nervous and attempted to hide behind a six-inch heating pipe. Because he called attention to himself, he was taken to a secondary inspection station, searched, and arrested. When questioned, he confessed immediately, stating that he really did not have enough money saved for retirement and so had decided to go to Colombia and bring in some drugs, just once, in order to set himself up financially.

---

24. Eric Lichtblau and Esther Schrader, "More Drugs Flow Into U.S. Than Estimated," *Los Angeles Times*, November 14, 1999: A1, 26, 28.

This man did not even live or work in close proximity to the temptations of the big money to be made in drugs. For people who do, the problem is even worse. Consider the arrests of a ring of fifty-nine American Airlines employees and food service workers at the Miami Airport in August 1999 for alleged drug smuggling.[25] Or the arrest of twenty-two Federal Express drivers, customer service representatives, and security agents in April 2000 for allegedly accepting bribes from a Jamaican drug lord to ship more than 121 tons of marijuana all over the country.[26] Temptation proved to be too much for these people.

Or take the situation involving the wife of a U.S. Army colonel who was the commanding officer of two hundred U.S. soldiers advising the Colombian military on counter-narcotics programs. This lady, a cocaine addict, was convicted and sentenced to five years in prison for smuggling six packages containing 2.6 pounds of cocaine each and worth about $30,000 apiece at the wholesale level, by mailing them to a friend in New York through the Air Force Postal Service. In addition, her husband, the commanding officer, pleaded guilty to a charge of money laundering and was sentenced to five months in federal prison for having continued to spend the money his wife had made from the drug sales even after he was aware of his wife's offenses.[27] The lure of easy money can strike anyone, anywhere, even the seventeen-year-old son of the cabinet minister responsible for law enforcement in Great Britain, who was arrested for selling hashish to a newspaper reporter.[28]

By no means is corruption like this limited solely to illegal drugs, of course. When I was assigned as a staff judge advocate to the U.S. Naval Air Station in Guam in the 1970s, I heard of a navy captain who was returning home from Guam to retire. Because the price of alcohol was so ridiculously low on the base in Guam, he gave in to temptation and

---

25. Mike Clary, "59 Workers Indicted in Drug Sting at Airport," *Los Angeles Times*, August 26, 1999, Orange County ed.: A1; David Kidwell, "Miami Sting a Tale of Corruption," *Orange County Register*, August 30, 1999: News 1, 6–7.

26. Esther Schrader, "22 FedEx Workers Arrested in L.A.-Based Marijuana Ring," *Los Angeles Times*, April 14, 2000: A19.

27. Norman Kempster, "U.S. Commander's Wife Arrested in Drug Case," *Los Angeles Times*, August 7, 1999, Orange County ed.: A1, 19; Associated Press, "Army Colonel's Wife Sent to Prison," *Los Angeles Daily Journal*, May 8, 2000: 4; Chronicle News Service, "Drug-War Leader Gets Jail Time for 'Betrayal of Trust,'" *San Francisco Chronicle*, July 14, 2000: A7.

28. Times Wire Reports, "Drug Suspect's Father Is Cabinet Minister," *Los Angeles Times*, January 3, 1998, Orange County ed.: A8.

filled his piano with bottles of booze and shipped them home with his personal effects. This was, of course, a violation of U.S. customs laws, and he was court-martialed and reduced in rank to a commander. We are all human, and when faced with such temptations, we sometimes succumb. And in this, we all should clearly be held accountable for our actions. But—at least with regard to our drug policy—wouldn't it be better to implement a policy that did not present such overwhelming and frequent temptations for corruption?

I once heard a story about forty prisoners who had been convicted of drug offenses were sitting around in a federal prison in California one evening, when the subject of "chickens" and "tickets" came up. In the jargon of drug dealers, a chicken is a kilogram of cocaine, and a ticket is a million dollars. One of them presented the question, "If after you served your time, you had a drug-dealer uncle who had decided that he no longer wanted to stay in the business, and he said he would give you 150 chickens which were worth three tickets, would you take them?" According to one of the prisoners present, who told me this story, thirty-seven of the forty said they would do it. There are simply too many "tickets" to be made in drug dealing for deterrence to work. The present situation is hopeless. Our communities are awash with illicit drugs, and things will simply never get any better under our current policy.

If the allure of these drug profits is so tempting that it corrupts even retired executives from our public utility companies, workers in our airports, and wives of our military officers, much less people who have already been convicted and served prison sentences for past drug violations, how will we ever control this problem? The answer is that in a free society we cannot. So ask yourself this question: if you had a roof that was keeping out only 10 percent of the rain (just as we are seizing only 10 percent—at most—of all illicit drugs in this country), wouldn't you decide to get a new roof? Wouldn't you call a different contractor? The drug situation is no different.

Has our new technology been able to overcome these basic problems? No, even our "high-tech" efforts to interdict the drugs being smuggled into this country are ineffective. From land, sea, air, and outer space, government agencies spend literally billions of our tax dollars in an effort to track and intercept illegal drugs. For example, the Relocatable Over the Horizon Radar (ROTHR) project, a radar system designed to detect potential drug smuggling airplanes along the 2,000-mile border with Mexico (at the cost of about $150 million to install and $1,500 per hour to run), was found to have a huge blind spot over northern and central Mexico. With some simple electronics gear, the pilots of the smuggling aircraft easily located these holes and went right through them without being detected.[29]

Similarly, the Customs Department had plans to purchase ten "backscatter" X-ray machines for about $38 million and use them to hunt for drugs in hidden compartments in vehicles coming across the border. These machines had been designed with Pentagon technology to detect Soviet missile warheads in trucks. Unfortunately, they were not powerful enough to see inside densely packed cargo. When drug smugglers made this discovery, they quickly adjusted their smuggling techniques and the expensive new machines were rendered ineffective.[30]

As evidence of the futility of our current efforts mounts, more and more law enforcement officials are privately and even publicly calling for a change. The authors of a news article reporting on these high-tech failures, for example, quoted a "longtime agent" of the Drug Enforcement Administration, who cited his agency's own widely published statistics about the flow of cocaine into the United States and stated, "The military is saying, 'Stop the flow of drugs.' But if 70% [of the cocaine] goes through Mexico and 95% of that gets through [to the United States], then stopping the flow is a failure. The more we seize, the more they produce—further evidence that the flow policy is a bust. In 30 years of anti-drug work, I can tell you that law enforcement is not the answer. You've got to reduce the demand. [If not], we [the DEA] will always have job security."[31]

In the meantime, the pervasive problems caused by the use and abuse of illicit drugs, and our efforts to combat these problems through the criminal justice system, continue unabated. As evidence of how widespread the problem is, in 1994, the United States Ninth Circuit Court of Appeals cited uncontradicted evidence presented in a money forfeiture trial that 75 percent of all currency in circulation in the Los Angeles area contained at least traces of cocaine or other illicit substances. The evidence disclosed that the percentage of drug-contaminated bills nationwide ranged from a low of 15 percent in Bozeman, Montana, to

---

29. Mark Fineman and Craig Pyes, "Cocaine Traffic to U.S. Finds Holes in High-Tech 'Fence,'" *Los Angeles Times*, June 9, 1996, Orange County ed.: A1, 8–9.
30. Ibid.
31. Ibid.

a high of 75 percent in Los Angeles and Las Vegas. Other researchers had found that of 135 bills gathered at random from cities around the country, all but four tested positive for traces of cocaine. The case was therefore dismissed by the appellate court, which said that based on this evidence "virtually everyone in Los Angeles is conceivably at risk of being barked at by drug-sniffing police dogs."[32]

The harmful effects of the enormous profits from illicit drugs are also spreading to smaller population centers around the country. Several years ago, the town of Yakima, Washington, became the heroin and cocaine trafficking capital of the Pacific Northwest, with all of the accompanying crime and violence. As a result, from 1984 to 1988 drug arrests increased from under three hundred to more than seven hundred, which quickly put the new county jail 30 percent over capacity, and the 1984 total of nine murders tripled to twenty-eight by 1988.[33] In Madison, Wisconsin, the purity of the heroin on the streets increased from around 3 or 4 percent during the 1970s and 1980s to about 35 percent in 1993. The DEA reports that the price of heroin has gone from an average of $3.90 per milligram in 1980 to 96 cents per milligram in early 2000. And even with this considerable drop in price, the purity of the heroin increased more than tenfold. This increase in strength, of course, has also increased the number of deaths by overdose.[34]

Small rural areas have also felt the effects of the profit motive for the sale of illicit drugs. In fact, a private study released in January 2000 said that young people in small-town and rural America are actually more likely to have used illicit drugs than their peers in the cities.[35] Long ago, Jamaican drug traffickers, Colombians, the Crips, the Bloods, and various biker gangs branched out their operations to include small towns in states like West Virginia, Iowa, Minnesota, and Oregon. Cocaine, LSD, and even crack cocaine became available to anyone who really wanted them, and undercover drug purchases were being made in towns with

---

32. Alan Abrahamson, "Drug Traces on Most Cash Voids Trafficking Case," *Los Angeles Times*, November 13, 1994, Orange County ed.: B13, 16.

33. Nicholas K. Geranios, "Quiet Town on Front Line of the Drug War," *Los Angeles Daily Journal*, March 8, 1990.

34. Jeff Richgels, "Powerful Heroin on Streets Here Causing Alarm," *Capital Times*, (Madison, Wisc.), August 20, 1993: 1A; Dena Bunis, "Drugs Happen Here, Too," *Orange County Register* May 10, 2000: News 1, 8.

35. Associated Press, "Rural Youth More Likely To Use Drugs," *San Francisco Chronicle*, January 27, 2000: A4.

populations as small as fifty. One federal prosecutor told the story of a pig farmer near Strawberry Point, Iowa, who was cited for a drug offense and attempted to flee with "his overalls in one hand [and] a kilo of cocaine in another arm." To compound the difficulties, it is harder in rural areas to uncover methamphetamine laboratories, which emit a cat-urine stench. The smell is not such a problem out in wooded areas, and the remoteness makes it easier for the operators to dump the toxic chem-icals on the ground and in streams—which also creates environmental hazards—without being detected.[36] About a year before I came out pub-licly in favor of investigating our drug policy options, I happened to be traveling on an airplane, and began talking to the woman sitting next to me. Since we had some time on our hands, I gave to her a copy of an outline I had prepared about problems with the "War on Drugs" and asked her if she would mind reading it and sharing her thoughts with me. After she read it she said that she agreed we had to change our approach and asked if I had heard about the problems they were having in her little town of Truckee, California. I had not. She told me that the town was suffering economically and that many of its folks had begun raising marijuana in their basements using heat lamps and hydroponics, and then selling their crops in order to get by. Unfortunately, many of these people had turned to violence, either in order to protect their own marijuana from theft or to muscle out the competition. The ease of growing the crop and the economic depression in the area, combined with the large-scale profits to be made, were undercutting the peace and stability of her small town. Wouldn't it be great, she said, if we could somehow do away with this huge economic incentive to violate the laws.

The only way this woman's hopes will possibly be realized is some-how to take the profit out of these drugs—to "de-profitize" them. Other-wise they will either be smuggled into the country or, as in Truckee, they will be grown here, both in large cities and small towns, in wealthy neighborhoods and poor ones, with all of the accompanying violence, crime, and corruption.[37] It is not only marijuana that will be grown here. For years the federal government has been trying to maintain the

---

36. Associated Press, "Not a Big City Business Anymore," *Los Angeles Daily Journal*, March 14, 1989, sec. 2: 1.

37. See Steven Pearlstein, "Marijuana Being Farmed in Vancouver's Best Neighborhoods," *San Francisco Chronicle*, May 13, 2000: C1, which described occasions on which violent gangs took over houses and planted, harvested, and sold large quantities of marijuana in very upscale neighborhoods.

fiction that opium poppies can be grown only in other countries, but this is simply not the case. As a gardener and editor-at-large of *Harper's Magazine* discovered, the seeds for opium poppies are easily available in at least half a dozen popular seed catalogs, including the breadseed poppy (*Papaver paconiflorum* and *Papaver somniferum*). In order to see if they would grow in cold climates like New England's, the editor ordered some and planted them in his own garden one summer. They grew beautifully.

In the April 1997 edition of *Harper's*, he described watching his poppies grow, harvesting them, brewing tea, and even slitting the bulbs in order to "milk" them for raw opium. He also recounted his adventures with the "poppy police," and passed along lessons he learned along the way, such as "that preparations made from opium were as common in the Victorian medicine cabinet as aspirin is in ours," and that similar poppies had been growing in the gardens of Thomas Jefferson's Monticello until the DEA ordered them uprooted. He concluded with the statement that he had found the U.S. government to be as concerned with people *writing* about poppies as *growing* them, and warned his readers about the threat to our Bill of Rights protections, both in the area of search and seizure and freedom of speech.[38] The point is that it is simply not possible to keep these dangerous drugs out of our communities, and our ineffective attempts to do so result in some very silly but also subversive results. So long as we pursue the failed policies of the past, the situation will never improve. It is time we confronted this truth and started taking positive steps to reduce both the devastating collateral harms of Drug Prohibition and the devastating effects of illegal drugs on our communities.

Stories about the terrible consequences of our drug policies are in the news every day. One that symbolizes the depth of the problem was set forth in a letter to the editor in a 1993 edition of the *Los Angeles Times*. It was written by a man who had watched a woman run out of her house by neighborhood drug dealers who had thrown a Molotov cocktail through her window. This woman had appeared anonymously on television to make a desperate plea for help from the blatant drug

---

38. Michael Pollan, "Opium, Made Easy," *Harper's Magazine*, April, 1997: 35–58. As an aside, the Veterans of Foreign Wars have been distributing "Buddy Poppies" since 1922, using them to raise many millions of dollars to benefit disabled and other needy veterans. Should the DEA "be consistent" with the zero tolerance program and force this wonderful group to change its symbol so we do not "send the wrong message" to our children?

dealing and gun battles among rival drug sellers on her street. This brave and law-abiding woman had taken a stand, and she was devastated at being forced out of her home. The writer said:

> I was also devastated. I am the patrol division commanding officer of the police division where this lady lived. I felt I should apologize for not providing better protection. There are similar problems to this lady's in other parts of my division, and it hurts all of the officers who work in the division. I know there are problems like this all over the city. We all want to provide safe streets for the people we serve. The fact is we can't. We might be able eventually to regain control of this lady's street; we will try. There will be other problems and we will try to solve them too.
>
> But I have to wonder what has happened to this city—or to our society as a whole—when criminals can make life so miserable that people, who only ask to be allowed to live in peace, have to run for their lives.
>
> I want you to realize there are not enough police officers to stop, let alone reverse, this unrelenting onslaught of criminality, lawlessness, violence and narcotics. Something has to be done for the law-abiding citizens of this city and country before long. I don't know what the answer is, but somehow the law-abiding people have to turn this descent around or the bad guys will win, if they haven't already.[39]

This police division commander had a right to be devastated and discouraged by our current drug policy. But we can all take heart—because we do have viable options.

Violence and Corruption
Domestic

I speak only as a 40 year veteran trial and appellate judge whose views are entirely my own, and carry no inference that I speak for the court with which I have been associated. . . . I have long shared your view that the present policies are doing far more harm than good. We are making criminals out of formerly decent police officers, turning local sheriffs into privateers looking for property to be forfeited, hardening the criminal tendencies of youthful offenders, making millionaires out of society's most conspicuous culls, and otherwise producing all the unintended consequences mentioned in the articles you sent.
Senior Judge Alfred T. Goodwin, United States Court of Appeals, Pasadena, California

Crime, particularly violent crime, has long been a major concern for Americans. It is difficult to find a public opinion survey that does not list crime as a chief public concern. What many people do not understand,

---

39. Roger D. Fox, "Lawlessness," *Los Angeles Times*, February 20, 1993, Orange County ed.: B 11.

however, is that our drug policy has a direct relationship to crime in our country. Despite the recent decline in crime rates, drug-related violence remains a major problem almost everywhere. As we have seen, the huge profits to be made by selling illicit drugs has a direct relation to the number of people willing to violate the drug laws. In addition, the sale of large quantities of illicit drugs can be a dangerous activity that generates violent crime. If a distributor of Coors beer were to have a dispute with a Budweiser distributor, it is most unlikely that they would resort to a shootout. They would both have the option of filing a complaint with the courts and having it heard by a judge. Sellers of illicit drugs, by contrast, are left to their own enforcement techniques, which frequently include intimidation and violence. In some places the situation has become so extreme that drug gangs now employ "enforcers" whose sole job is to kill rivals, potential witnesses, or others who cause them problems.[40] Add to this the further tragedy of police and even innocent bystanders being killed by drug dealers, and the tragedies, which are on the rise, of police mistakenly killing unarmed civilians in various drug operations, such as happened in the early part of 2000 both in Louisville and New York City.[41] Since prices of illicit drugs are artificially high, large numbers of drug users must resort to criminal behavior in order to get the money to buy their drugs. And large amounts of cash can and do buy large amounts of corruption.

The fact that the sale of large quantities of drugs is a dangerous activity was brought home to me years ago when I was stationed with the navy on the island of Guam. In 1972, a few months after I arrived on the island, the local newspaper ran big headlines about the first homicide Guam had experienced since the end of World War II. For weeks afterwards there were articles and editorials bemoaning the fact that such a thing could happen on their beautiful island. In time it was learned that this killing was related to a large drug transaction gone awry. Unfortunately, by the time my tour of duty was completed two years later, drug-related homicides were occurring on Guam every couple of months. These killings occurred not because of the drugs themselves, but because our drug laws had made drug trafficking so lucrative.

---

40. Pierre Thomas and Michael York, "Enforcers Are D.C.'s Dealers of Death: Drug Gangs Have Spawned Special Breed of Killer, Authorities Say," *Washington Post*, May 18, 1992: A1.

41. Ellis Cose, "Cracks in the Thin Blue Line," *Newsweek*, April 10, 2000: 33.

Another dangerous result of our drug prohibitionist policies is the likelihood of violence between rival drug dealers. There is both the immediate violence of a shooting or knifing, and also, on occasion, the danger that one dealer will try to ruin another by deliberately putting out a bad batch of drugs in his rival's territory. This happened in Philadelphia, with the result that several addicts died and hundreds more were hospitalized in a violently delirious condition.[42] Like most of the other social problems associated with drugs, this is the result of Drug Prohibition more than of the drugs themselves.

Another serious consequence of our drug prohibitionist policies is that entire blocks of our inner cities have been abandoned by the police because drug-related crime has made them too dangerous to enter except with heavily armed forces. As a result, drug dealers make and enforce their own laws in these ghetto neighborhoods, and the primary victims are women and children.[43] In addition to the general neglect and violence of these crime-ridden areas, and the threat of that violence to innocent bystanders, teenage girls are attracted to teenage drug dealers because of their money and "exciting" lifestyle, and are often sucked into drug use in this way.

U.S. drug policy also has other, more subtle influences on crime. Every dollar spent on the investigation, prosecution, and incarceration of drug users and drug dealers is a dollar that cannot be spent on the investigation, prosecution, and incarceration of other criminals. Getting "tough" on drugs inevitably translates into getting "soft" on all other offenses. The same thing happens when it comes to "plea bargaining" among prosecutors, defense counsel, and the courts. Our courts are so crowded with drug cases that other defendants, including rapists and murderers, can get away with "soft" plea bargains because prosecutors lack the time and resources to prosecute them more fully.

Try this experiment. Go to your local courthouse and take a seat in the courtroom where felony arraignments are held. (Defendants are informed officially of the charges they are facing and enter a plea at the arraignment.) You will very likely see that about 80 percent of all felony cases are drug-related. Of these, about half are straight drug cases, that

---

42. Associated Press, "Potent Heroin Brings Chaos to Philadelphia Hospitals," *Los Angeles Times*, May 11, 1996, Orange County ed.: A4.

43. See Victoria McKernan, "The Real War on Drugs," *Newsweek*, September 21, 1992: 14, which calls the War on Drugs "a scabby little affair where women and children are the foot soldiers."

is, people charged with possession or sale of drugs or with a violent act connected with their distribution. The other half are drug-related charges, namely, drug-addicted users who have perpetrated some offense in order to get money for drugs.

This was brought home to me one day in the Complaints Division of the U.S. Attorney's Office in Los Angeles. I was talking with an FBI agent about pursuing a grand jury indictment on one of his cases, when he happened to show me a bank surveillance picture of a bank robber and told me they were going to catch him the next day. This got my attention, and I asked him what he meant. The agent explained that they had identified the robber from pictures taken during prior robberies, and he was a man who always robbed banks in a particular area. On one occasion he had robbed a bank and escaped with about $900. Three days later, he robbed another bank in the area and took away $1,500. Five days after that he robbed a bank and got $1,200, and this was the day on which the new photograph had been taken, three days earlier. The agents deduced that this bank robber was probably a heroin addict with a $300 per day habit. So they were going to stake out all of the banks in the area the next day, because they reasoned that he would run out of money that day. I ran into this agent a few days later and asked if they had caught their man. Yes, they had, and yes, he was addicted to heroin. This pattern is repeated day in and day out, all across the United States.

Meanwhile, as police and law enforcement agencies devote scarce resources to the prosecution of drug crimes, other offenses are not even being investigated, much less resolved. In some communities 911 calls reporting household burglaries are not answered for hours, *if at all*, and police reports on vehicular burglaries are used by victims to process insurance claims instead of by police to pursue criminal investigations. Imagine the results we could get if even a small fraction of the drug enforcement budget was spent investigating and setting up sting operations for automobile thefts and burglaries.

The same problem even plagues the investigation and prosecution of willful homicides. A study by the *Los Angeles Times* revealed that only about 47 percent of all slayings from 1990 to 1994 were even prosecuted in Los Angeles County, compared with about 80 percent in the late 1960s. Of this 47 percent, only 16 percent resulted in actual murder convictions, and 14 percent in convictions for the lesser charge of manslaughter. The county had too few detectives to follow all credible leads, the study found, as well as inadequate investigations, allowing many murder charges to be dismissed, or prosecutors being forced to offer a plea to reduced charges because they did not detect the weaknesses in their cases until they were too close to trial.[44]

Several years ago, upon returning from a two-week vacation, I asked my court reporter what she had done during my absence. "Reporting felony preliminary hearings," she replied. These are mini-trials to ascertain whether there is sufficient evidence to determine both that a felony offense has been committed and that the defendant was the perpetrator. I asked her about how many of these hearings she had worked on, and she said about twenty-five. When I asked her how many of those had been drug-related offenses, she answered, "About twenty-one." And then she volunteered that the last one was really pathetic. It involved a homeless man, one who pushed a shopping cart filled with aluminum cans and his worldly belongings through the streets. He was arrested while selling a ten-dollar bindle of cocaine to an undercover police officer. That is about one dosage unit. A courtroom, judge, clerk, court reporter, and two bailiffs were taken up by this hearing for half a day, which did not include all of the preparation, reports, and efforts of a prosecutor, public defender, and four police witnesses. This was a complete waste of time and tax dollars, with no real benefit of any kind.

Most people simply do not realize that this kind of thing is exceedingly common and that this is how our system *operates* (I cannot say "works"). In spite of what we may see on TV, in cop shows and lawyer shows, our resources are not being spent in bringing large-scale drug offenders to justice. The desire is there, but "drug lords" are almost always shielded from conviction by layers of lower-ranking offenders. Instead we routinely spend scarce resources churning low-level, nonviolent drug offenders like the homeless man through the system, to no effective purpose. If the same resources were used to investigate and prosecute homicides, rapes, robberies, and automobile and home burglaries, crime rates would drop dramatically, both because the perpetrators could be removed from society and because the higher prosecution rate really would have a deterrent effect.[45]

---

44. Frederic N. Tulsky and Ted Rohrlich, "1 in 3 Killers in L.A. County Are Punished," *Los Angeles Times*, December 1, 1996, Orange County ed.: A1.

45. "The High Cost of War: A New Look at Crime Statistics," *Prevention File* (winter 1997): 2–6.

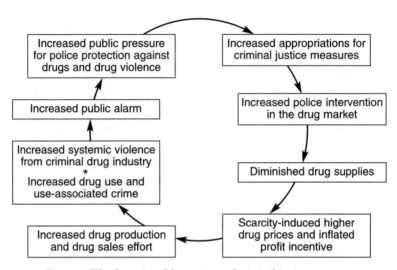

Figure 1. The dynamics of drug crime and criminal justice measures.

Another subtle reason why more resources are spent on drug investigation and prosecution than on other crimes is our asset forfeiture laws. Since these laws allow both police departments and prosecutors' offices to retain and spend a percentage of the seized drug money and other assets, these agencies have a logical economic incentive to concentrate on drug cases. Unfortunately, these laws have forced many police departments to adopt policies mandating that if officers must choose between following the money from a transaction or following the drugs, they are ordered to follow the money. Drugs are a liability because they must be guarded and then destroyed in a special incinerator; money can be spent. Regardless of one's view of the appropriateness of drug forfeiture laws, amending them to allow seized funds to go only into the general public accounts would restore a proper balance to prosecutorial incentives and policies.

A third subtle reason why our drug policy has increased violent crime is best represented by this diagram of a vicious circle (see Figure 1). The dynamics of drug crime and the criminal justice response to it actually increase violence in our communities. With increased public alarm over violence comes public pressure for more funding for more police protection. With more funding comes more police resources, which results in more successful arrests and drug seizures. This serves temporarily to diminish drug supplies. As a result of this drug scarcity, the price for illicit drugs goes up. This directly results in even greater economic incentives for people to sell drugs at the higher profit margin. Accordingly, there is both a greater incentive for drug sellers to employ violent measures to protect themselves and their even higher profits, and also for the drug customers to involve themselves in greater criminal acts in order to get money for the now higher-priced drugs. With higher crime levels comes another public outcry for more police protection. And so we are back where we started. In a very real sense, our drug policy has been increasing crime in our country for decades, to the extent that, according to author William F. Buckley, Jr., "More people die every year as a result of the war against drugs than die from what we call, generically, overdosing."[46] In other words, the cure is worse than the disease.

Similar results were seen during this country's experience with the prohibition of alcohol. Rates for both murder and assaults with a firearm increased with the onset of Alcohol Prohibition, remained high while it was in effect, and then declined for ten straight years after it was repealed. Similarly, although the years of Alcohol Prohibition saw continual increases in the length of prison sentences and in law enforcement budgets, the number of illegal alcohol stills rose from about 18,000 in 1921 to almost 282,000 in 1930.[47] The more the government tried to enforce these prohibitionist laws, the worse the problem became.

Almost everyone in the legal profession knows someone who has succumbed to the temptation of large amounts of "easy" drug money. In my case, I was appointed to a seat on the municipal court bench that had been vacated by a fairly young man who, for reasons unknown to me, no longer wanted to be a judge and had resigned. Eight years later, former Judge Alan A. Plaia was convicted in federal court for conspiracy to distribute 220 pounds of cocaine.[48] In addition, a former federal prosecutor with whom I served in the U.S. Attorney's Office was subsequently convicted, as a practicing criminal defense attorney, of stealing his client's cocaine and drug money and then attempting to arrange for his client's murder.

---

46. David G. Savage, "Views on the Drug War," *Los Angeles Times*, September 13, 1996.

47. Steven B. Duke and Albert C. Gross, *America's Longest War: Rethinking Our Tragic Crusade against Drugs* (New York: G. P. Putnam's Sons).

48. Susan Seager, "Ex-Judge Admits Drug Conspiracy," *Los Angeles Daily Journal*, December 23, 1991, Part 1: 2.

Stories like this abound in the legal and law enforcement communities. Law enforcement corruption, sparked mostly by illicit drugs, has become so chronic that the number of federal, state, and local police and law enforcement officials serving terms in federal prisons increased fivefold in four years, from 107 in 1994 to 548 in 1998. In Los Angeles, twenty-six members of the sheriff's office were convicted after a six-year investigation for skimming drug money they had seized. In Philadelphia, a judge threw out nine drug convictions after he found that six police officers had planted drugs on the suspects, stolen their money, and falsified police reports. In Fort Lauderdale, Florida, five years after DEA supervisor Rene de la Cova had received great notoriety for taking former Panamanian strongman Manuel Noriega into custody, de la Cova pleaded guilty to stealing $760,000 in laundered drug money and was sentenced to prison. In New Orleans, eleven police officers and a civilian employee were convicted and about two hundred police officers were fired after an FBI sting operation disclosed that they were involved in widespread violence and theft of cocaine from drug dealers. In Los Angeles a veteran state narcotics agent with twenty-one years of law enforcement experience was found with $600,000 in cash in his home and garage, and was eventually convicted of stealing 650 pounds of cocaine from a Riverside County evidence locker and conspiring to sell it in the community.[49]

In the case of the Los Angeles sheriff's office convictions, their federal prosecutor later made a statement about his involvement in the investigations that everyone in this country should hear:

> As the months passed and I spent many days listening to [one of the Sheriff's deputies who had decided to cooperate], I realized how much of the story of police corruption revolved around drugs. The temptation to skim came from the constant contact with outlandish sums of untraceable drug proceeds. The temptation to take "extraordinary measures" to put away dope dealers came, in part, from the intensity of the rhetoric about the "war on drugs." Narco-wars require narco-warriors. . . .
>
> Finally, there is this: If you ask enough people—good, bad, or indifferent people—to go into a room with a bag of apparently untraceable cash, sooner

---

49. Jack Nelson and Ronald J. Ostrow, "Illegal Drug Scene Spurs Rise in Police Corruption," *Los Angeles Times*, June 13, 1998, Orange County ed.: A1, 16; Associated Press, "Police Admit Planting Evidence," *Los Angeles Daily Journal*, October 12, 1995, 4; Hudson Sangree, "Ex-Agent Convicted in Drug Case," *Los Angeles Times*, October 22, 1999, Orange County ed.: B3–4.

or later, someone will unzip the bag and take a bundle. . . . That is no excuse; that is, however, a fact. That is a bell tolling; ask not for whom, L.A.

And, regrettably, those are things we must ask some people to do every day.[50]

Not only is this drug-money corruption problem of enormous concern in its own right, but additional lawless behavior often is derived from it as well. For example, the entire southern California area was shocked in September 1999 when a former officer of the Rampart Division of the LAPD who had been convicted of stealing eight pounds of cocaine started testifying about drug-related offenses. He confessed that he and fellow officers had been stealing drugs and drug money from drug dealers, using prostitutes to sell the drugs for them, planting evidence, and committing perjury repeatedly in court. He further testified that he and a fellow officer had shot and killed an alleged drug dealer for simply leaning into their undercover police car. On another occasion they had shot an unarmed black man they believed was a drug dealer, after he was in handcuffs, and then framed him by planting a sawed-off .22 rifle on him and testifying falsely that the man had assaulted them with it. That young man was convicted, and had already served three years of his twenty-three-year sentence before the truth came out. Worse yet, the police bullets will keep this man in a wheelchair for the rest of his life.[51]

Subsequent investigations stemming from this police officer's testimony, in what has become known as the "Rampart Scandal," have led to evidence that at least twenty-eight LAPD officers have been involved in similar illegal conduct. This in turn has resulted in the LAPD's public acknowledgment that about ninety-nine defendants have been wrongly convicted of felonies, and many more wrongly convicted of misdemeanors.[52] Now, it may very well be that many of these defendants

---

50. Thomas A. Hagemann, "The Thin Blue Lie," *Los Angeles Daily Journal*, October 27, 1999: 6.

51. Matt Lait, "Ex-Officer Says He Shot Unarmed Man," *Los Angeles Times*, September 16, 1999, Orange County ed.: A1; Scott Glover and Matt Lait, "2nd LAPD Shooting Targeted as Corruption Probe Widens," *Los Angeles Times*, September 17, 1999, Orange County ed.: A1, 22; Andrew Murr, "L.A.'s Dirty War on Gangs," *Newsweek*, October 11, 1999: 72; Matt Lait and Scott Glover, "LAPD Corruption Probe Expands to Seven Shootings," *Los Angeles Times*, October 22, 1999, Orange County ed.: A1, 33.

52. Matt Lait and Scott Glover, "71 More Cases May Be Voided Due to Rampart," *Los Angeles Times*, April 18, 2000, Orange County ed.: A3; Michael D. Harris, "Secret DA Memo Names 28 Officers," *Los Angeles Daily Journal*, May 25, 2000: 1, 9.

were guilty of some of these offenses, regardless of the perjured testimony that put them away, but our system of justice simply must
be better than that. Official corruption is one of the most invidious
crimes against any society. In addition, although money cannot com-
pensate an innocent person who was wrongly convicted and imprisoned, there are many attorneys who will give it a good effort. And
because of these lawsuits, lots of roads will go unpaved, libraries will
not be opened, and parks not improved for years to come, while state
and local governments pay for these tragedies caused by our War on
Drugs.

We all know that sometimes there is a "bad apple" in the barrel,
but it is our drug laws that often put the initial bruises upon otherwise good apples by exposing them to unimaginable amounts of cash
from drug transactions. Between 1993 and 2000, the number of law
enforcement officers convicted and sentenced to federal prison rose
to 668, an increase of almost 600 percent.[53] In our attempts to reduce
the overall harm caused by dangerous drugs, we must also consider
the corruption of our law enforcement officers, which will inevitably
continue so long as we pursue our current drug policy of Drug Prohibition.

Highly placed officials from other segments of society have shown
themselves to be just as vulnerable as police officers to the allure of easy
drug money. These include judges, police commissioners and chiefs of
police, mayors, former Justice Department lawyers, FBI agents, border guards, military personnel, airline employees, immigration inspectors, criminal prosecutors, and even a Roman Catholic priest.[54] The

---

53. Richard A. Serrano, "Battle against Bad Cops Isn't Fought Only in L.A.," *Los Angeles Times*, May 28, 2000, Orange County ed.: A1, 30–31.

54. See, for example, Tom Morganthau, "Why Good Cops Go Bad," *Newsweek*, Decem-
ber 19, 1994: 30–34; Victor Merina, "The Slide from Cop to Criminal," *Los Angeles Times*,
December 1, 1993, Orange County ed.: A1; Mark Fineman, "Dealer Goes Undercover on
Underworld Odyssey," *Los Angeles Times*, November 22, 1998, Orange County ed.: A1;
Michael York, "D.C. Jail Officers Admit Smuggling: Drug Sting Caught Seven Guards,"
Washington Post, April 28, 1992: B1; Anne-Marie O'Connor, "Border Agent Arrested with
550 Pounds of Pot," *Los Angeles Times*, August 7, 1997, Washington ed.: A8; Jim McGee,
"3 Ex-Justice Dept. Lawyers Indicted in Huge Drug Case," *Los Angeles Times*, June 6, 1995,
Orange County ed.: A10; Associated Press, "FBI Agent Accused in Efforts to Sell Stolen
Heroin," *Los Angeles Times*, June 5, 1994, Orange County ed.: A23; "2 City Officials Arrested
in Alleged Bid to Buy Pot," *Dallas Morning News*, April 15, 1992: 34A; Matt O'Connor,
"Ford Heights Ex-Police Chief Guilty of Corruption," *Chicago Tribune*, February 12, 1997:
Sec. 2, 1; Chip Brown, "Ex-Sheriff Sentenced to Life in Drug Case," *The Dallas Morning*

head of the DEA testified before Congress that Mexican drug cartels were corrupting U.S. police agencies "on a systematic basis" with bribes of about $1 million *per week*. And following the arrest on drug bribery charges of an INS inspector in Nogales, Arizona, where authorities seized $300,000 in cash from the home of this $30,000-per-year agent, Tucson FBI Chief Steve McCraw said that border corruption was so "pervasive . . . it's a national disgrace."[55]

We should not be surprised by this corruption in high places, which, of course, breeds disrespect for our governments and institutions along the way. Long ago, no less an intellect than Albert Einstein, *Time Magazine*'s "Man of the Century," warned us that this problem was directly linked to laws of prohibition: "The prestige of government has undoubtedly been lowered considerably by the Prohibition law. For nothing is more destructive of respect for the government and the law of the land than passing laws which cannot be enforced. It is an open secret that the dangerous increase of crime in this country is closely connected with this."

Nor have our young people escaped the net of corruption brought about by the temptation of large amounts of cash. Surveys conducted by the National Youth Gang Center report that youth gangs are responsible for about 70 percent of all illicit drugs sold by juveniles and somewhere between 25 and 43 percent of *all* illegal drug sales in our country. Fully 28 percent of the youth gangs in our country are identified as "drug gangs," or gangs that are *organized specifically for the purpose of trafficking in illicit drugs*.[56] Many of our young people join gangs just so they can be a "part of the action" in drug sales, and gang

---

News, May 9, 1992: 33A; Associated Press, "Five Marines in Brig on Drug-Smuggling Charges," *Los Angeles Daily Journal*, December 31, 1998: 9: Christopher Wren, "Nine at Delta Are Seized in Smuggling of Cocaine," *New York Times*, July 31, 1997: A23; David Johnston, "U.S. Customs Admits Its Own Drug Corruption," *New York Times*, February 17, 1999: A13; Scott Martelle, Daniel Yi, and Phil Willon, "How Rising Prosecutor Became Defendant," *Los Angeles Times*, June 9, 1999, Orange County ed.: A1; "Dutch Priest Arrested Carrying Cocaine," *Denver Post*, February 19, 1997: 17A; Dara Akiko Williams, "Veteran Inspector Found Guilty Of Smuggling Drugs, Immigrants," *Los Angeles Daily Journal*, April 11, 2000: 5.

55. Dan McGraw, "The Corrupting Allure of Dirty Drug Money," *U.S. News and World Report*, March 8, 1999: 28.

56. John P. Moore and Ivan L. Cook, "Highlights of the 1998 National Youth Gang Survey," *OJJDP Fact Sheet* (December 1999); Shay Bilchik, "Highlights of the 1996 National Youth Gang Survey," *OJJDP Fact Sheet* 86 (November 1998): 1–2 (U.S. Department of Justice, Office of Juvenile Justice and Delinquency Prevention).

influence is spreading.[57] The Office of Justice Programs of the U.S. Department of Justice reported:

> Against a backdrop of escalating violence, declining drug prices, and inten-sified law enforcement, Los Angeles area gang-related drug dealers are seek-ing new venues to sell the Midas product—crack cocaine. . . . Respondents claim to have either participated in or have knowledge of Blood or Crip crack operations in 22 states and at least 27 cities. In fact, it appears difficult to over-state the penetration of Blood and Crip members into other states.[58]

Those of us in the criminal justice system see daily that the allure of easy drug money is corrupting our youth and destroying their work ethic. Young people who have honest jobs are frequently asked by drug dealers how much money they made in the last month. When they answer, the dealer sneers, "Why, you're a real sucker. I can easily make

---

57. According to the Juvenile Justice Bulletin of June 1997, which was written by the U.S. Department of Justice's Office of Justice Programs, gang members account for 70 percent of all illicit drugs sold by juveniles. In other words, young people are in gangs in order to get "a piece of the action."

One day when I was in the complaints department of the U.S. Attorney's Office in Los Angeles, an FBI agent sought prosecution of a group of gang members in South Central Los Angeles. He said that the federal government had sponsored a program to try to deter-mine why juveniles joined gangs. So some bureaucrats decided that they would invite some gang members to come to their office and "rap" about all of the reasons why they had joined their gangs. They knew that the gang members would not come without incentives, so they decided to pay them for their time. Then they decided that the juveniles would not really "open up" if actual adults were present in the meetings, so they left them alone and simply asked them to bring in other members and prepare a final report. The gang members were so enthusiastic, and said they had been so successful, that they threw a party for themselves at a local hotel. Then, of course, they failed to pay the bill, and destroyed quite a bit of furniture along the way. Finally, after all of this was over, the bureaucrats were left with a bill for the furniture, as well as a telephone bill for thousands of dollars of calls made by the gang mem-bers from government offices to numbers all over the world.

I told the agent that the only people that really deserved to be prosecuted were the ones who had come up with such a stupid program in the first place. But I was told by the same agent a few months later that as a direct result of the program, gang membership in this area of Los Angeles had actually increased substantially during this time period. It seemed that everyone wanted to be paid to have parties and talk on the telephone.

In a similar vein, I heard not long ago that a young prosecutor in the Boston area had been gunned down by a young male who was heard to be shouting gang slogans just before he fired. To my knowledge, the murder has never been solved. But it was revealed that at the time he was killed, the young prosecutor was working on cases involving a gang that called itself "Koz," which stood for "Kilos and Ounces." This gang had been organized expressly to sell drugs.

58. Cheryl L. Maxson, "Gang Members on the Move," *OJJDP Juvenile Justice Bulletin* (October 1998): 5.

that much money in an afternoon selling drugs." The dealer is right; and our children know it.

Weapons offenses by our young people have also increased dramatically thanks to our War on Drugs. Since drug dealing can be a dangerous activity, more young dealers, like their adult counterparts, are arming themselves in order to do business. As a result many users, and even many young people who are not even involved with drugs, now carry weapons in order to protect themselves. People who say they are willing to continue with our present drug policy, "for all of its defects," in order to protect our children, should look at what our drug policy is actually doing to them. It is not a pretty sight.

Foreign

It is clear to me that the difference between Europe and the U.S. is that here the terms "war on drugs" and "hard v. soft on crime" have become political swords and few are willing to risk the blows of those swords by criticizing the efficacy of present process and procedures. Perhaps what is needed is a grassroots approach. . . . In any event, the attack on drugs through heavy sentences of "mules" and filling our jails with young, predominately black, men and women is clearly a failed approach. While I have no ready answers, I am willing to pursue new initiatives.
Judge David A. Katz, United States District Court, Toledo, Ohio

The fact that our nation's drug policy is based on attempts to repeal the law of supply and demand is transparently evident in the development of the drug production cultures of other nations. We have already seen the futility of trying to persuade the peasants of underdeveloped countries not to grow their largest cash crop. As we now know, if one could eliminate Colombia and Mexico as havens for drug-supplying middlemen, their lucrative businesses would quickly be replaced by distribution systems already in place in places like Nigeria, the Caribbean, and elsewhere.[59] And their work will only continue to get easier and less risky as entities like the World Trade Organization do away with restrictions on trade among nations under agreements like NAFTA, GATT, and the European Common Market.[60]

---

59. Juanita Darling, "Newest Cocaine Route to States: East Caribbean," *Los Angeles Times*, April 27, 1997, Orange County ed.: A1, 12-13; Mark Fineman, "In Court: Cocaine, Caribbean, Conspiracy," *Los Angeles Times*, October 22, 1997, Orange County ed.: A10, 12; Joshua Hammer, "The Nigerian Connection," *Newsweek*, October 7, 1991: 43; Scott Kraft, "A Gaping Gateway for Drugs," *Los Angeles Times*, February 17, 1994, Orange County ed.: A1, 8-9.

60. Frank Viviano, "Drug Rings Thrive as EC Eases Border Controls," *Orange County Register*, December 21, 1992: A20.

According to a United Nations International Drug Control Program report, *world trafficking in illicit drugs made up about 8 percent of all world trade as of 1995.* This figure represents about $400 billion of international drug transactions per year.[61] The report goes on to say that nearly 140 million people (about 2.5 percent of the world's population) smoke marijuana and hashish; 13 million people use cocaine, 8 million use heroin, and 30 million use stimulants such as amphetamines. Illegal drugs are a bigger business than all exports of automobiles, and about equal to the international textile trade. The report estimates, moreover, that seizures worldwide amount to only a third of all cocaine, and from 10 to 15 percent of all heroin, being sold and consumed. This means that the profits to be made from selling on a mere fraction of the unseized drugs easily cover the costs of the drugs that are seized. Our supermarkets would be overjoyed if they lost only this percentage of their fruits and vegetables to spoilage. Once again, because these drugs are ridiculously easy and cheap to grow and process, the enormous profits and corruption brought about by their sale is a Drug Prohibition problem, not a drug problem. In essence, we have made a plague out of disease.

The adverse impact that drug money has had on developing countries is simply impossible to measure. One thing is clear, however: drug money from the United States has substantially corrupted the entire governments of Colombia, Peru, and Bolivia, and has come dangerously close to corrupting the government of Mexico.[62] To gauge the depth of the problem, consider that on November 6, 1985, the Medillin drug cartel in Colombia attacked and actually captured the Colombian Palace of Justice in Bogota. By the time the shooting stopped, they had killed ninety-five people, including the chief justice of the country and eleven of the twenty-four justices.[63]

While this kind of thing goes on, the U.S. government continues to play politics. The Foreign Assistance Act requires our president to

---

61. Mark Porubcansky, "Drug Trafficking Equals 8 Percent of All World Trade, the U.N. Reports," *Philadelphia Inquirer,* June 27, 1997: A7.

62. For an in-depth account of the corrupting influences of our drug policy on the Andean countries of South America and elsewhere, see Kevin Jack Riley, *Snow Job? The War against International Cocaine Trafficking* (New Brunswick, N.J.: Transaction Publishers, 1996); and Rachel Ehrenfeld, *Narco Terrorism: How Governments Around the World Have Used the Drug Trade to Finance and Further Terrorist Activities* (New York: Basic Books, 1990).

63. Jill Jonnes, *Hep-Cats, Narcs, and Pipe Dreams: A History of America's Romance with Illegal Drugs* (New York: Scribner, 1996), 358.

compile a list of major drug trafficking countries each year, and then to assess them as to their cooperation with us in our anti-drug efforts. Should we "certify" or "decertify" various countries as cooperating with our anti-drug efforts? If a country is decertified, all U.S. aid except anti-drug assistance will be withdrawn, and the United States will vote against that country's receiving loans from any international lending institution. But this device has little to do with reality and instead has become a device for politics and posturing.

For example, in March 2000, President Clinton again certified that Colombia and Mexico had "fully cooperated" with our War on Drugs, even though Colombian cocaine cultivation was up a full 20 percent from the year before.[64] In 1998, President Clinton had similarly certified Mexican and Colombian cooperation, even though his own "Drug Czar" Barry McCaffrey had just told Congress that "There is massive [drug-related] corruption and violence directed at Mexican institutions in general and law enforcement and the military in particular." Congressman John Mica (R-Fla.), chairman of the subcommittee General McCaffrey was addressing, said in response that some of Mexico's law enforcement officers, including some trained by the United States, had helped drug traffickers and participated in drug-related violence. "Now I'm concerned," Mica concluded, "that the people we're training may be involved in some of the terrorism. We've gone from corruption to terrorism, and this concerns me."[65] Congressman Mica had every reason to be concerned, since even the chief of the DEA was quoted at the same time as saying that Mexico is losing the drug war and that Mexican drug traffickers' penetration of the United States has increased dramatically.[66]

All of those comments were made "on the record." Off the record, U.S. officials were saying things like, "This is not about what Mexico has done, this is about convincing the Hill that whatever Mexico has done is enough." As two writers for the *New York Times* put it, "This simply underscores that the 'certification' process has become more of

64. Esther Schrader, "White House Certifies Colombia, Mexico Anti-Drug Efforts," *Los Angeles Times*, March 2, 2000, Orange County ed.: A6.

65. Cassandra Burrell, "Mexico Engaged in War vs. Drugs, McCaffrey Says," *Orange County Register*, February 26, 1999: News 33.

66. Paul de la Garza, "Mexico's Drug War Draws Ire, Praise," *Orange County Register*, February 26, 1999: News 29, 33.

a joint public-relations campaign aimed at the Congress than an objective appraisal."[67]

Those public relations efforts, of course, are also aimed at the American people. After President Clinton again certified the Mexican government on February 26, 1999, he had his Secretary of State, Attorney General and Drug Czar jointly publish a letter in many of our nation's newspapers trying to justify the action, while acknowledging that "serious problems remain."[68] Among the problems these three top leaders mentioned were that in Mexico "crime is increasingly violent and better organized," that "impunity and inefficiency are found in law enforcement," that "the administration of justice is inadequate," and that "sixty percent of the cocaine sold on American streets comes through Mexico, even while Mexico's cocaine seizures sharply declined last year." They finished by stating that "Mexico also must continue to confront pervasive corruption driven by the enormous illicit wealth of the drug kingpins."[69] Since these leaders acknowledge publicly how desperate the Mexican situation is, and since it is directly caused by our drug money, one would think that they could at least bring themselves to agree to discuss some options to our nation's drug policy that has inflicted such untold damage upon the government and people of our neighbors to the south. But do they? Of course not.

One newspaper captured the essence of this silly and self-deceptive ritual in 1998, when it editorialized, "President Clinton announced on Friday that he will participate in the annual game of 'Let's Pretend.' The president will pretend that Mexico is a cooperating partner in the War on Drugs, the United States will continue to send Mexico aid that it and the Mexican government will pretend will help to win the war, and citizens will pretend that it all is helping the cause."[70]

Such political exercises and self-righteous pronouncements are just part of a larger package of self-deception that our War on Drugs is doing any good whatsoever. The message this country is really sending the rest of the world is that *we in the United States are simply unable to*

---

67. Tim Golden and Christopher S. Wren, "U.S. Officials: Mexico's War on Drugs Is a Bust," *San Francisco Chronicle*, February 14, 1999: A17, 19.

68. John C. Henry and Bennett Roth, "Mexico Passes U.S. Drug Test," *Houston Chronicle*, February 27, 1999: 1A.

69. Madeleine Albright, Janet Reno, and Barry McCaffrey, "Clinton Was Right to Certify Mexico," *Los Angeles Times*, March 19, 1999, Orange County ed.: B9.

70. Editorial, "Drug War Pretenses," *Orange County Register*, March 2, 1998: Metro 6.

stop our people from using these drugs, so the rest of the world must stop their people from producing them. This is especially hard for others to swallow when they understand that the largest cash crop in the state of California is marijuana. To be consistent, our federal government should require that all federal funds be cut off from our largest state because its government has failed to eliminate or even reduce marijuana farming.

Following our government's lead, the United Nations held a special session on drugs in New York and passed a program, touted to be effective worldwide, to rid the world of illicit drugs. Here is what the editors of the *Ottawa Citizen* had to say about this exercise in political self-deception:

> Today in New York City, an act of almost indescribable stupidity will be committed. Eighteen years after Ronald Reagan announced he would stamp out drugs, the "War on Drugs" will be declared once again.
>
> This time the United Nations will play the fool, with an announcement of the most ambitious international anti-drug program ever. Representatives from 130 nations, plus 30 heads of state, including President Bill Clinton, will be there to applaud.
>
> The cornerstone of the UN plan will be a program to get farmers in the eight major drug-producing nations—Afghanistan, Burma, Laos, Colombia, India, Mexico, Pakistan, and Vietnam—to switch from growing plants that produce illegal drugs to other crops. The stated goal of the UN plan: To eradicate the world's entire production of heroin, cocaine, and marijuana in 10 years.
>
> *Bonne chance, nos amis.* The nations being targeted range from merely corrupt to tyrannical to anarchic. Authority, where it exists, is often intimately involved in the production and transportation of drugs. Unless the UN is prepared to pay every farmer to grow soybeans and send peacekeepers to fight off the guerrillas, police, and soldiers who will be displeased that their cash-cow has dried up, its war will be lost. But assume the UN could manage the impossible and turn the nations now producing the bulk of the world's drugs into exporters of soybeans. Would that mean victory in the War on Drugs?
>
> Not at all. Cutting the supply of drugs does nothing to reduce the demand for them. It would mean, however, that some of that demand wouldn't be met, which would push the value of drugs skyward. That in turn would tempt criminals, soldiers, police, guerrillas, and farmers in nations elsewhere in the world to produce their own supply. If it's not Afghanistan and Burma supplying the drug markets, it will be Nigeria, or Peru, or somewhere else. Unless the UN can afford to put every farmer in the world on the anti-drug dole, crop substitution won't work. . . .
>
> What about Canada? As always, the federal government is clambering onto the bandwagon and cheering on the war. Since the Trudeau years, it has

seldom given serious thought to drug policy, preferring instead to follow whatever variation on failure is being proposed.

That, sadly, is true of most of the world's nations. Sense and experience are ignored, folly is repeated, and the War on Drugs becomes a war on reason itself.[71]

Playing politics is not, of course, limited just to governments of drug-consuming countries like ours. Governments of drug-supplying countries, such as Bolivia, for example, have been playing politics for years. That is, they try to do just enough to look like they are cooperating with the United States in order to receive our foreign aid. They arrest a few foreigners and minor drug dealers in their country with much fanfare, while allowing large-scale drug transactions to go undisturbed. In fact, government officials themselves often make big money by selling drugs, or by protecting the ones who are doing the selling. It is simply not possible to close down the drug-growing and distribution business in these countries because their economies are far too dependent upon this revenue.[72]

Nor have the world's financial institutions been immune from corruption by these large amounts of money. A major banking disaster several years ago involving the Bank of Credit and Commerce International and its "loss" of billions of dollars ("the BCCI scandal") almost entirely involved the laundering of drug money. In addition, the head of the DEA has openly charged Mexico's banks with laundering millions of dollars in drug profits.[73] Thereafter, two of Mexico's largest banks pleaded guilty, and three Mexican businessmen were convicted of laundering tens of millions of dollars for a Colombian drug cartel.[74] Furthermore, it was no coincidence that many of the world's banks opened branches in Miami because of the large amounts of drug money being laundered through that city—or that many banks large and small simply "forgot," in violation of federal law, to notify the government of financial transactions involving cash transactions of amounts greater than $10,000.[75]

---

71. Editorial, "War on Reason," *Ottawa Citizen*, June 8, 1998.

72. Andrew A. Reding, "Why Zedillo Is Slow to Curb the Drug Lords," *Los Angeles Times*, March 26, 1995, Orange County ed.: M2.

73. Mary Beth Sheridan and Mark Fineman, "Mexico Bristles at U.S. Charge on Drug Money," *Los Angeles Times*, April 26, 1996, Orange County ed.: A10.

74. Dara Akiko Williams, "3 Guilty of Laundering for Drug Cartel," *Orange County Register*, June 11, 1999: News 4.

75. Jonnes, *Hep-Cats, Narcs, and Pipe Dreams, supra,* at 344–45, 349, 439.

The laundering of large amounts of money can be quite complex, but the payouts are enormous, and deeply corrupting.[76] In June 1999, the U.S. Treasury undersecretary for the enforcement of money-laundering laws told the Senate's informal Caucus on International Narcotics Control that the "black-market peso exchange system" in itself actually launders approximately $5 billion per year in drug profits, with which they purchase American goods and export them to Colombia. He went on to warn our companies that they should be on the lookout for laundered money that was being used to purchase their products, such as household appliances and cigarettes.[77] How effective do you suppose this warning not to allow any purchases to be made with drug money will be?

Just as in the United States, victory in the War on Drugs in developing nations is increasingly being defined as simply slowing down the pace of defeat, and once again the reason is money. We have seen the financial incentives behind large-scale transactions, where organized and violent men make tens of millions of dollars per month in this illicit activity. When we are finally able to destroy and disband major drug organizations, like the Cali Cartel in Columbia, which was "the biggest, most powerful crime syndicate we've ever known," according to DEA chief Thomas Constantine, new "baby cartels" sprang up almost overnight. The Cali Cartel, which emerged when the Medellin Cartel was eradicated, was thought to have supplied about 80 percent of our nation's cocaine. But it made no difference. People who once worked with the Cali Cartel had at least one hundred *tons* of cocaine already warehoused near the Mexican border. As Mr. Constantine told the U.S. Senate, "It's entirely possible that these newly emerging groups could rise to an equal or superior footing with the Cali mafia."[78]

The same hopeless situation that prevails at the top of the illicit drug distribution network prevails at the bottom at the campesino or peasant level. In the Chapare region of Bolivia, which is a jungle valley about the size of New Jersey, about 25 percent of the world's cocaine is grown by peasants. And why not? The peasants quickly found that they could quadruple their incomes by harvesting the coca leaf without working any harder than before. Naturally the peasants organized themselves

---

76. Mark Schapiro, "Doing the Wash: Inside a Colombian Cartel's Money-Laundering Machine," *Harper's Magazine*, February 1997: 56–59.

77. Associated Press, "Money-Laundering Warning Issued," *Los Angeles Daily Journal*, June 22, 1999: 4.

78. David Schrieberg, "Birth of the Baby Cartels," *Newsweek*, August 21, 1995: 37.

militarily to protect their largest cash crop.[79] As a result, about 300,000 out of a Bolivian population of about 7 million are employed in the cocaine industry. That is enormously significant in a country with a 20 percent unemployment rate. With such numbers, cocaine has become the largest earner of foreign exchange, replacing the mining of tin.[80]

For a while, a man named Evo Morales was the leader of a confederation of about 31,800 peasant coca growers in Bolivia. He was actually elected to Congress, along with three other allies, and others in his organization were also elected to village councils. The United States has been combating the growth of the coca leaf by Morales's organization with helicopters that spray chemical defoliants over the jungle, and by paying the peasants $2,500 per 2.4 acres to let their coca be eradicated and alternate crops planted. The peasants accept our tax dollars, and alternate their crops where it is visible, then continue to plant their coca out in the hills. Should we be surprised? This "cat and mouse" game has been going on for decades, with the peasants replanting their coca about as fast as the police eradicate it.

Another problem that gets very little attention is that our drug policy has taken a terrible toll on the environment. The United States government has polluted the countryside of Latin American countries like Colombia with herbicides such as tebuthiuron, which, incidentally, frequently kills legitimate crops such as beans and potatoes, and this has been done despite public warnings from the chemical's manufacturer against its usage. In this country, tebuthiuron is used mainly as a potent weed killer on railroad beds and under high-voltage lines that are far removed from food crops and people. The EPA has stated that this agent can contaminate ground water and could have a lasting effect on the soil where the coca once grew.[81]

The peasants growing the coca crops are also using large amounts of often carcinogenic pesticides, without even protecting themselves or their families from their harmful effects, much less their land and the groundwater.[82] Similarly, drug traffickers, who are obviously not

79. Sebastian Rotella, "Bolivia Held Hostage by Cocaine," *Los Angeles Times*, September 29, 1997, Orange County ed.: A1. See also William R. Long, " 'Coca Power' Winning Drug War in Bolivia," *Los Angeles Times*, September 24, 1995, Orange County ed.: A1.

80. Ehrenfeld, *supra*, at 131.

81. Diana Jean Schemo, *New York Times*, "Colombia to Test Coca Herbicide," *Orange County Register*, June 20, 1998: News 29.

82. Juanita Darling, "Researchers See Another Victim in Cocaine Chain," *Los Angeles Times*, June 23, 2000, Orange County ed.: A5.

concerned with the environment or environmental laws, often use a cyanide-based chemical to mark ocean drop-off sites that guide low-flying aircraft to bales of drugs that are intentionally dumped overboard by passing ships along the west coast of Mexico. These phosphorescent chemicals, known as Natural Killer-19, or NK-19, are suspected in the deaths of large numbers of whales, dolphins, and fish.[83] Furthermore, illegal growers of marijuana on public lands in this country frequently use pesticides that poison wildlife, groundwater, and waterways, not to mention creating booby traps that can injure the occasional legitimate visitor to the areas.[84]

But small-scale peasant operations growing these illicit crops quickly add up to a large-scale business throughout the developing world. It is estimated that in 1997 the peasants of Peru, which was then the world's top producer of cocaine, harvested about 192,570 tons of coca; Bolivia harvested about 82,780 tons, and Colombia about 44,970.[85] The U.S. government estimates that between $3 billion and $5 billion was injected into the economy of Colombia in 1998 as a result of the illicit coca trade. This makes drugs Colombia's top export, far ahead of oil and "Juan Valdez's" coffee.[86]

The governments of these developing countries have little choice but to allow the growing and distribution of these drugs to continue. Peasants, much of the wealthy upper class, and the governments themselves all rely on the foreign currency generated by this lucrative business. Furthermore, if a Latin American government cooperates too closely with the United States, as the government of Peru once did with a coca bush fumigation and eradication program, it discovers that its peasants will simply switch their allegiance to the guerrillas. Peru's high-ranking military leaders were quoted as saying that they simply could not afford to let that happen again.[87]

---

83. Associated Press, "Traffickers Tied to Sea Die-Off," *Los Angeles Times*, February 15, 1997, Orange County ed.: A5.

84. Pauline Arrillaga, "Marijuana Growers Ravage U.S. Forests," *Los Angeles Times*, March 26, 2000, Orange County ed.: A33.

85. Sebastian Rotella, *supra*, at 12.

86. Reuters, "Drug Hauls and Kidnappings in Colombia Surged in 1998," *Los Angeles Times*, December 20, 1998, Orange County ed.: A4.

87. Brook Larmer, "The Gateway to Heaven: A Trip Inside Peru's Perilous Cocaine Valley," *Newsweek*, January 20, 1992: 41; Alan Weisman, "The Cocaine Conundrum: Can Colombia Finally Win the War on Drugs? Better to Ask Can It Survive if It Does Win?" *Los Angeles Times Magazine*, September 24, 1995: 14.

The situation for these countries in trying to combat unimaginably large profits is so grim that Dr. Gustavo de Greiff, the prosecutor general of Colombia from 1991 to 1994, said publicly that the drug war will never work and that the world must begin to investigate other options. De Greiff's statement was all the more significant in that he was the drug warrior who had been able to increase the conviction rate of drug traffickers from 20 percent when he took office to 75 percent when he left, and whose strategy arguably coaxed the cocaine kingpin Pablo Escobar out of hiding and resulted in his death. Nevertheless, the response of the U.S. government was to oppose de Greiff and to imply that he was a corrupt tool of the Colombian drug cartels—a demonstrably ridiculous accusation, since many of the options de Greiff proposed to investigate would put all the cartels out of business.[88]

While South American countries are flooding the United States with cocaine, Afghanistan and the Southeast Asian countries of the so-called Golden Triangle, where Burma, Laos and Thailand come together, are doing the same thing with heroin. And for all of our efforts at interdiction, the street prices of all these drugs continue to fall, while their purity has increased from about 5 to 10 percent in President Nixon's time to up to almost 90 percent now.[89]

By no means is this problem unique to the United States or other Western developing nations. Other countries, even those with repressive regimes like Vietnam and Iran have major problems with other drug-supplying countries like Burma and Thailand, on the one hand, and with Afghanistan and Pakistan, on the other. And all of them have significant problems with the corruption of their own police and military officers stemming from large amounts of drug money.[90] Even Ireland has increasingly had a large dose of drug-money corruption. In the mid-1980s, two investigative journalists began to document the rise of heroin traffickers in that country. For a while, politicians and chiefs of police either ignored the reports or accused the writers of sensationalism. Then

88. Kevin B. Zeese, "A Colombian Prosecutor's Crusade against War on Drugs," *Los Angeles Daily Journal*, July 21, 1994: 6.

89. Peter Maas, "The Menace of China White," *Parade Magazine*, September 18, 1994: 4–6.

90. Andy Soloman, "Vietnam's New Drug of Choice: Heroin," *Orange County Register*, July 25, 1999: News 37; Greg Torode, "Heroin in Hanoi Leads to the Top," *Orange County Register*, December 26, 1996: News 29, 35; John Daniszewski, "Iran's Own Desert Storm," *Los Angeles Times*, March 21, 2000, Orange County ed.: A1, 18.

in 1994, one of the reporters was murdered in his car while waiting at a traffic light. At that point, the Irish government got the message.[91]

Irish reporters are not the only innocent victims of the drug wars. What happened to the Tarahumara Indians in the Mexican mountains, about 250 miles south of El Paso, Texas, is even more tragic. These people lived in peace and seclusion in the mountains for about six thousand years. Then in the 1980s, they were set upon by "narcotraficos" who cleared their land of timber and planted opium poppies and marijuana. At the beginning, the Tarahumaras who protested were routinely shot with AK-47s, and the local authorities were powerless to protect them. As time passed, the Tarahumaras were killed even if they refused to raise the illicit crops for these invaders.[92]

In the case of the Tarahumara homeland, it was estimated that the brown gum garnered by slitting the opium poppy was worth more than $3 per gram. It takes about ten poppy bulbs to yield one gram, and each bulb can be milked from three to ten times. At about ten poppy bulbs per square yard of land, one harvest results in a return of about 12,500 grams of opium gum per acre, which would be worth about $37,500 in even this remotest of regions.[93] Profits like this cannot be combated successfully.

But even the violence against the Tarajumara Indians pales in comparison to the violent upheavals caused by drug money used to finance revolutionary groups throughout the world. It is universally understood that three accepted currencies finance violent revolutions: dollars, guns, and illicit drugs. The U.S. drug policy helps furnish them all. Repressive regimes and terrorist and revolutionary groups around the world use the sale of illegal drugs to advance their political objectives and to finance their bloody works. These include Fidel Castro's government in Cuba, Manuel Noriega's former government in Panama, Erich Honecker's former government in East Germany, Muammar Kaddafi's government in Libya, and the late Ayatollah Khomeini's government in Iran. The government of Bulgaria has used the sale of drugs effectively in its attempts to dislodge the government of neighboring Turkey. Much of the civil war in Lebanon was fought

---

91. Sebastian Rotella, "Tentacles of Latin Drug Lords Extend Well Beyond Borders," *Los Angeles Times*, June 12, 1999, Orange County ed.: A2.

92. Alan Weisman, "The Drug Lords vs. the Tarahumara," *Los Angeles Times Magazine*, January 9, 1994: 10.

93. Ibid., at 33–34.

over who would control the profits of the production, refining, and distribution of hashish, heroin, and cocaine. The Shining Path ("Sendero Luminoso") guerrilla movement in Peru is almost completely financed by the sale of illicit drugs,[94] and both the Serbs and the Kosovo Liberation Army (which the United States supported) financed much of their black-market gun purchases by trafficking in drugs.[95] George Shultz summarized the situation succinctly:

> Money from drug smuggling supports terrorists. Terrorists provide assistance to drug traffickers. Organized crime works hand in hand with these other outlaws for their own profit. And what may be most disturbing is the mounting evidence that some governments are involved, too, for their own diverse reasons. Cuba and Nicaragua are prime examples of communist countries involved in drug trafficking to support guerrillas in Central America. . . . The link between narcotics, terrorism and communism is not confined to Latin America, but also exists in Italy, Turkey and Burma.[96]

No discussion of violence caused by drug money can be complete without specifically addressing its damaging effects on Mexico. Whatever harm and corruption drug money has caused in other countries of the developing world, we can live with them if we must. But U.S. interests are substantially affected by the economic and social stability of our neighbor to the south. And things do not look good. The Mexican government has been infiltrated and corrupted by U.S. drug money to the extent that corruption was alleged "at the highest levels" of the country's government during the presidency of Carlos Salinas de Gortari, including the president's own brother;[97] and Mexico's own "Drug Czar" was arrested, convicted, and sentenced to fourteen years in prison for corruption.[98] In addition, Mexico's former deputy attorney general was indicted for laundering more than $9 million in drug

---

94. See Ehrenfeld, *supra*, at 53.

95. Mark Hosenball and Daniel Klaidman, "Deadly Mix of Drugs and Firepower," *Newsweek*, April 19, 1999: 27.

96. Ehrenfeld, *supra*, at xxii.

97. Mark Fineman, "Smuggler May Shed Light on Level of Corruption," *Los Angeles Times*, March 4, 1997, Orange County ed.: A4; "Salinas Kin Linked to Cocaine," *Los Angeles Times*, September 20, 1998, Orange County ed.: A8.

98. Mark Fineman, "Mexico Fires Drug Czar; Ties to Cartel Alleged," *Los Angeles Times*, February 19, 1997, Orange County ed.: A1; Mary Beth Sheridan and Jodi Wilgoren, "Ex-Leader of Mexico's War on Drugs Sentenced," *Los Angeles Times*, March 4, 1998, Orange County ed.: A16; Esther Schrader, "Drug Cartels Seizing Mexico," *Phoenix Gazette*, November 18, 1994: A1.

money payoffs through a Houston bank. According to the indictment, the deputy attorney general and an associate made deposits in amounts between $40,000 and $800,000 every few weeks during 1994 and 1995, most of which were in the form of $20 bills taken from suitcases. After his arrest, he apparently committed suicide.[99] The Mexican state of Baja California lost two attorneys general in only nineteen months due to allegations of drug money corruption and large numbers of homicides were linked to the drug trade.[100] The military and police are unreliable at best and, by most interpretations, thoroughly corrupted by U.S. drug money.[101]

Through all of this, the United States government has self-righteously and hypocritically criticized Mexico for not working harder to combat these major problems caused by *our* drug money. But it is the Mexicans who are bleeding heavily from the violence caused by our drug policy. Journalists have been killed and prosecutors, the chief of police of Tijuana, and many other government officials assassinated.[102] Crime stemming from drug trafficking is abounding; and atrocities have become commonplace.[103] In September 1998 in Ensenada, which is about 80 miles south of San Diego, there was a turf battle linked directly to the drug trade in which armed gunmen who were looking for a rival drug lord invaded a cluster of three country houses, roused the families from their sleep, and killed ten adults and eight children, execution-style,

---

99. Esther Schrader and James F. Smith, "U.S. Indicts Ex-Mexico Prosecutor in Drug Case," *Los Angeles Times*, August 28, 1999, Orange County ed.: A1; Esther Schrader, Mary Beth-Sheridan, and James F. Smith, "Mexico's Ex-Drug Enforcer an Apparent Suicide," *Los Angeles Times*, September 16, 1999, Orange County ed.: A12; Alan Zarembo and Mark Hosenball, "Dead Men Don't Talk," *Newsweek*, September 27, 1999: 37.

100. Associated Press, "Crime, Corruption Controversies Lead to Resignation of Baja AG," *Los Angeles Daily Journal*, July 16, 1999: 5.

101. Tim Golden, "U.S. War on Drugs in Mexico Faltering," *The Orange County Register*, December 23, 1998: News 22; Andrew Downie, "Mexico Says 34 in Military Accused of Drug Crimes," *Houston Chronicle*, July 29, 1997: A8; Eva Bertram and Kenneth E. Sharpe, "U.S. Policy Corrupting Mexico Army," *Los Angeles Times*, August 10, 1997, Orange County ed.: M1.

102. Anita Snow, "Mexican Journalist Fatally Beaten," *Orange County Register*, December 7, 1996: News 29; Anne-Marie O'Conner and Mark Fineman, "Anti-Drug Chief, 3 Aides Found Slain in Mexico," *Los Angeles Times*, September 23, 1996, Orange County ed.: A1; Ken Ellingwood, "6 Held in Deaths of Tijuana Police Chief, 14 Others," *Los Angeles Times*, March 9, 2000, Orange County ed.: A1, 33; Ken Ellingwood, "Agents' Deaths Underscore Peril of Mexican Drug War," *Los Angeles Times*, May 2, 2000, Orange County ed.: A1, 18.

103. Michelle Ray Ortiz, "Crime Keeps Tijuana on Edge," *Orange County Register*, December 13, 1998: News 37.

as a warning to others who would protect this drug lord.[104] The killings caused by drug feuds in Mexico are estimated to be several thousand per year.[105]

Much of this violence is spilling across the border into the United States. Since about 70 percent of all illicit drugs smuggled into this country come across the Mexican border, federal border authorities concentrate much of their efforts on the border crossings. As a result, the rural part of Texas, with its 1,268 miles of border, has become a major arena of smuggling activity. Ranchers claim that gangs of Mexican drug traffickers bring tons of marijuana, cocaine, heroin, and amphetamines across the Rio Grande with impunity. On the cattle ranches that stretch for miles along both sides of the river, gangs have torn down fences, scattered cattle, commandeered houses, and threatened citizens who have gotten in their way. One rancher was sitting in a deer-hunting blind when he saw a man dressed in camouflage and carrying an AK-47 assault rifle emerge from the vegetation by the river in broad daylight. Close behind him was a column of men who were carrying packages of drugs, with another armed escort close behind.[106] Often the porters of the drugs are illegal aliens who pay for their passage this way. In many instances these heavily armed gangs are so frightening that many Texas ranchers are selling off their land, frequently to buyers who are a front for the drug lords, who then get a stronger foothold in our country.

A steep increase in violence against our federal agents has also accompanied this drug trafficking along the southwestern border. The U.S. Border Patrol agents' union believes that drug traffickers have actually offered a bounty to people who kill U.S. law officers. Incidents of violent attacks on our agents increased from 156 in 1992 to more than 500 in 1999. Since 1992, two agents have been killed, and in 1997 alone, agents were shot at ninety-seven times. In addition, they were rammed

---

104. Sam Dillon, "Drug Gangs' Deadly Toll: Indian Villagers in Baja," *New York Times*, September 26, 1998: A4; Tony Saavedra, "U.S. Experts Sure Mexico Massacre Work of Druglords," *Orange County Register*, September 19, 1998: A1.

105. Mary Beth Sheridan, "Drug Feud Slayings Taking Toll on Mexico," *Los Angeles Times*, October 16, 1998, Orange County ed.: A1.

106. William Branigin, "Drug Gangs Terrorize the Texas Border," *Washington Post*, September 25, 1996: A1; Mark Fineman and Craig Pyes, "Border Ranchers Losing Drug War," *Los Angeles Times*, July 7, 1996, Orange County ed.: A1, 11.

with cars or trucks sixty-four times, and on twenty separate occasions bombs were found in places frequented by U.S. agents.[107]

In short, nothing good is happening on the foreign front as a result of our drug prohibitionist laws. The peasants of developing countries are still harvesting coca, opium poppies, and marijuana. The drug lords are getting more and more organized, violent, and wealthy. Violence and corruption stemming from drug money are rampant in foreign countries, as they are in the United States. In many countries drug lords are respected for their money and influence,[108] while the United States is hated for its politics, arrogance, helicopters, and the defoliants our agents spray on the people's villages and crops.[109] Our communities remain awash in illegal drugs in spite of every enforcement effort, and there is no progress in sight.

And so, as one political commentator from Colombia put it, a new narco-reality is dawning. The cry that "we are becoming Colombia" is being heard from the developing nations:

> In every Latin American country, from Mexico on south, "becoming Colombia" is a buzz-phrase among commentators and officials, the threatening prophecy or terrifying diagnosis of what the nation has become or soon will be: a stinking bog of corruption, violence and immorality—the demons that assemble around the expanding, unstoppable and most profitable business in the world: drug trafficking.[110]

---

107. Esther Schrader, "War on Drugs Taking Toll on Border Agents," *Los Angeles Times*, March 12, 2000, Orange County ed.: A1, 30; "Mexicans Targeted Agents, Union Says," *Los Angeles Times*, March 21, 2000, Orange County ed.: A5.

108. Anita Snow, "Kingpins Are Saints to Many in Drug Culture of Culiacan," *Orange County Register*, September 4, 1995: News 10.

109. In 1998, our government caused the fumigation of at least 145,000 acres of land in Colombia, up from about 125,000 acres in 1997. Reuters, "Drug Hauls and Kidnappings in Colombia Surged in 1998," *supra*.

110. Cecilia Rodriguez, "A New Narco-Reality Dawns in Latin America," *Los Angeles Times*, February 2, 1996, Orange County ed.: B11.

3

Erosion of Protections of the Bill of Rights

Many thanks for your letter. I certainly share your concern about the current "war" on drugs. If you like, you may say that I said that many of our drug laws are scandalously draconian and the sentences are often savage. You may also quote me as saying that the war on drugs has done considerable damage to the fourth amendment and that something is very wrong indeed when a person gets a longer sentence for marijuana than for espionage.
Judge Morris S. Arnold, United States Court of Appeals, Little Rock, Arkansas

I would contribute a short quote from a fellow by the name of Thomas Jefferson. He said, "The natural progress of things is for government to gain ground and for liberty to yield." Given enough time and enough government, eventually we'll have no freedom left at all.
Judge Francisco Firmat, Superior Court, Santa Ana, California

Nothing in the history of the United States of America has eroded the protections of our Bill of Rights nearly as much as our government's War on Drugs. There are at least two major reasons for this. The first, as we have seen, is that the enormous amount of money to be made from the sale of illegal drugs has resulted in large-scale criminal organization and violence, which makes the drug problem continually outstrip all efforts to contain or control it. Conventional wisdom says that the only way to stem the tide is to grant law enforcement agencies greater and greater powers and to let them intrude more and more completely into the private lives of our people. The second reason is that since drug use is consensual, "victims" do not file complaints and are not inclined to testify voluntarily. As a result, law enforcement has been forced to utilize different tactics from those pursued in crimes like burglary, rape, and assault. These tactics necessarily result in greater intrusions into people's private lives.

"Undercover" operations are the chief method used by law enforcement in the War on Drugs. Undercover police officers pretend to participate in drug deals, use informants or "snitches," and cause the wiretapping of telephones and surreptitious recording of private conversations. Faced with an ever-worsening drug problem, and the public alarm that accompanies it, the courts, albeit without design, have grudgingly but consistently allowed our Bill of Rights protections to be eroded in exchange for what is hoped to be progress in the war against drugs. Judges are human, and when faced with a choice between weakening the protections of the law "just a little bit" in order to make progress against this overwhelming problem, they unconsciously have been "doing their part."

Many people, if faced with a choice that would allow true progress to be made against this persistent drug problem in exchange for giving up some of our Bill of Rights protections, would probably reluctantly choose the progress against drugs. And that is what has happened. We have lost many of our protections in the last thirty years— and since this erosion has always been incremental, we have allowed it to occur. For example, when faced with the alternative of "doing something" rather than simply allowing a cocaine-dealing street gang to take over a Los Angeles neighborhood, a prominent Los Angeles radio station editorialized in 1993 that it was "grudgingly supportive" of the police department's request for court orders allowing them to arrest gang members on sight, regardless of whether or not they had actually witnessed any illegal activity. The radio station concluded that "with [police] resources already spread too thin, the options are 'arrest first, ask questions later.' It's a hell of a solution; but to the beleaguered residents of [that particular] street, it's better than nothing."[1]

But this "solution" has not worked; and it has become a civil liberties disaster. Our civil rights protections have been demonstrably reduced, while the availability of dangerous drugs is now greater than

---

1. KNX Radio (Los Angeles), "Arrest First, Question Later," *Los Angeles Daily Journal*, January 29, 1993: 6.

ever before, and at a lower cost. And for this loss of our civil liberties we have no legitimate excuse. We in the Western world have been warned for centuries about the perils of failing to protect our freedoms:

> The true danger is when liberty is nibbled away, for expedients. (Edmund Burke)

> The public good is in nothing more essentially interested, than in the protection of every individual's private rights. (Sir William Blackstone)

> Necessity is the plea for every infringement of human freedom. It is the argument of tyrants; it is the creed of slaves. (William Pitt)

> Those who would give up essential Liberty, to purchase a little temporary Safety, deserve neither Liberty nor Safety. (Benjamin Franklin)

> Those who deny freedom to others deserve it not for themselves. (Abraham Lincoln)

> Our freedoms must be defended over and over again. (Ronald Reagan)

> Republic ... it means people can live free, talk free, go or come, buy or sell, be drunk or sober, however they choose. (John Wayne)

When I graduated from law school in 1971, the law as set forth by the U.S. Supreme Court was that an anonymous tip was of no value in an attempt to obtain a search warrant unless there was independent corroboration, so that warrants could not be issued merely on the basis of unsubstantiated rumors or false accusations.[2] A search incident to an arrest was limited to the area within the arrestee's immediate control at the time of the arrest;[3] a search warrant was necessary in order to search a person's automobile if it was already in the custody of the police;[4] and a search warrant was required in order to search any place in which an individual had a "reasonable expectation of privacy."[5]

All of these protections have now been greatly reduced as a result of drug cases. In fact, it is widely understood by attorneys and legal commentators that there is a "drugs exception" to the Bill of Rights. Since 1971, for example, search warrants have been upheld on the basis of partially corroborated *anonymous* tips, if the tip itself contained "sufficient

---

2. See *Spinelli v. United States*, 393 U.S. 410 (1969), and *Aguilar v. Texas*, 378 U.S. 108 (1964).

3. See *Chimel v. California*, 395 U.S. 752 (1969).

4. See *Preston v. United States*, 376 U.S. 364, 368 (1964).

5. See *Katz v. United States*, 389 U.S. 347 (1967).

detail" based on the "totality of the circumstances."[6] A warrant is no longer required for the search of an automobile, even for the search of the glove compartment or the locked trunk, after an arrest or after the car has been impounded.[7] It is even legal to search any containers located within a car that might possibly conceal the object of the search, even though the containers may be locked and even if the police had time to apply for a warrant.[8] The Supreme Court has further held that a person has no greater expectation of privacy in a motor home (i.e., a house on wheels) than she would in an automobile;[9] and if there is probable cause to search an automobile, the police may search all of the personal effects of the *passengers* as well as of the driver.[10] The Supreme Court also unanimously held that evidence seized during a traffic stop can be used in court, even if the traffic stop was only a *pretext* to look for drugs or evidence of other illegal activities,[11] and the Court further held that the police can seize an automobile without a warrant as being subject to civil forfeiture if they have probable cause to believe the vehicle has been used previously for the transportation of drugs.[12]

In 1983, the Court made a major effort to help the police get illegal drugs off the streets and put and keep drug dealers in prison when it decided the case of *United States v. Leon*.[13] The ruling in this case stated that even if a magistrate made a mistake and issued a search warrant without probable cause, if the police relied on the warrant in good faith the evidence could still be admitted at trial. The rationale for this ruling was that the exclusionary rule (the principle that evidence seized by police in violation of the Fourth Amendment may not be used against a defendant at trial) was intended to deter police misconduct rather than to punish the errors of judges and magistrates. What the Court did not take into account, however, was that trial judges and magistrates, at

---

6. See *Illinois v. Gates*, 462 U.S. 213 (1983), which also stated that an anonymous tip could, by itself, support a finding of probable cause if it contained "sufficient detail" based on a "totality of the circumstances." See also *Alabama v. White*, 496 U.S. 325 (1990), which held that an anonymous tip accompanied by "sufficient indicia of reliability . . . provide[s] reasonable suspicion to make the investigatory stop."

7. See *South Dakota v. Opperman*, 428 U.S. 364 (1976).

8. See *United States v. Ross*, 456 U.S. 798 (1982).

9. See *California v. Carney*, 471 U.S. 386, 393–94 (1985).

10. See *Wyoming v. Houghton*, 526 U.S. 295 (1999).

11. See *Whren v. United States*, 517 U.S. 806 (1996).

12. See *Florida v. White*, 526 U.S. 559 (1999).

13. 468 U.S. 897 (1983).

least subconsciously, also want to get these drugs off the streets. If no appellate court is "grading their papers," judicial officers are more likely to sign search and arrest warrants even when the requisite probable cause is missing. As much as individual appellate review itself, it was the institutional safeguard of the exclusionary rule that protected society from the mistakes and excesses of law enforcement.

In many cases, the doctrines protecting individual rights have not themselves been changed, but the interpretation of them has. In 1984, for example, in *Oliver v. United States*,[14] the Supreme Court decided that police who walked around a locked gate and a "No Trespassing" sign onto defendant's farm and down the road, where they found a field of marijuana about a mile from the his house, were not in an area in which the defendant had a reasonable "expectation of privacy." This was considered to be an "open field" which was accessible to the public and open to view. However, the Court said, if the police had gone "inside the curtilage," which was defined as the land immediately surrounding and associated with the home, the search would have been impermissible.

Two years later, the Court heard and decided *California v. Ciraolo*.[15] This was a case in which the police received an anonymous tip that someone was growing marijuana in the backyard of his suburban house, which was completely enclosed by a six-foot outer fence and a ten-foot inner fence. The police secured a private airplane, flew over the defendant's house at 1,000 feet, and took pictures of marijuana growing in a fifteen-by-twenty-five-foot plot in the backyard. The Court found the plot to be "within the curtilage," but nevertheless found that the police had a right to fly over the house and therefore approved of the search. Three years later the ceiling at which the police were allowed to fly in conducting warrantless searches was reduced to four hundred feet.[16]

On December 1, 1998, the Court in *Minnesota v. Carter* further reduced the protections of the Constitution and overturned the Minnesota Supreme Court by holding that the Fourth Amendment does not protect a houseguest who does not stay overnight. A visitor who was involved in packaging cocaine in an apartment was held to be involved in a commercial transaction, and therefore could not have had a reasonable expectation of privacy. Justice Ruth Bader Ginsburg sounded

---

14. 466 U.S. 170 (1984).
15. 476 U.S. 207 (1986).
16. See *Florida v. Riley*, 488 U.S. 445 (1989).

the alarm in dissent, saying that the Court's decision "undermines not only the security of short-term guests, but also the security of the home resident herself. . . . As I see it, people are not genuinely 'secure in their . . . houses' . . . against unreasonable searches and seizures . . . if their invitations to others increase the risk of unwarranted governmental peering and prying into their dwelling places. . . . When a homeowner . . . personally invites a guest into her home . . . that guest should share his host's shelter against unreasonable searches and seizures."[17]

One of the clearest cases of the Supreme Court's losing its moral compass and sense of direction as to the principles on which this country was founded as a "land under the law" has to be the infamous case involving Dr. Humberto Alvarez-Machain. This Mexican gynecologist was suspected of prolonging the life of DEA Agent Enrique Camarena expressly so that Camarena's kidnappers could continue to torture and question him. U.S. government agents first tried to extradite Alvarez-Machain so that he could be tried in this country. When that failed, they simply paid some mercenaries $20,000 to kidnap him and bring him to Texas to stand trial. Chief Justice William Rehnquist, writing for the majority, found that this kidnapping violated no express treaty language, declined to utilize the Court's inherent supervisory powers to deter such conduct in the future, and ordered him held.

Joined in dissent by Justices Harry A. Blackman and Sandra Day O'Connor, Justice John Paul Stevens showed genuine concern about this decision, writing, "I suspect that most courts throughout the civilized world . . . will be deeply disturbed by the 'monstrous' decision the Court announces today. For every nation that has an interest in preserving the Rule of Law is affected, directly or indirectly, by a decision of this character. As Thomas Paine warned, an 'avidity to punish is always dangerous to liberty' because it leads a nation 'to stretch, to misinterpret and to misapply even the best of laws.' To counter that tendency, he reminds us: 'He that would make his own liberty secure must guard even his enemy from oppression; for if he violates this duty, he establishes a precedent that will reach to himself.'"[18]

---

17. 525 U.S. 83 (1998).

18. 504 U.S. 655 (1992). See also Bob Cohn and Tim Padgett, "Nabbed in the Name of the Law," *Newsweek*, June 29, 1992: 68; Ruth Marcus, "Kidnapping Outside U.S. Is Upheld: Supreme Court Rules Government Can Seize Foreigners for Trial," *Washington Post*, June 16, 1992: A1.

The end of the story is that Alvarez-Machain was acquitted at trial and allowed to bring a lawsuit against both the U.S. Government and the law enforcement officers involved under the doctrine that "pretrial detainees have a clearly established right to be free from punishment."[19]

In our society, it is left to the courts to curb the excesses of legislative and executive acts. Without court sanctions, there is no deterrence to such actions as the kidnapping of Alvarez-Machain. And so the same thing happened again. In 1994, Juan Matta-Ballesteros was forcibly abducted from his home in Honduras by Honduran special troops and four U.S. marshals and brought to this country for trial. But first, he said, he was hooded, beaten, burned, and tortured with a stun gun that was applied to various parts of his body, including his feet and genitals. He denied being involved in Agent Camarena's torture and killing but did acknowledge having some information about it. Eventually, Matta-Ballesteros was convicted of numerous narcotic violations, and his kidnapping and conviction were upheld on appeal by the Ninth Circuit Court of Appeals, following the Alvarez-Machain precedent.[20]

Why our courts and our people fail to condemn agents of our government who kidnap foreign nationals can only be explained by the frustration we all feel about the lack of progress in the nation's War on Drugs. The killing of DEA Agent Camarena was horrendous, and he must have suffered horribly before he finally died. But how would we respond as a court system and as a country if agents of a foreign nation decided that, for example, the directors of one of our large tobacco corporations should be tried in their country for manslaughter or worse as a result of the cancer deaths from our exported cigarettes? How would we like it if they kidnapped the tobacco company CEO and took him to their country for trial? I submit that we would be so outraged that we would seriously consider military action against the offending country. And yet our War on Drugs has made our country and its institutions so desperate that our judgment and our reason have been seriously clouded.

The problem is that every law-abiding person wants to be rid of this all-pervasive drug problem, and the defendants are frequently not

---

19. Henry Weinstein, "Suit Over Camarena Case Gains," *Los Angeles Times*, September 25, 1996, Orange County ed.: A3.

20. *U.S. v. Matta-Ballesteros*, 71 F.3d 754 (9th Cir. 1995).

sympathetic individuals. Nevertheless, our Founding Fathers recognized that we must have a Bill of Rights to protect us from the excesses of government. It was John Adams who said that a major force behind the American Revolution was the British use of "carte blanche" search warrants on the colonists in an effort to collect taxes on illegally imported goods.[21] This is strikingly similar to what is happening today.

People should be concerned about the loss of their Constitutional safeguards. It is not possible to have one Constitution for the "good guys" and another for the "bad guys." It is said only half in jest that a conservative is a liberal who just got mugged, and a liberal is a conservative who just got indicted.

These things can happen to any of us. We too can be the recipients of an inappropriate stop by the police, or a search of our home based upon an anonymous tip. We too can be detained on the highway or at an airport because a police officer suspects for some reason that we may be carrying drugs. It is so easy to lose our Bill of Rights protections, and so very difficult to get them back.

At one of my talks about our nation's failed drug policy at an exclusive country club in Orange County, California, a man in his forties stood up and said, "I hate the War on Drugs!" He was a successful land developer and often had occasion to travel by air on the spur of the moment, without luggage, and he tended to pay for his ticket in cash. He fits the standard profile of a drug courier, and has been stopped and strip-searched on a number of occasions. No wonder he hates the War on Drugs. And so should we all. Former Hall of Fame baseball player Joe Morgan, who is black, also fit the drug courier profile for the same reason as the land developer, and with the same results. On one occasion Morgan was arrested at Los Angeles International Airport, thrown to the floor, and handcuffed. The officers who did this to him had received a tip that a known drug dealer who was black would be at the airport accompanied by another black male. When Morgan appeared to look directly at the officers and turn abruptly around, they jumped to the conclusion that he was their man. Morgan brought a civil action against the officers and the police department and was awarded com-

---

21. See Jeremy M. Miller, "Nation's War on Drugs Is Clearly Unconstitutional," *Los Angeles Daily Journal*, November 17, 1992: 7; and Daniel J. Larkosh, Esq., "The Shrinking Scope of Individual Privacy: Drug Cases Make Bad Law," *Suffolk University Law Review* 24, no. 4 (winter 1990): 1009–42.

pensatory as well as punitive damages—money that was, of course, paid by the taxpayers.[22]

As a result of what they have seen on the bench, many judges around the country have spread the alarm that our country's drug policy must be changed. The comments of only a small number of those judges are included in these pages, but they are representative of a much wider sample.

What have these judges seen? They have seen people like Fidel Salem, age twenty-one, and Mohammad Khalid, age eighteen, who were arrested on cocaine charges and spent two days in jail before police confirmed that the white powder they were arrested with was yogurt.[23] They have seen people like Purdue University freshman Jarrod Allan Eskew, who shot and killed Jay Severson, the student dormitory counselor who had discovered cocaine in Eskew's possession the day before, and then killed himself.[24]

And then these judges have seen cases like the one involving the death of Donald Scott. Scott was shot and killed by Los Angeles sheriff's deputies in the early morning of October 2, 1992, when government agents attempted to serve a search warrant upon him at his Trail's End Ranch in the Santa Monica Mountains region of Malibu. Scott, a reclusive millionaire, had first come under suspicion when an informant told the Los Angeles authorities that Scott had been seen paying for small purchases with hundred-dollar bills and flashing a very large bundle of currency. Another informant reported that he was growing 3,000 to 4,000 marijuana plants on his two-hundred-acre ranch.[25]

To pursue the case, a DEA agent got an airplane and flew over Scott's ranch at an elevation of 1,000 feet. He reported in a sworn declaration that he spotted about fifty marijuana plants growing around some large trees near a house on the property. Even though a U.S. Border Patrol team had entered the ranch a few days before and had not found any marijuana, and even though a pilot from the California National Guard had photographed the ranch from the air without confirming any marijuana,

---

22. See Brenda L. Hunt, "Civil Rights," *Los Angeles Daily Journal*, September 16, 1992: 4.

23. "Police Find 'Cocaine' Was Yogurt; 2 Freed," *Washington Post*, November 4, 1996: A7.

24. Associated Press, "Purdue Student Kills Counselor, Then Self," *Chicago Tribune*, October 17, 1996: sec. 1, 2.

25. John Dillin, "Citizens Caught in the Cross-Fire," *Christian Science Monitor*, October 1, 1993: 6–7; Matthew Heller, "A Death in 'Shangri-La,'" *Los Angeles Daily Journal*, February 11, 1993: 1, 16.

the Los Angeles authorities sought the warrant based on the DEA pilot's "observations."

The Los Angeles deputies obtained a search warrant from a Ventura judge because, although the entrance to the ranch was in Los Angeles County, the buildings were actually in Ventura County. A brigade of twenty-seven government agents from the Los Angeles sheriff's office, LAPD, DEA, National Park Service, and the California National Guard served the warrant. Although accounts of the incident differ, when Donald Scott was abruptly awakened that morning by the yelling and entry into his home of these officers and the screams of his wife, he grabbed a handgun from his nightstand and pointed it toward the officers, whereupon he was shot dead in his own bedroom. A complete search revealed no marijuana whatsoever to be on the property.

Ventura County District Attorney Michael Bradbury conducted a six-month investigation into Mr. Scott's death. After interviewing forty-nine witnesses, Bradbury issued a report in which he concluded that the raid conducted by these twenty-seven government agents was motivated, at least in part, by a desire to seize and forfeit Scott's $5 million ranch. The report also concluded that the declaration upon which the search warrant was based contained "misstatements" and serious omissions that invalidated the warrant, that the Border Patrol agents committed civil trespass by entering the ranch without authority a few days before the raid, and that "probably" the Los Angeles authorities did not notify the Ventura authorities about the raid so that they would not have to share the forfeiture with Ventura County.[26] Los Angeles County taxpayers were forced to pay $4 million to Mr. Scott's family for the county's part in this tragedy, and the federal taxpayers were forced to pay an additional $1 million.[27]

The mistakes that resulted in the death of Donald Scott were by no means unique. In San Diego, agents of the DEA and the Customs Department used a battering ram and concussion grenades to break into the home of Donald Carlson, an assistant vice president of a computer company. The agents were acting on the tip of a paid informant who told them that the house was vacant but that the garage was being used to store large quantities of cocaine. Carlson, who was later found

---

26. Daryl Kelley, "Ventura D.A. Calls Fatal Raid Unjustified," *Los Angeles Times*, March 30, 1993, Orange County ed.: A3, 19.

27. Editorial, "Drug War Toll," *Orange County Register*, April 4, 2000: Local News 8.

by the U.S. Attorney in San Diego to be "wholly innocent," was shot and seriously injured by the agents after they broke in. No drugs were found at this location, nor at another equally innocent location the same informant had fingered. Carlson, who lost one-quarter of his lung capacity to the federal bullets, was paid $2.75 million of our tax dollars for this tragic mistake.[28]

It is critically important to keep in mind that the general fault for these terrible situations is not with law enforcement. Many of these raids take place as planned, and many "bad guys" are arrested and large amounts of drugs are appropriately seized. But too often things go wrong, and once again the fault lies with our underlying drug policy. This is a dangerous business, and to be involved one must deal with shady and dangerous people. It is inevitable that mistakes and deceptions will occur, and that tragedies will happen. This was the case on May 1, 1998, when New York narcotics police officers mistakenly raided the Brooklyn apartment of a family of four. After throwing a concussion grenade into the apartment and keeping the family, including a mentally retarded girl whom they pulled from the shower, handcuffed for more than an hour, the officers found no drugs or contraband at all. The police had raided the wrong house.[29] On another occasion, an undercover police officer in New York shot and killed an unarmed black security guard in a drug "buy and bust" operation that went very wrong. The dead man was later discovered not to have any drugs on him at all. Hundreds of people rioted and smashed store windows on the day of his funeral, complaining that he was the third innocent black man to be killed by police within thirteen months.[30]

In the summer of 1998, police in Houston acted on the uncorroborated statement of an arrestee who was already on probation for a previous drug offense, and went to the apartment of Pedro Oregon Navarro, whom they suspected of being a drug dealer. When Oregon's brother-in-law answered the door, the police rushed in. Oregon, who

28. Sacramento Bee, "On Overzealousness, Another Drug War Travesty," *Los Angeles Daily Journal*, May 6, 1994: 6; John Dillin, "It Was the Perfect Drug Raid . . . but the Wrong House," *The Christian Science Monitor*, October 1, 1993: 6; Peter Katel, "Justice: The Trouble with Informants," *Newsweek*, January 30, 1995: 48.

29. Michael Cooper, "Scared Family Says Police Raided the Wrong Home," *New York Times*, May 8, 1998: B1.

30. John J. Goldman, "Protesters, N.Y. Police Clash After Funeral," *Los Angeles Times*, March 26, 2000, Orange County ed.: A11.

was asleep, was awakened by the commotion and grabbed a handgun that he kept in the bedroom. The police shot him twelve times and killed him. It was subsequently learned that the informant's statements were self-serving lies and that Oregon had nothing whatsoever to do with drug dealing.[31]

A similar tragedy occurred in El Monte, California, when police with a search warrant shot their way through the back and front doors of the home of a sixty-five-year-old man they knew to be a neighbor of a drug dealer, and shot him in the back, killing him, in full view of his wife while they were both still in their bedroom. The raid took place in the middle of the night and the family had been asleep when the police shot their way into the house. The police request for the warrant was based on the fact that the known drug dealer had been found to have some telephone bills, motor vehicle records, and other mail bearing the neighbor's address. So the police wanted to find evidence in the neighbor's home to use against the dealer. But they had no information at all that the man they killed had been involved in drug dealing.[32]

Even when police do have evidence of illicit drug involvement, one must wonder if consequences such as these can ever justify their actions. In Bangor, Maine, six masked police officers on a "special response team," brandishing guns and dressed in riot gear that made them look like "giant gray and black Ninja Turtles," forced their way into a residence to conduct a search for marijuana at about 10:30 at night. The officers found marijuana paraphernalia and $500 in cash. Along the way, they traumatized five young children ranging in age from three to ten years. Nine-year-old Danielle Mason, who had participated in a police-taught D.A.R.E. program, was quoted as saying, "I can't trust them anymore." Her six-year-old brother Carlie was quoted as saying, "Big guys pointed guns at us and told us to shut up." Their mother acknowledged smoking marijuana, but "we don't smoke in front of the kids," and said that the cash was taken from her bureau drawer where it was being saved for her family's planned move to Ohio.[33]

---

31. Timothy Lynch, "'Drug War' Is Slowly Diluting Constitutional Safeguards," *Los Angeles Daily Journal*, December 12, 1998: 6.

32. Anne-Marie O'Connor, "No Drug Link to Family in Fatal Raid, Police Say," *Los Angeles Times*, August 28, 1999, Orange County ed.: A1.

33. Susan Young, "Parents Claim Police Terrorized Their Children," *Bangor Daily News*, August 4, 1994: A1, 3.

Remember the picture on the front page of every paper in the country of the INS agent pointing an automatic weapon at the head of the man holding little Elian Gonzalez, during the raid on the household in Miami to seize Elian and return him to the custody of his Cuban father? Remember the look of terror on Elian's face, and the near-universal consensus on how traumatic this experience must have been for the child? The very same trauma is being inflicted each year on hundreds of small children throughout the United States, children who are exposed to paramilitary police tactics in their homes because someone living there is suspected, rightly or wrongly, of some form of drug offense. The trauma caused to these young children is yet another cost of our policy of Drug Prohibition.

Our society experiences more than enough tragedies involving *trained* police officers fighting the War on Drugs. But in ever more desperate attempts to make an unworkable policy work, some people are seriously suggesting the domestic use of American military forces inside our country in the drug war effort. The fact is, this is already happening. On May 20, 1997, eighteen-year-old Esequiel Hernandez was tending his family's goats near his home in Redford, Texas, along the U.S.-Mexican border, when a heavily camouflaged marine corps patrol fatally shot him. Hernandez frequently carried an antique rifle to target shoot and to protect his goats from coyotes and snakes, and the marines later stated that he had fired two shots in their direction before he was killed while preparing to fire a third.[34]

We must be clear, again, that the inherent problem is not with the military, but with the system. This country was founded, in part, on the principle of keeping our military forces out of our domestic affairs, and this is a fundamentally important issue on a philosophical level. But even beyond its philosophical importance—even if we were to reverse ourselves on this crucial point—it is simply not feasible adequately to train our armed forces in the complicated issues of search and seizure, probable cause for arrest, and the complexities of the criminal law. In the case of Esequiel Hernandez, a military board of inquiry exonerated the marine patrol; but Congress subsequently issued several reports that were highly critical of the training received by the patrol, as well

---

34. Anne Presley, "Year Later, Marine Killing of Goatherd Remains in Dispute," *Washington Post*, June 14, 1998: A3; Steve Lash, "Official Hits Agencies in Killing by Marine," *Houston Chronicle*, November 13, 1998.

as of the chain of command. And, a little more than a year after the killing, the federal taxpayers paid the goatherd's family $1.9 million as a "humanitarian gesture" to settle the wrongful death case.[35]

In many ways our criminal justice system has been crippled and discredited by its large-scale use of "snitches" and paid informants in its attempts to win the War on Drugs. The Honorable Stephen Trott, U.S. Ninth Circuit Judge and former head of the Justice Department's Criminal Division during the Reagan administration, has warned that given long mandatory sentences, many informants will do anything to stay out of jail, including "lying, committing perjury, manufacturing evidence, soliciting others to corroborate their lies with more lies, and double-crossing anyone with whom they come into contact, including—and especially—the prosecutor."[36] And this problem is growing. Federal law enforcement agencies paid $97 million of our tax dollars to informants in 1993, almost four times what they spent in 1985. Often, according to Michael Levine, who served as an agent in the DEA and U.S. Customs Service for twenty-five years, federal agents have allowed "about 15,000 wild, out-of-control informants" to take control of investigations, and, according to U.S. District Judge Marvin H. Shoob of Atlanta, the informants are often worse criminals than the defendants on trial.[37]

Juries have also spoken out about the practice of using informants in drug cases. In a case in Florida in which the defendants were charged with leading a $2 billion cocaine smuggling and distribution operation and smuggling seventy-five tons of cocaine into the United States between 1978 and 1991, the jury found the defendants not guilty. The jury foreman stated after the trial that one of the key factors in the decision to acquit was the suspicion that the twenty-seven informants, who had previously worked for the defendants and were called to testify by the prosecution, were lying in order to strike deals

---

35. Associated Press, "U.S. to Pay $1.9M to Family of Teen Slain by Marine," *USA Today*, August 12, 1998: 8A. In addition to the trauma to the individuals involved, these cases are almost always very expensive to the taxpayers, and reports of large payments being made by governments to claimants are increasingly common. See, for example, Anne La Jeunesse, "City Pays $775,000 For Bungled Search," *Los Angeles Daily Journal*, June 21, 2000: 2.

36. Reuters, "Use of Snitches Out of Control, Study Finds," *Los Angeles Times*, February 13, 1995, Orange County ed.: A23.

37. Wire Reports, "Spending on Informants Increases," *Los Angeles Daily Journal*, February 14, 1995: 4.

with the government.[38] That was not the end of the story, however, because the jury foreman himself was later convicted and sentenced to seventeen years in prison for accepting $500,000 in bribes for his vote in acquitting the defendants. Of course, eleven other jurors, against whom there were no allegations of bribery, also voted to acquit these defendants.[39] But the case simply underscores that with all of the big money involved in drug cases, there is a huge potential for bribery, corruption, and injustice of many kinds.

Probably the most notorious drug case involving paid informants was the prosecution of Manuel Antonio Noriega, the former "Maximum Leader" of Panama. In a trial that took seven months and cost taxpayers $164 million, prosecutors obtained their conviction only by making deals with more than twelve felony drug traffickers. One of them was Carlos Lehder, the co-founder of the Medellin cartel in Colombia who had already been convicted and sentenced to life plus 135 years in prison.[40] In exchange for his testimony that his cartel paid Noriega millions of dollars to permit their drug-filled airplanes to stop and refuel in Panama on their way to the United States, Lehder was moved to the federal witness-protection program, and his family was also moved to the safety of the United States. Another man named Max Mermelstein, who faced a ninety-year sentence for transporting large quantities of drugs, was released from custody after two years and twenty-one days and was paid $700,000 in reward money in exchange for his testimony. Luis del Cid faced seventy years in prison, but government prosecutors agreed that he would receive a maximum sentence of ten years, that they would release $94,000 in pension funds, and that he would not be deported. A pilot named Floyd Carlton, who was charged with flying 880 pounds of cocaine into our country, was given a suspended sentence and was freed on three years' probation.[41] In a footnote to the story, in March 1999 the federal sentencing judge reduced Noriega's sentence

---

38. Associated Press, "Prosecutors Stunned as Jury Clears Duo in $2.1 Billion Cocaine Scheme," *Philadelphia Inquirer,* February 18, 1996: A24.

39. Associated Press, "Jury Foreman on Trial for Taking Bribe for Acquittal," *Los Angeles Daily Journal,* January 7, 1999: 4; "Juror Sentenced," *Los Angeles Daily Journal,* March 6, 2000: 1.

40. You will recall that Carlos Lehder was the "connection" of the drug smuggler whose story was told by Bruce Porter in *Blow, supra.*

41. Bob Cohn and Spencer Reiss, "Noriega: How the Feds Got Their Man," *Newsweek,* April 29, 1992: 37.

by ten years, which will make him eligible for parole in 2007. The reason given by the judge for this reduction was the "disparity between the defendant's sentence and the sentences served by his co-conspirators."[42] It seems that under our current system, the "heavies" usually come out ahead eventually.

Even more directly, in *United States v. Cuellar*, when the government paid an informant a $580,000 fee (consisting of a percentage of laundered drug money recovered and a $400,000 bonus paid after his testimony), this was found not to have been a bribe or an "improper inducement for perjury or fabricated evidence."[43] Given the promise of substantially reduced sentences, and of hundreds of thousands of taxpayer dollars as a fee for services, informing has become a growth industry. Of course the price paid for this weapon in the War on Drugs is not only millions in tax dollars but the integrity of our criminal justice system itself.

On July 1, 1998, the Tenth Circuit U.S. Court of Appeals found the practice of "paying" informants with reduced sentences in criminal cases in exchange for their cooperation and testimony in drug money-laundering cases constituted a violation of federal laws prohibiting the bribery of witnesses—and it ordered the practice stopped.[44] Given the long history of this practice in virtually all criminal courts in the nation and the uproar that followed, the full court vacated this ruling nine days later. Congress also joined the fray, and within days several amendments were offered to the federal bribery law that would allow prosecutors to offer leniency in exchange for testimony. This proved to be unnecessary, however, because six months after issuing the initial ruling, the Tenth Circuit held in a nine-to-three vote that federal prosecutors were exempt from the federal bribery statute and thus were free to continue to offer leniency in exchange for testimony.[45]

Law enforcement agencies are not to blame for this sad state of affairs. The individuals who staff and oversee these agencies are saddled with the impossible task of making a hopeless system work, and they feel legitimate frustration that they simply cannot accomplish that task.

---

42. Associated Press, "Judge Reduces Noriega's Sentence," *Los Angeles Daily Journal*, March 5, 1999: 4.

43. *U.S. v. Cuellar*, 96 F.3d 1179 (9th Cir. 1996).

44. *United States v. Singleton*, CA10, No. 97-3178, 63 CrL 451, 7-1-98, vacated 7-10-98. The criminal law prohibiting the bribery of witnesses is 18 U.S.C. 201(c)(2).

45. *United States v. Singleton*, 165 F.3d 1297 (10th Cir. 1999).

In their attempts to succeed, they try ever more creative and desperate ways of "making a round peg fit into a square hole." And they deal with low-life "snitches," which almost everyone in law enforcement finds quite distasteful.

Abuses of the system, and there are many, almost always begin incrementally. They start out slowly and progress over time. In Chicago in 1993, for example, six drug-based gang convictions were reversed and new trials ordered because the federal prosecutor was alleged to have "paid" informants for their testimony by allowing them to have heroin and cocaine in prison, and to have sex with their wives and girlfriends, sometimes in the privacy of government offices.[46] These "payments" were preceded by simpler and less egregious attempts to keep their witnesses happy, but gradually and inexorably the favors snowballed until finally resulting in this unacceptable situation.

An even worse instance of the same kind of corruption involved the trial of a man accused and later convicted of the killing of a police officer. In this case, in which an informant later produced photographs of himself and his wife having sex in the San Diego district attorney's office, the trial judge criticized the prosecutors for allowing the informant to have sex with "any woman he could convince to join him during his incarceration." For obvious reasons, none of these "payments" were disclosed to the defense, the court, or the jury during the trial.[47] When the facts came to light at the superior court level, all of the convictions were reversed—and so, at great effort and expense to everyone, the defendants will have to be retried.[48]

There is also, of course, a major concern about wide-scale corruption from within the system, some of which we have already seen. This often takes the form of fabricated testimony by police officers about arrests of drug offenders. During the 1990s alone, many police departments, including those in Los Angeles, Boston, New Orleans, San Francisco, Denver, and New York have been involved in scandals in which police personnel were found to have committed perjury about how they obtained evidence in drug cases. Joseph D. McNamara, the former chief of police of both San Jose and Kansas City, expressed his concern about

---

46. John McCormick, "Good Times, Not Hard Time," *Newsweek*, July 19, 1993: 58.

47. Brae Canlen, "Prosecutorial Zeal," *California Lawyer*, March 1999: 34.

48. Tony Perry, "Convictions Overturned in Policeman's Slaying," *Los Angeles Times*, July 21, 1999, Orange County ed.: A3.

this kind of corruption in a 1996 editorial comment entitled "Has the Drug War Created an Officer Liars' Club?":

> As someone who spent 35 years wearing a police uniform, I've come to believe that hundreds of thousands of law-enforcement officers commit felony perjury every year testifying about drug arrests.
>
> These are not cops who take bribes or commit other crimes. Other than routinely lying, they are law-abiding and dedicated. They don't feel lying under oath is wrong because politicians tell them they are engaged in a "holy war" fighting evil. Then, too, the "enemy" these mostly white cops are testifying against are poor blacks and Latinos. . . .
>
> [Every year], hundreds of thousands of police officers swear under oath that the drugs were in plain view or that the defendant gave consent to a search. This may happen occasionally but it defies belief that so many drug users are careless enough to leave illegal drugs where the police can see them or so dumb as to give cops consent to search them when they possess drugs.[49]

All of these matters are significant threats to our civil liberties. Abuses and mistakes in governmental law enforcement will always be a fact of life to some extent, just as abuses and errors will always play a role in the private sector. But these abuses are heightened enormously by this country's unworkable drug policy. Governmental wiretapping of our telephones increased significantly during the last two decades, predominantly due to the War on Drugs. The number of federal wiretaps grew from 106 in 1981 to 554 in 1994, the vast majority being for suspected drug crimes. As of that time, federal judges had not refused a wiretap for six years. Even so, only 17 percent of all of the intercepted conversations produced any incriminating evidence; and the cost to the taxpayers averaged $66,783 per wiretap.[50] And this governmental intrusion and use of tax dollars has continued to grow. The FBI reported that in 1997, 1,080 telephone lines were actually tapped on *one busy day* in Los Angeles County alone. The number of wiretaps for the busiest day in San Diego County was 263, and for Orange County 116. Government wiretapping is clearly becoming a widespread activity and, with a $500 million annual expenditure authorized by Congress, an expensive one.[51]

---

49. Dr. Joseph D. McNamara, "Has the Drug War Created an Officer Liars' Club?" *Los Angeles Times*, February 11, 1996, Orange County ed.: Opinion 1.

50. Electronic Privacy Information Center, "Listening In—Selectively," *Newsweek*, May 15, 1995: 22.

51. Stephen Lynch, "Agents Tap up to 116 Phones a Day in O.C." *Orange County Register*, January 25, 1997: A1.

Other intrusions into private lives that have resulted directly from the War on Drugs include the prohibition on participating in any kind of financial transaction involving more than $10,000 in cash. To do so is now a violation of our federal "structuring" laws, which are trying to control and detect drug-money laundering.[52] On October 27, 1998, the Federal Deposit Insurance Corporation (FDIC) proposed regulations called "Know Your Customer" that would have greatly expanded intrusions into private financial transactions. These regulations would have required insured banks to develop and maintain programs to monitor and report on their customers, and were "designed to reduce the likelihood that insured nonmember banks will become unwitting participants in illicit activities."[53] Had they been put into effect, it would have been simply a logical extension of the federal structuring laws. Fortunately the proposed regulations were withdrawn after the FDIC received a large number of complaints about financial privacy and the danger of turning bank tellers into police officers.[54]

The drug wars have spawned other kinds of intrusions into our privacy as well. Many citizens who live in mountainous areas must now put up with the noise and annoyance of police helicopters flying at low altitudes over their homes while searching for marijuana fields. As one resident put it, "It's noisy, it's scary, there's dust flying—it's ridiculous and very frustrating." Others say that the low-flying helicopters routinely kill birds, stampede farm animals, violate environmental laws, and terrify innocent homeowners.[55] These intrusions may not rival the ones in which a person's house is mistakenly raided by police, but tell that to the affected residents and their children.

In other cases, people are unaware that they are being observed in their homes. When police in Wisconsin use heat-sensing devices on helicopters to detect the heat from "grow lights," which are commonly used

---

52. See 31 U.S.C. 5311, et seq.

53. Michael Allen, "Privacy Concerns Spark Criticism of Bank Rule," *Wall Street Journal*, December 10, 1998: B1.

54. "Outcry Beats Back Banking Proposal," *Arizona Republic*, March 24, 1999; Editorial, "Banking Privacy: Congress Should Prevent Tellers from Being Made into Cops," *Houston Chronicle*, February 8, 1999.

55. Lisa M. Krieger, "Pot Spies in the Sky Irk Locals," *San Francisco Examiner*, July 6, 1997: A13; Hohn Howard, "Residents Criticize Federal Pot Raids," *Orange County Register*, January 19, 1999: News 4.

to grow marijuana in residential basements, this is still a significant intrusion into citizens' private lives caused by the War on Drugs.[56]

Many Americans are deeply concerned about the increasing intrusion of governmental agencies into our personal lives. Some of the more outspoken of these adhere to a libertarian philosophy, which holds that their choice, as adults, about what to put into their bodies is simply not the business of government. Governmental involvement is appropriate only when the conduct of one person harms or threatens to harm someone else. Many judges and appellate justices have published opinions and dissents based on this right of personal autonomy, or individual privacy. Such an opinion was written by Justice Steven H. Levinson of the Supreme Court of Hawaii. In his dissent in *State v. Mallan* (86 Hawaii 440, 454 [1998]), he argued extensively, citing the U.S. Supreme Court case of *Griswold v. Connecticut* (381 U.S. 479 [1965]) and numerous other cases, that these fundamental rights of citizens should be afforded the highest consideration under the law. People should be free from prosecution, he argued, for choosing to put even such things as mind-altering drugs into their bodies, as long as no other person is harmed by this action.

In such a large and sensitive area as this, emotions are bound to run high. Steven Loza, an associate professor of ethnomusicology at UCLA, for one, felt compelled to write a letter to the *Los Angeles Times* entitled "Why Does Customs Pick on Me?" Loza is a third-generation Mexican American and a U.S. citizen, but almost every time he returns from a trip to Latin America or Japan he is singled out and questioned by U.S. Customs and his luggage is searched. "All the while I am watching scores of other travelers, especially Asians and whites, pass through Customs without so much as a look their way." During one of these searches, an agent told Loza that customs inspectors are instructed to look more closely at Latinos because they are more likely than Asians or whites to be bringing in drugs. In the normal course of his life, Mr. Loza does not trade on his UCLA affiliation, but he uses it now to get these people "off my back." His letter to the editor expressed a view held by many minorities in this country: "When you challenge these officials, you run the risk of upsetting them and who knows what they could do to you. Even I have been at the point of fearing they might plant something on me if I asked too many questions. . . . When people are sin-

---

56. Associated Press, "Copters Sniff for Drugs," *Sheboygan Press*, May 31, 1992.

gled out because of their ethnic characteristics, we are running into grave danger."[57]

Legitimate fears are also raised by the intrusion of governmental drug warriors into people's religious lives. It is common knowledge that many people arrested for using illicit drugs claim that they are taking them for religious reasons—or for any other reason that might get them off the hook. But sometimes these claims are legitimate, as in the case of Robert Lawrence Boyll, a non-Native American member of the Native American Church. On May 10, 1990, he was indicted by a federal grand jury for unlawfully importing peyote through the U.S. mail and for possessing peyote with the intent to distribute it. Mr. Boyll had gone to Mexico to obtain peyote for himself and members of his congregation. In September 1991, Judge Juan Burciaga, Chief Judge of the U.S. District Court for New Mexico, granted Boyll's motion to dismiss the indictment. Judge Burciaga's action was upheld by a three-judge court on the Tenth Circuit Court of Appeals. Exhibit "A" was Dr. Omar Stewart's book *The Peyote Religion* (University of Oklahoma Press, 1987). In his Memorandum Opinion and Order dismissing the indictment, Judge Burciaga said:

> There is a genius to our Constitution. Its genius is that it speaks to the freedoms of the individual. It is this genius that brings the present matter before the Court. More specifically, this matter concerns a freedom that was a natural idea whose genesis was in the Plymouth Charter, and finds its present form in the First Amendment to the United States Constitution—the freedom of religion.
>
> The Government's "war on drugs" has become a wildfire that threatens to consume those fundamental rights of the individual deliberately enshrined in our Constitution. Ironically, as we celebrate the 200th anniversary of the Bill of Rights, the tattered Fourth Amendment right to be free from unreasonable searches and seizures and the now frail Fifth Amendment right against self-incrimination or deprivation of liberty without due process have fallen as casualties in this "war on drugs." It was naive of this Court to hope that this erosion of constitutional protections would stop at the Fourth and Fifth Amendments. But today, the "war" targets one of the most deeply held fundamental rights—the First Amendment right to freely exercise one's religion.
>
> To us in the Southwest, this freedom of religion has singular significance because it affects diverse cultures. It is as much of us as the rain on our hair,

---

57. Steven Loza, "Why Does Customs Pick on Me?" *Los Angeles Times,* January 16, 1999, Orange County ed.: B9.

the wind on the grass, and the sun on our faces. It is so naturally a part of us that when the joy of this beautiful freedom sings in our soul, we find it hard to conceive that it could ever be imperiled. Yet today . . . the free spirit of the individual once again is threatened by the arrogance of Government.

The issue presented is the recurring conflict between the Native American Church members' right to freely exercise their religion through the ceremonial use of peyote and the Government's efforts to eradicate illegal drugs. To the Government, peyote is a dangerous hallucinogen. To Robert Boyll, peyote is both a sacrament and a deity essential to his religion. But this matter concerns competing interests far greater than those relating to this small, spineless cactus having psychedelic properties. It draws forth a troublesome constitutional conflict which arises from fundamentally different perspectives of peyote.

In its "war" to free our society of the devastating effects of drugs, the Government slights its duty to observe the fundamental freedom of individuals to practice the religion of their choice, regardless of race. Simply put, the Court is faced with the quintessential constitutional conflict between an inalienable right upon which this country was founded and the response by the Government to the swelling political passions of the day. In this fray, the Court is compelled to halt this menacing attack on our constitutional freedoms.

Apart from religious significance, there is a large body of evidence that many currently illicit drugs have widespread medicinal and cultural value. For centuries cultures, ranging from the hunter-gatherers to complex ancient civilizations such as the Incas, have used hallucinogens and other mind-altering plants as a beneficial part of their experience.[58] The major universal and critical difference between those societies and ours, however, is that their systems kept the distribution and use of the substances under the control of their "medicine man" or tribal elders, while under our system the distribution and use is in the hands of drug dealers, gangs, and children.

On the subject of emotion, but at the opposite end of the spectrum, on January 24, 1996, when U.S. District Judge Harold Baer, Jr. threw out thirty-six kilograms of seized drug evidence as well as a confession in a New York case because they were obtained illegally, there was an

---

58. See Marlene Dobkin De Rios, *Hallucinogens: Cross-Cultural Perspectives* (Bridgeport, Dorset, Great Britain: Prism Press, 1990); Michael Winkelman, "Therapeutic Effects of Hallucinogens," *The Anthropology of Consciousness, Society for the Anthropology of Consciousness* (September–December 1991): 15–19; Huston Smith and Jeremy P. Tarcher, *Cleansing the Doors of Perception* (New York: Putnam, 2000); Charles S. Grob, M.D., et al., "Human Psychopharmacology of Hoasea, A Plant Hallucinogen Used in Ritual Context in Brazil," *Journal of Nervous and Mental Disease* 184, no. 2 (1996).

enormous outcry from law enforcement, Capitol Hill, and the White House.[59] Then Senate majority leader and Republican presidential candidate Robert Dole immediately criticized President Clinton for appointing "liberal judges who bend the laws to let drug dealers go free" and called for Judge Baer's impeachment. Not wanting to be outdone by the uproar, the Clinton administration, through President Clinton's press secretary, Mike McCurry, announced that Clinton regretted his decision to appoint Baer to the federal bench and called his ruling "obviously a wrongheaded decision." On April 1 (fittingly?), and for "undisclosed reasons," Judge Baer reversed his decision and actually apologized to the "law-abiding men and women who make [the subject community] their home and the vast majority of the dedicated men and women in blue who patrol the streets of our great city."

Before the decision was reversed, however, the threat to the independence of the nation's judiciary was seen as so great that four judges from the U.S. Court of Appeals for the Second Circuit issued a statement on March 28 defending the trial judge, saying, "The recent attacks on a trial judge of our circuit have gone too far. They threaten to weaken the constitutional structure of this Nation, which has well served our citizens for more than 200 years.... These attacks do a grave disservice to the principle of an independent judiciary, and, more significantly, mislead the public as to the role of judges in a constitutional democracy."[60]

Regardless of the merits of that particular decision, drug cases by their very nature almost always have search-and-seizure and other constitutional implications, and these often give rise to emotional misunderstandings and resentments. If we could find a way to reduce the number of these cases, our country would not be facing such a large threat to its individual liberties and independent judiciary.

One of the largest and most invasive challenges to our Bill of Rights protections remains to be discussed, and that is the civil asset forfeiture laws. These laws permit governments to bring suits to recover instrumentalities, proceeds, and the substituted proceeds of crime. The major difference between these and other laws is that the action is brought

---

59. See *U.S. v. Bayless*, 913 Fed. Supp. 232 (S.D.N.Y. 1996).

60. Don Van Natta, Jr., "Judge Assailed Over Drug Case Issues Reversal and an Apology," *New York Times*, April 2, 1996: 1; Verbatim, "Judges: Attacks on Baer Go Too Far," *Legal Times*, April 1, 1996: 12.

in rem, which is to say, against the property itself, and is not considered to be a punishment of an individual.[61] This is, of course, a legal fiction, because individuals own the property and its loss certainly feels like a punishment. But under these forfeiture laws, if it is shown, for example, by a "preponderance of the evidence" (that is, if it is shown to be more likely than not) that illicit drugs were transported in a particular automobile, airplane, or by other means, or that identifiable money was received from the sale of illicit drugs, or that drugs were stored at a particular house, or particular jewelry was purchased with drug money, any of these assets—the automobile, cash, house, or jewelry—can be forfeited to the government.

The statutory scheme involving asset forfeiture is unprecedented in U.S. legal history. Not only can property be forfeited without a criminal conviction, it is estimated that about 80 percent of the people whose property is taken are not even charged with a criminal offense. Further, these laws require that the people from whom the property is seized have the burden to prove that it was *not* used to facilitate the sale of drugs or purchased with drug money. In other words, the property owners are presumed to be guilty. Never before in the history of U.S. jurisprudence has the burden been placed on individual citizens to prove their innocence. As every schoolchild knows—or should know—it is supposed to be the other way around. And if that is not bad enough, in order to attempt to reclaim their property, they must file a petition to the government within a very short period of time, along with a 10 percent bond—and the government is not even obliged to furnish instructions about how this can be done.[62] Even if the claimants are eventually successful in having their property returned, the government is not required to pay any interest on the money impounded—nor is the government responsible for any injuries that may have been done to the property while it was in the government's possession.[63]

From the time that I became a judge in December 1983, I have kept a hand-printed sign posted on my bench that reads, "There can be no peace in a land without justice." I keep it there to remind myself that

61. See *U.S. v. Ursery*, 518 U.S. 217 (1996); and Linda Greenhouse, "Justices Uphold Civil Forfeiture as Anti-Drug Tool," *New York Times*, June 25, 1996: A1.

62. See *City of West Covina v. Perkins*, 525 U.S. 234 (1999).

63. Charles Levendosky, "Forfeiture Reform Would Stop Law Enforcement Piracy," *Los Angeles Daily Journal*, July 22, 1999: 6; Editorial by the San Jose Mercury News, "End to Forfeiture Abuse," *Los Angeles Daily Journal*, June 29, 1999: 6.

each decision a judge makes is important to somebody and, therefore, to the system of justice as a whole. If justice is not done as much as is humanly possible, we put our way of life and system of government at risk. The manner in which asset forfeiture has been implemented is not at all consistent with our traditional system of justice. In fact it turns our system of justice on its head, and if we continue to implement statutory schemes of this kind, it is only a question of time before we pay an exorbitant price for our shortsightedness.

From the standpoint of law enforcement, however, probably no other procedure accomplishes so many objectives simultaneously as civil asset forfeiture. Removal of assets interferes with the illegal activity itself, weakens the people engaging in that activity, deters others by reducing the profits to be realized, punishes the wrongdoer and denies him the enjoyment and use of the assets gained from his illegal behavior, satisfies the claims of possible victims of the crimes, and raises money for law enforcement agencies.

As one would expect, however, with so much money at stake a great many abuses of this system have been reported. Since law enforcement agencies profit from the assets seized, they have come to depend on this cash flow as part of their budgets, which gives them an added incentive to go after potentially forfeitable property (recall the case of Donald Scott and his two-hundred-acre ranch). As a result, large numbers of automobiles, pieces of real estate, yachts, businesses, jewelry, and other commodities have been seized and forfeited from some big-time drug dealers. But because it is so easy for the government to file a forfeiture case—no conviction is necessary and no drugs need be found—and because it is difficult for people to learn how to defend themselves, and expensive once they learn, many of the forfeitures come from people never intended by Congress to be the subjects of these actions.[64]

And for every big-time drug dealer who loses an estate to the forfeiture laws, there are many, many more small-time crooks who are routinely stopped by the police, relieved of $50 or $100 from their wallets, and then released without any charges ever being filed. Since it costs around $200 in filing fees to seek redress in court and there is a ten percent bond, subjects, whether involved in the selling of drugs or not, almost never try to get the money back.

---

64. For a detailed discussion of this area, see Andrew Schneider and Mary Pat Flaherty, *Presumed Guilty* (Pittsburgh: Pittsburgh Press Co., 1991).

Then there are those whose property is impounded and forfeited who are never even suspected of involvement in illicit drugs. In the town of Fillmore, California, Pat and Bud Untiedt sold their pet-grooming shop and took back a second mortgage. The shop was later seized by the government because it said the new owner was using it to sell cocaine. But even though the government kicked the new owner out, it would not let the Untiedts back in so they could protect their second mortgage, and it would not keep up the payments on the first mortgage, which caused the Untiedts to lose their investment.[65] Similar cases in which innocent people are wronged by our government at all levels are widespread.[66]

Other victims include people who have had their homes and other property seized because of the activities of their children or house-guests. In Hamden, Connecticut, Paul and Ruth Derbacher lost their home to the government because their grandson, whom they had raised from the age of ten, was found to have some marijuana and cocaine in his room. A state judge told the Derbachers, who were by then living in an apartment, "You are probably only guilty of being too tolerant of a criminal grandson."[67] Similar forfeitures were made of three Virginia fraternity houses, worth about a million dollars, where some form of drug dealing allegedly took place.[68] A mother who was a retired cafe-teria worker from the local school district in Roseville, California, had to fight for three years to get her home back after her son was convicted for the possession of methamphetamines with the intent to sell them.[69]

Almost everyone agrees that drug dealers should not be able to profit by their illegal acts, and that the profits and even the instruments, such as the automobiles and airplanes, used to transport the drugs, are rightly subjects of forfeiture. But these goods and assets should be able to be forfeited only *after* a conviction for selling or the intention to sell an

---

65. Jim Newton, "Seizure of Assets Leaves Casualties in War on Drugs," *Los Angeles Times*, October 14, 1992, Orange County ed.: A3.

66. See David A. Kaplan, "Where Innocents Lose," *Newsweek*, January 4, 1993: 42–43; John Dillin, "When Federal Drug Laws Create Havoc For Citizens," *Christian Science Monitor*, September 28, 1993: 10–11; Gary Webb, "Are Police Abusing Asset-Forfeiture Law?" *Orange County Register*, September 5, 1993: State 1.

67. Dillin, ibid. at 10.

68. *New York Times* Editorial, "Are Narcs Swayed by Booty?" *Los Angeles Daily Journal*, May 6, 1991: 6.

69. Art Campos, "After a 3-Year Forfeiture Fight, Home Is Hers to Keep," *The Sacramento Bee*, February 7, 1994: B1.

illicit drug. Once a jury has convicted, evidence can be submitted to the same jury about any proceeds or instruments and the jury can decide what forfeiture is appropriate. In addition to this safeguard, the forfeited assets must not go to law enforcement agencies. We certainly must fund our law enforcement agencies appropriately; but to allow them a share of the booty is an invitation to abuse. Under many of our asset forfeiture laws, the first line of defense for a citizen who believes he has suffered an improper forfeiture is to appeal to the local district attorney. But since the laws frequently allow the same district attorney to keep 13.5 cents of every dollar forfeited, there is an undeniable incentive for (frequently cash-strapped) district attorneys to uphold the forfeiture.[70]

One more problem deserves attention: asset forfeiture programs, such as those in California, have traditionally not required an accounting of what the money from forfeited assets were used for. Since these assets are not always inventoried, it is difficult to trace exactly how much was confiscated and where it went. Between 1986 and 1993, for example, law enforcement agencies in California received $590 million in forfeited assets. For the most part, no one knows where it all went. The Los Angeles sheriff's officers who were convicted of skimming drug money later made comments such as, "We were told, basically, if you want cars, you should go out and seize them. So we would just go out and get them." Former San Diego Sheriff John F. Duffy put more than $300,000 into a secret bank account and said that he would spend the money any way he saw fit. In 1993, an internal audit of the Los Angeles Police Department disclosed that $714,696 in forfeited money was spent for "logistical support" without any further accounting or the approval of the chief of police or any of the fiscal managers. In Marin County, the county counsel decided that the use of $300,000 of forfeited money to settle a sexual harassment suit brought against two county detectives was an appropriate use of the funds—the grand jury disagreed.[71] The stories go on and on, but when the dust settles, the fact remains that large amounts of cash inevitably corrupt. If prohibition laws actually worked, people might be willing to trade some of their civil liberties in exchange for results. But we have already given up civil liberties, and it has been a one-sided trade. Our Drug Prohibition laws

---

70. See Gary Webb, "People Victimized by the Law Can't Do Very Much About It," *Orange County Register,* September 5, 1993: State 4.

71. Sarah Henry, "The Thin Green Line," *California Lawyer,* September 1994: 46.

have not worked, but we have lost, perhaps irretrievably, valuable civil liberties in our futile and expensive attempts to stem the flow of illegal drugs. Long ago, Abraham Lincoln told us what would happen with laws of this kind: "Prohibition goes beyond the bounds of reason in that it attempts to control a man's appetite by legislation and makes crimes out of things that are not crimes. A prohibition law strikes a blow at the very principles upon which our government was founded." We should have heeded Lincoln's warning.

4

Increased Harm to Drug Users

Demonization

Like you, I think our federal and state drug policy has been counterproductive, not to mention horribly expensive. After twenty years of experiencing our myopic drug war, with its enormous expenditures and without any successful reduction in drug use, I have come to the reluctant conclusion that the criminal law remedy is worse than the disease, and that we should explore means other than draconian criminalization to alleviate the drug menace.

Judge Rudolph J. Gerber, Arizona Court of Appeals, Phoenix, Arizona

A good friend of mine who is a federal district court judge teaches a class about the War on Drugs to upper-division students at the University of California at Irvine. Each year he invites ten residents of a live-in drug treatment facility to come to the class. Then he divides the class into ten sections, pairs each section with one of the residents, and leaves them alone for an hour to talk.

This experience allows the students to see the drug problem in a wholly differently light. For the first time they see the problem in human terms rather than in terms of crime and punishment. They learn, in one hour, that these drug-addicted people are human beings like themselves. They have needs and desires, goals and failings, just like everyone else.

Unfortunately, most Americans have not learned this lesson, and they continue to allow people who take illegal drugs to be stereotyped, demonized, prosecuted, and jailed. Remember Billie Holiday, a tortured soul who was arguably the

123

greatest jazz singer of all time? She died in 1959 at the age of forty-four, ravaged from the devastating effects of heroin and alcohol. But when she was literally on her deathbed in a hospital, she was arrested for possession of heroin, fingerprinted, and photographed for a mug shot.[1] This is the depth to which our current drug policy has taken us! Most people do not even distinguish between drug use and drug abuse, or, often enough, between the different drugs themselves. If a drug is "illegal," the people taking it must be "trash," or "crazed addicts" or any number of other stereotypes. Only be demonizing people like Billie Holiday in this way do we allow them to be treated so callously and inhumanely.

Of course, at one time these things were said of people who drank alcohol, a similarly dangerous and sometimes addicting drug. Fortunately this is less the case now than it used to be. Not only have more and more people realized that alcoholism really is a disease, but the legal system has also stated clearly in the California Supreme Court case of *Sundance v. Municipal Court* that people who are addicted to alcohol cannot be punished merely for their addiction. Alcoholics, like the rest of us, will be held accountable for their conduct, and if they cause an accident or kill someone while driving drunk, or assault someone in a bar because they are intoxicated, they will pay the price. But for simply using alcohol, even if they are addicted to it, they cannot be involuntarily confined in a place that does not provide "the minimum requisites of proper treatment and rehabilitation services."[2]

What difference is there between alcohol and any other dangerous and sometimes addictive drug? The primary difference is that one is legal while the others are not. And the U.S. Supreme Court has said as much on at least two occasions, finding both in 1925 and in 1962 that to punish a person for the disease of drug addiction violated the Constitution's prohibition on cruel and unusual punishment.[3] If that is true, why do we

---

1. Francis Davis, "Our Lady of Sorrows," *Atlantic Monthly*, November 2000: 104–8.

2. *Sundance v. The Municipal Court for the Los Angeles Judicial District of the County of Los Angeles*, 42 Cal. 3d 1101, 1155 (1986).

3. See *Linder v. United States*, 268 U.S. 5, 18 (1925), and *Robinson v. United States*, 370 U.S. 660 (1962). The Supreme Court upheld the same principle in *Powell v. Texas*, 392 U.S. 514 (1968), when Justice White said in a concurring opinion that "Unless *Robinson* is to be abandoned, the use of narcotics by an addict must be beyond the reach of the criminal law. Similarly, the chronic alcoholic with an irresistible urge to consume alcohol should not be punishable for drinking or for being drunk." In effect, this "forgotten precedent" says that one can only be constitutionally punishable for one's *conduct*, such as assaults, burglary, and driving under the influence, and not simply for what one puts into one's own body.

continue to prosecute addicted people for taking these drugs, when it would be unconstitutional to prosecute them for their addiction?

The reason is that people who are invested in current U.S. drug policy do not allow these kinds of questions or this kind of analysis. It remains a critical part of our zero-tolerance policy that people who use illegal drugs cannot be considered in human terms. They must be treated as demons and we must contrast "drug cultures," on the one hand, with "decent" people, on the other. We are also led to assume that these "junkies" are always dangerous. It was no slip of the tongue when Daryl Gates, former chief of police of Los Angeles, said that "casual drug users should just be taken out and shot,"[4] or when "Judge Judy" is reported to have said while on a speaking tour in Australia that her answer to the free needle program, which was trying to reduce the spread of disease associated with intravenous drug use, was to "give them dirty needles and hope they die."[5] The unmistakable message to the public is that drug users are to be feared and scorned.

But why are these drug prohibitionists so successful in what amounts to public deception, whether this deception is organized or not, deliberate or not, even conscious or not? Why is there any question in anyone's mind about whether drug addicts should really be treated at all? Why is it so difficult to educate people in this area—especially when study after study shows that treatment for substance abuse is at least as effective as treatment for some forms of heart disease, diabetes, and mental illnesses, and that it reduces drug use by more than 40 percent? When it has been statistically proven that about half the people who receive drug treatment go on to gainful employment, whereas before treatment they were unable to hold a job, why do people still believe that punishment, not treatment, is the answer?[6] Why do our "leaders"

---

4. Joseph D. McNamara, "We're Fighting a No-Win War against Drugs," *Orange County Register*, April 20, 1993: Metro 11.

5. Mike Farrell, "There's Disorder in the Court—and Television Stands Accused," *Los Angeles Times*, May 31, 2000, Orange County ed.: B13. In this article, the well-known actor of *MASH* fame rightfully complains, as a member of the California Judicial Performance Commission, that the public is left with the mistaken impression after watching Judge Judy that it is common and even appropriate for a judge to act in such a "thoughtless, mean-spirited and destructive" manner. He cringes at the thought (so do we all!), but because Judge Judy is no longer a practicing judge, she is beyond the control of any public disciplinary body.

6. Alan I. Leshner, Director of the National Institute on Drug Abuse at the National Institutes of Health, "Why Shouldn't Society Treat Substance Abusers?" *Los Angeles Times*, June 11, 1999, Orange County ed.: B9.

pay lip service to the effectiveness of drug treatment, while carrying on business as usual?

One major reason is that in the degraded political arena of five-second sound bites, most politicians dare not be labeled "soft on drugs." Moreover, and equally important, one does not get elected by taking positions that run counter to the numerous, wealthy, and well-established vested interests, both inside and outside government. As the lyrics of "Politics, the Art of the Possible," from the great Andrew Lloyd Webber musical *Evita*, say, politicians always try to "pick the easy fight" and "take their stand" when the "risk is slight." For people who occupy or are seeking to occupy elective office, it is much easier to declare war on "disgusting drug addicts" and "evil drug pushers" who are "corrupting and threatening our children." The immediate and tangible results can be seen on Election Day. Drug users are not politically organized and cannot fight back. So there is no risk in taking a "hard line" against these "enemies," these "demons."

Whose fault is this? It is our fault. It is our country, and we are the voters. Politicians are great at "followership." They would not campaign on a platform of zero tolerance if it would not help them get elected. It might even be said that politicians do not have to deal with reality, just with voters' perception of reality. If politicians were forced to deal with reality, then they would have gotten "real" on the drug problem long ago.

Deterioration of Health

There are many devastating results of the "War on Drugs." One which is especially cruel and will have a terrible impact on American life for many generations is the large increase in the number of women incarcerated for drug violations. From 1980 to 1996, there has been over a 400 percent increase in the number of women prisoners. Many of those jailed for drug violations were mules or assistants. I venture that none was a principal organizer. Many are mothers of small children who will be left without maternal care, and most probably without any parental care at all. Leaving these children adrift will sow the seed for future lawbreakers. The engine of punitive punishment of mothers will haunt this nation for many years to come. There must be a better way.

Judge John T. Curtin, United States District Court, Buffalo, New York

The effects of our drug policy on the health of people who use illicit drugs stem from four basic problems: (1) a lack of information about medical hygiene, because our laws push drug users away from the medical professionals who can help them; (2) no quality control regarding either the strength or purity of illicit drugs; (3) the inability of many drug users to prepare and use injectable drugs under more medically hygienic conditions (San Francisco spends up to $40 million per year treating abscesses in heroin users, which are usually caused by injecting heroin into muscles instead of veins; and about half of the twelve patients per day who are admitted into the general hospital emergency room require surgery, which frequently results in extensive scarring or amputation);[7] and (4) the enormous pressure on drug addicts to engage in dangerous criminal activity, such as prostitution, burglary and drug dealing, in order to get the money to purchase these artificially expensive drugs. As we will see, these issues are addressed much more effectively by the governments of Switzerland, Holland, and Germany, which are far more practical than we are in our doctrinaire approach.

The results of violence are one obvious medical problem that result from the War on Drugs, violence to both to drug users and non-users alike. I recall the story of an innocent bystander who was shot in the chest during a drug war shootout. As he was being screened and prepared for emergency surgery, he was asked if he suffered from any allergies. "Yes," he responded, "I'm allergic to bullets." This is an allergy we all share, to the extent that Milton Friedman, the Nobel-prize-winning economist, has estimated that an average of 10,000 people are killed each year in the United States as a direct result of the high price of buying and selling illegal drugs.[8]

But there are other, more subtle medical threats as well. Methamphetamine laboratories, for instance, sometimes blow up, killing everyone inside, including innocent children who happen to be in the same building. These labs can be found not only in "ghetto" areas but also in upscale neighborhoods.[9] Even when they do not explode, tests have

---

7. Edward Epstein, "Treatment of Heroin Users' Sores Cost S.F. Up To $40 Million Yearly," *San Francisco Chronicle*, March 24, 2000: A20.

8. Milton Friedman and Thomas S. Szasz, *On Liberty and Drugs* (Washington D.C.: The Drug Policy Foundation Press, 1992): 71.

9. Matthew Heller, "Mother Guilty in Drug Lab Deaths," *Los Angeles Daily Journal*, December 2, 1996: 2. One evening several years ago I was invited to a dinner party given at the home of a fellow judge in Seal Beach, California. When we arrived in the neighborhood, several blocks were closed off because a methamphetamine lab had been found in one of the neighboring houses. I later heard that the owners of the home had gone on an extended vacation. When they returned, they found an unknown man living in their house and manufacturing these drugs. He simply fled and the owners called the police, who called the fire department, who closed off the entire area. Similar illegal and volatile labs have been discovered in hotel rooms and office buildings.

shown that about one-quarter of all children who are taken out of these labs have methamphetamines, or other caustic chemicals or dangerous substances used to make that drug, in their systems. Often the fumes from these drugs are inhaled by the "chemist's" children, who play and in some cases live in these illegal laboratories, and these substances have been known to cause harm to the brain, liver, kidneys, lungs, and eyes, and to cause learning disabilities, emotional and behavioral problems, or even death.[10]

And then there is the reluctance to seek medical help out of fear or prosecution. In the town of Plano, Texas, a suburb of Dallas with a population of 200,000, about twenty teenagers died of drug overdoses in one year. The friends of these teens did not seek medical help until it was too late because they were afraid that they would be arrested for using illegal drugs. When he heard about this tragedy, author Mike Gray asked the local authorities in Plano why they did not announce that anyone reporting a drug overdose would be guaranteed safe passage, with no questions asked. The authorities responded that this "would send the wrong message." Apparently they prefer to send the message that it is better to let your friends die than to get them to a hospital to save their lives.[11]

Another drug victim in Plano, Texas, was Mark Tuinei, a former offensive lineman for the Dallas Cowboys. He died in May 1999 from a combination of heroin and a stimulant. At the time of his death, a running back with the Cowboys named Nicky Sualua was with him but also did not seek immediate medical attention.[12] This was also apparently the case in the highly publicized drug death of Len Bias in 1986. As sports fans know, Bias was an outstanding basketball player for the University of Maryland, so exceptional that he was drafted in the first round by the Boston Celtics. Bias was so excited at having been drafted that night that he tried some cocaine for the first time in his life. He had an allergic reaction to the drug and died. What is not widely known, however, is that Bias was having his third convulsion before his friends sought medical attention. They were too afraid that Bias or they them-

---

10. Bill Rams, "Kids Taken from Meth-Lab Homes Show Internal Levels of Drug," *Orange County Register,* December 22, 1998: Metro 1.

11. Mike Gray, oral testimony before the Los Angeles Citizens' Commission on U.S. Drug Policy, May 23, 1999, University of Southern California.

12. Staff and Wire Reports, "Examiner Says Tuinei Died of Drug Overdose," *Los Angeles Times,* May 12, 1999, Orange County ed.: D12.

selves would be arrested that they did not take him to a hospital. If not for our drug prohibitionist laws, Len Bias, Mark Tuinei, those twenty teenagers in Plano, and many more people just like them would probably still be alive today.

One of the most emotional and perplexing problems in this entire area is drug use by pregnant women. It appears that all pregnant women—not just poor women—are routinely denied access to the limited drug treatment that is available in this country. In an important study finished in 1990, Dr. Wendy Chavkin discovered that fully 54 percent of the drug treatment facilities in New York City actually refused to accept pregnant women at all. She further found that 67 percent of the facilities refused to take pregnant women who were on Medicaid, and 84 percent of these facilities refused to take pregnant women who were addicted to crack cocaine.[13] When we add to this problem the natural tendency in our society to demonize drug-addicted women, punish them through the criminal justice system, and try to get them off drugs at the earliest opportunity, we begin to see why many of these women give in to despair—which of course often increases their drug usage.

Almost all drug-addicted pregnant women are concerned about the harmful effects their drug usage will have on their unborn child, and most of them try, within their limits, to engage in their own type of "harm reduction." Most try to cut down on their drug consumption, or change to what they perceive to be a less harmful drug during pregnancy. Some utilize various home remedies, such as "cleansing their system" by drinking vinegar or pickle juice, and many take vitamin pills. But these measures are no match for a regular dose of crack or some other harmful drug.

The high cost of their drug habit also often has a direct effect on their ability to take care of themselves and the fetus, and their well-founded fear of punishment—or of having their babies taken away if their drug use is discovered—means that many of these pregnant mothers forego even the prenatal care that is available to them, or even decide to have the baby at home or to have an abortion. Our policy of Drug Prohibition is pushing pregnant women away from getting professional help at exactly the time when they—and their unborn children—need it most.[14]

---

13. Dr. Wendy Chavkin, "Drug Addiction and Pregnancy: Policy Crossroads," *American Journal of Public Health* 80, no. 4, (April 1990): 483–87.

14. See Sheigla Murphy and Marsha Rosenbaum, *Pregnant Women on Drugs, Combating Stereotypes and Stigma* (New Brunswick, N.J.: Rutgers University Press, 1999).

The relief of pain by marijuana in cases of cancer, AIDS, arthritis, and other diseases where conventional pain remedies have proved ineffective has been fairly well documented, and people seem to be beginning to understand this, as the medical use of this drug has been approved by many state ballot initiatives, and a bill providing for the possession and use of marijuana for medical purposes was signed into law by the governor of Hawaii in June 2000.[15] But in some cases, because these state measures conflict with the federal law, the "will of the people" has yet to be put into effect. In any case, the medical use of beneficial drugs is certainly an area in which health concerns have been adversely affected by our blind addiction to failed drug prohibitionist policies. If you have doubts about this issue, consider the words of this woman from Santa Barbara, California:

> I am a cancer survivor who has firsthand knowledge of a treatment option that should be freely available but is not: marijuana.
>
> Although I grew up in the decade that made marijuana famous, I never smoked it. I never smoked anything; I didn't even know how to use a lighter. But when I underwent chemotherapy for ovarian cancer, and the prescribed anti-nausea medications didn't work, and my doctor refused to prescribe marinol (the pills with the active ingredient from marijuana), I resorted to the herb. A young man had to teach me what to do. Friends had to risk legal repercussions to provide me with it.
>
> I never smoked enough to get high—smoking was an exhausting challenge in itself. But I got enough in me so I could force myself to drink liquids. Before marijuana, I'd become dangerously de-hydrated. I would use enough so that I could finally sleep a few hours. Previously, I'd been awake nonstop and so miserable I wished I'd just die. Unlike with the doctor's pharmaceuticals, there were no side effects—like dopey drowsiness, constipation or depression. . . .
>
> Every useful substance can be used for harm. But prejudice, a tremendous fear and lack of big profits for corporations has us by the throat when it comes to this humble servant from God's pharmacy. Let us have mercy: Marijuana isn't just for potheads. It is good medicine.[16]

---

15. Chronicle News Service, "Governor Signs Hawaiian Law on Medical Pot," *San Francisco Chronicle*, June 15, 2000: A6.

16. Ruth Barnett, "Marijuana: Good Medicine," *Los Angeles Times*, October 23, 1999, Orange County ed.: B6. For an overall history of the medical uses of marijuana, with numerous anecdotal evidence of its beneficial effects, see Martin Martinez, *The New Prescription: Marijuana As Medicine*, ed. Francis Podrebarac, M.D. (Oakland, Calif.: Quick American Archives, 2000), and Alan Bock, *Waiting to Inhale, The Politics of Medical Marijuana* (Santa Ana, Calif.: Seven Locks Press: 2000).

Rather than persist in staunch, self-defeating opposition to the medical use of marijuana, under a doctor's supervision, for people with cancer and other diseases, the federal government should, at the very least, change marijuana from a Schedule I drug (one known to have no beneficial medical properties), to a Schedule II drug, which, like cocaine, can be prescribed when a licensed physician believes it is medically appropriate. When General Barry McCaffrey spoke before my local chapter of the World Affairs Council in February 2000, I asked him if, in light of the state initiatives on medical marijuana that had been passed in seven states and the District of Columbia, he would now do what he could to allow the will of the voters to prevail. The Drug Czar's answer was that since he himself did not believe that marijuana was a viable medicine, he would try to keep the federal government from changing its policy.[17]

A drug-related problem that seems even more clearly to defy progress is presented by mentally disabled people who "self-medicate" with illicit street drugs. But the policy of Drug Prohibition is aggravating this difficult problem. What the answer is to the problems of these troubled people, I do not know. But what the answer is *not* is to put them in jail, which is what we are doing in large measure. To my knowledge the Los Angeles County Jail is the largest mental facility in the world. Since any drugs that a mentally disabled person could want are easily available on the streets, for a price, and since they frequently do not have sufficient knowledge or strength to resist them, a large number of these emotionally fragile people end up in jail, where they get very little beneficial attention or treatment, to put it mildly. This also puts their loved ones and care providers in a difficult situation, as we see in the case of an Australian mother of a twenty-five-year-old schizophrenic son who had been dependent on heroin for three years. This brave mother described her course of action: "Trauma is finding a solution when faced with a life and death situation. I had to gain control of the heroin, which was spiralling out of control and heading down the crime road unless I intervened. My 'harm minimisation' was to 'do a deal' with him. I paid for the heroin on the condition that I kept it and meted out the doses. Gradually we were able to reduce it. What wouldn't a parent do to save their child?"[18]

---

17. See James P. Gray, "Is Our Drug Policy Failing? Don't Ask," *Los Angeles Times*, March 29, 2000, Orange County ed.: B11.

18. Family Drug Support, *heroInsight* (April/May 2000), 1–2. This support group can be located at P.O. Box 226, Willoughby, New South Wales, Australia 2068, e-mail <trimmo@tig.com.au>

What would you do if it were your son? What do you think General McCaffrey would do if that young man were his son? This mother needs and deserves all the help she can get, and the last thing she needs is that her mentally disabled son be locked in jail for his drug addiction.

It is a great irony of this country's so-called War on Drugs that prescription drugs kill more Americans each year than AIDS and homicides combined.[19] In fact, the DEA estimates that the black market in prescription drugs totaled $25 billion in 1993, compared to an estimated $31 billion spent the same year for cocaine. The National Institute on Drug Abuse estimates that 2.6 million Americans use prescription drugs for "non-medical reasons," which is more than the estimated number of users of heroin, crack, and powder cocaine. The Drug Abuse Warning Network estimates that prescription painkillers, sedatives, stimulants, and tranquilizers account for 75 percent of the top twenty drugs that bring people to the emergency room each year.[20] This is also becoming a major problem area for teenagers. Abuse of medication and painkillers sent hundreds of youngsters to hospital emergency rooms in 1999, and the U.S. Department of Health and Human Services estimates that the number of teenagers nationwide who abuse prescription painkillers alone rose from 125,000 in 1990 to 718,000 in 1998.[21] Prescription drugs are often over-prescribed by doctors, or prescriptions are forged by the sometimes addicted users, or the drugs are smuggled into the United States from other countries, such as Mexico, and sold from the trunks of cars or at swap meets.[22] But even though the magnitude of this problem far exceeds that of illicit drugs, our current drug policy leaves prescription drugs almost entirely out of the picture.

After his death, Congressman Sonny Bono's widow stated publicly for the first time that her husband had been hooked on valium and percodan, taking twenty of those pills *each day*. Why get so tough on a substance like marijuana, and overlook the abuse of valium or percodan? No one who wanted seriously to address the medical and social problems of our communities would allow such a policy to exist. But the drug

---

19. "Test Your Health IQ," *Newsweek*, August 2, 1999: 53.

20. Dan Weikel, "Prescription Fraud: Abusing the System," *Los Angeles Times*, August 18, 1996, Orange County ed.: A1.

21. Richard Marosi and Theresa Morlau, "Teens' Abuse of Legal Drugs on the Rise," *Los Angeles Times*, October 23, 2000, Orange County ed.: A1, 20.

22. Editorial, "Illegal Health Care Crackdown," *Los Angeles Times*, August 1, 1999, Orange County ed.: B6.

warriors, and all those with vested interests in maintaining the status quo, have no room for reason or common sense. And let's not forget the power of the pharmaceutical lobby, which contributed $9.5 million to candidates of both political parties in the 1998 election cycle, according to the Center for Responsive Politics.[23] It is evidently much easier for our elected officials to lock up defenseless drug addicts than to take on such a powerful organized interest.

Fortunately, however, other people are beginning to focus on the problem. In an editorial on the Sonny Bono story, the *San Francisco Examiner* wrote:

> This level of medication made [Congressman Bono] part of a huge, silent epidemic that neither Gen. Barry McCaffrey nor DARE nor conservative politicians spend much time bemoaning, let alone fighting. But legal mood drugs and painkillers are abused more widely in this country than heroin, cocaine or just about any other illegal drug you can name. Statistics are hard to come by, but one study this year estimated that 2.8 million American women over age 59 were addicted to prescription drugs. Instead of combating this real peril, the federal government is filing suit to stop AIDS sufferers from enjoying a joint, and pouring billions of dollars into the eradication of coca fields in South America.[24]

If anyone needs more evidence of the severity of the prescription drug problem, they should consider that after film producer Don Simpson died from overdosing on cocaine and twenty prescription drugs, police found more than 2,200 pills and tablets stockpiled in his bedroom closet. Subsequent investigation disclosed that about 15,000 sedatives, amphetamines, tranquilizers, anti-psychotics, narcotics, and other medications had been provided to Simpson in the three years before his death by fifteen local doctors and pharmacies.[25] Similarly, the last prescription that was filled for Elvis Presley before he died in August 1977 included 50 tablets of Dilaudid, 150 Quaeludes, 100 Dexedrines, 100 Percodans, 100 Amytals, and 100 Biphetamines. Were the doctors and pharmacists who wrote and filled these prescriptions, and made a nice profit doing so, arrested for pushing these dangerous drugs? Obviously not. If you are looking for a consistent, commonsense approach to

---

23. Arianna Huffington, *How to Overthrow the Government* (New York: ReganBooks, 2000), 149.

24. Editorial, "Dangerous *Legal* Drugs," *San Francisco Examiner*, November 22, 1998.

25. Chuck Philips, "Don Simpson's Death Showed Depth of Abuse," *Los Angeles Times*, August 18, 1996, Orange County ed.: A26.

health policy in the United States, do not look at the actions of the federal government. Although a five-year federally funded program existed to spend a *billion dollars* to get our children to swear off "drugs,"[26] a congressional committee voted against adding alcohol to the anti-drug message, for fear that it would "water down" their message against the "illicit" drugs.[27] They did this even though underage drinking of alcohol is easily a larger health threat to our children than the use of all illegal drugs combined. And to this irresponsibility can be added the vote in the Senate and the House on July 23 and 24, 1997, against an amendment to end the $34 million subsidy by the federal government to tobacco.[28]

Another problem cries out to be discussed. Clearly there is a place for prisons in our society, even though one of the necessary evils of imprisonment is that it can embitter and demoralize people. And of course convicted felons face serious obstacles in finding meaningful employment once they are released. We must also understand that imprisonment all too frequently causes severe physical and emotional damage to people. Chief Judge Donald P. Lay of the U.S. Court of Appeals in St. Paul, Minnesota, has addressed this problem, adding his voice to the growing chorus demanding a change in our policy:

> In an effort to fight crime, we aimlessly set goals of putting more and more people into jails and prisons, regardless of consequential costs or the complete denigration of dignity and resulting human sacrifice. As a nation, we countenance, without apparent concern, increasing episodes of temporary banishment of individuals to horrific and indecent environs in our jails and prisons, and falsely assume on their return to society that they will become useful citizens bearing no resentment. . . .
>
> The atrocities that take place within jails and prisons are commonplace. A few years ago, I visited a correctional institution in a southern state. A 19-year-old farm boy had just been sentenced for one year for possession of marijuana. He was received in their central processing unit, designed to hold 120 prisoners. At that time there were 465 prisoners incarcerated in small cells in a four level building that afforded little ventilation and no recreational area.
>
> The young man was sent to a psychological evaluation unit. After two hours they picked up his exam papers and he had written only two words:

---

26. Frank Rich, "Just Say $1 Billion," *New York Times,* July 15, 1998: A19.

27. Lisa Keck, "Federal Anti-Drug Campaign Omits Alcohol Abuse," *Orange County Register,* August 22, 1999: Commentary 4.

28. "Tobacco Subsidy Survives," *Washington Post,* July 25, 1997: A16.

"Help Me. Help Me." Officials discovered that he had been put in a small cell block containing four beds with 11 other inmates who had sexually assaulted him for 48 hours, every hour on the hour. . . .

The resulting approach is accomplishing nothing more than exorbitantly wasting tax dollars, creating a warehouse of human degradation and in the long run breeding societal resentment that causes more crime. . . .

Punishment is one thing, but our incarceration policies are wasteful and should be changed. Present policies breed further crime, dehumanize individuals and require gross expenditures of tax dollars needed for other purposes. With our nation facing both societal and fiscal crises of unrivaled proportions, we must move quickly and forcefully to overhaul the current system.[29]

Finally, the federal government continues to turn a deaf ear to the cries of chronic pain from the sick and dying. Morphine has been shown to be one of the most effective substances known to mankind for the relief of severe pain. But doctors are legitimately wary of prescribing this drug, even for the dying, because of the Drug Enforcement Administration, who can seize the doctors' property and destroy their careers over even one questionable prescription. This has left approximately one in four elderly cancer patients in nursing homes receiving no treatment for daily pain, and approximately 34 million people in this country who suffer chronic but treatable pain without relief. As a practical matter, if a person is dying, what difference does it make if she might become addicted to a narcotic drug, a drug that could make her last days on earth free from unnecessary pain? Further, it is estimated that one-quarter of all sick days taken from employment and school, or approximately 50 million days per year, are taken because of the absence of pain relief.[30] Many Americans are still not aware that we have this problem, but, especially as they get older, they will learn.

In reality, drugs in themselves are neither "bad" nor "good." It depends on how and under what circumstances they are used. In some circumstances, obviously, the use of a particular drug can be quite beneficial; in other circumstances the same drug may be quite harmful. But our current drug policy has focused arbitrarily on only some drugs,

---

29. Chief Judge Donald P. Lay, U.S. Court of Appeals for the Eighth Circuit, "Our Justice System, So-Called," *New York Times*, October 22, 1990.

30. Shannon Brownlee and Joannie M. Schrof, "The Quality of Mercy—Effective Pain Treatments Already Exist. Why Aren't Doctors Using Them?" *U.S. News & World Report*, March 17, 1997: 54–67; Lauran Neergaard, "New Law Could Ease Pain-Racked Deaths," *Orange County Register*, October 16, 1999: News 12.

often making their use illegal in all or almost all circumstances. Not only has this approach not worked, and not only has it caused an enormous amount of unintended hardship, crime, and misery along the way, it has also resulted in other—and sometimes more harmful—drug use being almost completely ignored.

Our myopia on the drug question can be seen when we reflect on the fact that our children are now consuming caffeine earlier and more often than ever before. According to a 1994 survey by the U.S. Department of Agriculture, children and teens are consuming on average more than 64 *gallons* of soda each year. This amount has tripled since 1978, doubling for children between the ages of six and eleven and even increasing by one-quarter for children under the age of five. This has made soda the best-selling product at our nation's grocery stores.[31] But is caffeine a "good" drug or a "bad" drug? According to several medical reports, caffeine poses some worrisome health threats, especially for children, and can produce dependency and withdrawal symptoms when taken away. Where does caffeine fit into America's drug policy? Why isn't it illegal for children under eighteen, as alcohol is? A thoughtful, rational drug policy would address and educate about the use of all of these drugs, instead of moralistically addressing only the ones that have arbitrarily been made illegal.

---

31. Helen Cordes, "Generation Wired: Caffeine Is the New Drug of Choice for Kids," *The Nation*, April 27, 1998; A. Goldstein and M. E. Wallace, "Caffeine Dependence in Schoolchildren," *Experimental and Clinical Psychopharmacology* 5 (1997): 388–92.

5

Increased Harm for the Future

Conspiracy Theories

I applaud your efforts to bring the light of reason to this subject.
I seriously doubt that our politicians have the will to accept a
dispassionate solution, however.
Justice Byron J. Johnson, Idaho Supreme Court, Boise, Idaho

n August 1991, while attending a reunion of my Peace Corps
Costa Rica group in San Francisco, I went with some friends
to a service at the Glide Methodist Church. This is a fa-
mously successful church in one of the poorer areas of the
city, where people from all walks of life attend a rousing
church service full of love, brotherhood, and rock music.
Although there is normally a wide variety of people in atten-
dance—rich and poor, young and old, healthy and sickly,
educated and streetwise, and people of all races—the majority are black. That Sunday, the senior pastor was absent,
and the sermon was delivered by a young, articulate, well-
dressed black man.

The thrust of this man's sermon was that after the riots
in 1965 in Los Angeles, Detroit, and Chicago, the federal
government plotted to keep blacks in city ghettos under
control either by sedating them or by incarcerating them on
drug charges. This scheme was put into effect, he said, by
FBI agents who drove into ghetto areas, opened the trunks
of their cars, and gave out free samples of heroin to the local
residents. Many poor blacks became addicted as a result,
and others became "addicted" to selling heroin and other

narcotics. This articulate and intense young man said that he had proof that this had happened, in the form of the names of people who themselves had witnessed the giveaway of drugs by federal agents.

If this story were true, it would be an immoral and despicable if not treasonous act. I myself do not believe it; I regard conspiracy theories with suspicion. But whether this story, and others like it, are true or not is irrelevant, at least in one respect. What is important is that many people believe they are true. Their cynicism and anger erode the confidence and adherence of many people to our government and our way of life.

Since the prohibition of drugs involves so much money and so much organized illegal activity, it naturally gives rise to speculation about conspiracies such as the one the young black man described. As a result, even legitimate and proper government programs and actions come to be tainted, in the minds of many Americans, with some kind of ulterior motive. Take, for example, the disparity in criminal sentences for powder and crack cocaine. Under our current laws, a crack dealer (usually black) who is arrested for the first time with five grams of crack must serve a five-year mandatory minimum sentence, whereas a first-time seller of powder cocaine (more often white) would not receive this mandatory sentence unless he had at least five *hundred* grams. This disparity—some would say obvious injustice—has placed significantly more blacks than whites in federal prison for longer periods of time, and is widely considered to be deliberately racist.[1]

More fuel for the argument that our drug policy may be a racist conspiracy was provided in the small town of Tulia, Texas, where a sting operation in July 1999 resulted in the arrest and indictment of forty-three people on charges of drug dealing based on the testimony of one undercover deputy sheriff. Fully one-sixth of all the black residents in the town were indicted, and one of them received a sentence of sixty years for selling about $150 worth of cocaine. The prosecutions began

---

1. See Dan Weikel, "War on Crack Targets Minorities Over Whites," *Los Angeles Times,* May 21, 1995, Orange County ed.: A1; Greg Krikorian, "Study Spotlights Justice System's Racial Disparity," *Los Angeles Times,* February 13, 1996, Orange County ed.: A1; Sam Vincent Meddis, "Is the Drug War Racist? Disparities Suggest the Answer Is Yes," *USA Today,* July 23–25, 1993: 1A; Sam Vincent Meddis, "Is the Drug War Racist? In Twin Cities, a Tale of Two Standards," *USA Today,* July 26, 1993: 6A; Susan Seager, "A Matter of Race, Study Says Whites Elude Federal Court in Crack Cases," *Los Angeles Daily Journal,* August 25, 1993: 1.

to unravel, however, when it was learned that the deputy sheriff had an undisclosed background of theft and lying, leaving many people with the belief that the entire episode been designed to get rid of an undesirable racial element.[2]

Conspiracy theories about the U.S. government's involvement with major drug traffickers outside the country are rampant. For one thing, it would be difficult to deny that during the Cold War the United States cared more about fighting communism than about fighting drug trafficking. Indeed, the U.S. government supported a number of "anticommunist" foreign leaders and agents who also happened to be making huge amounts of money from the shipping of illegal drugs. Manuel Noriega of Panama was one of the better known of these people, but there were many others throughout Southeast Asia during the Vietnam War, in Afghanistan during its war with the Soviet Union, and elsewhere around the globe.

One of the severest charges of U.S. government alliance with foreign drug traffickers—and one that provides fertile ground for conspiracy theorists—was an allegation made by Gary Webb of the *San Jose Mercury News*. On August 18, 1996, Webb reported that a Colombia–to–San Francisco Bay area drug pipeline had helped finance the CIA-backed Contras in their fight against the Sandinistas in Nicaragua.

> For the better part of a decade, a San Francisco Bay Area drug ring sold tons of cocaine to the Crips and Bloods street gangs of Los Angeles and funneled millions in drug profits to a Latin American guerrilla army run by the U.S. Central Intelligence Agency, a *Mercury News* investigation has found.
>
> This drug network opened the first pipeline between Colombia's cocaine cartels and the black neighborhoods of Los Angeles, a city now known as the "crack" capital of the world. The cocaine that flooded in helped spark a crack explosion in urban America . . . and provided the cash and connections needed for L.A.'s gangs to buy automatic weapons.
>
> It is one of the most bizarre alliances in modern history: the union of a U.S.-backed army attempting to overthrow a revolutionary socialist government and the Uzi-toting 'gangstas' of Compton and South-Central Los Angeles.[3]

---

2. Hector Tobar, "Big Drug Bust in Small Town: A Race Question," *Los Angeles Times*, October 7, 2000, Orange County ed.: A1, 27; Arianna Huffington, "Texas Town Is a Crucible for Today's Witch Hunt," *Los Angeles Times*, October 10, 2000, Orange County ed.: B11.

3. Gary Webb, "'Crack' Plague's Roots Are In Nicaraguan War," *San Jose Mercury News*, August 18, 1996: 1.

After that article appeared, other publications investigated Webb's charges and found that many of them were unsubstantiated.[4] The *Mercury News* in turn defended itself by publishing an analysis of the criticism of its series.[5] But whether some or all of Webb's allegations are true, the fact remains that our drug laws have made it appear to the world that the U.S. government itself is intimately associated with bigtime drug dealers and thugs.

There's an old saying that if you lie down in the gutter with dogs, you will get up with fleas. Because we have chosen to make these drugs illegal, and therefore obscenely lucrative, we have made it inevitable that politics in much of the world centers on drug wealth. There is simply no way for our government to be involved with corrupt people, people who control hundreds of millions of drug dollars, without dirtying itself in the process.

Since Gary Webb's series, the CIA itself has officially acknowledged that CIA personnel worked with about two dozen members of Nicaraguan rebel organizations involved in narcotics trafficking while the U.S.-financed war against the Sandinistas was underway in the 1980s. One CIA official said, "We dealt with them nonetheless because of the value they brought. In other cases, the allegations appear simply to have dropped through cracks in the bureaucracy."[6] Even Robert C. Bonner, the head of the DEA under President George Bush, acknowledged that there was "at least some participation in approving or condoning" drug smuggling by the CIA.[7] Unofficially, many books and hundreds of articles have alleged the involvement of the U.S. government with acknowledged drug traffickers in connection with the Contras and similar groups, each one weaving a plot in which the United States either dealt actively with the exchange of drugs for guns that would then be used by groups like the Contras, or turned a "blind eye" to these transactions being performed by others. I have no particular information about

---

4. See Doyle McManus, "Examining Charges of CIA Role in Crack Sales," *Los Angeles Times*, October 21, 1996, Orange County ed.: A1; Robert Suro and Walter Pincus, "The CIA and Crack: Evidence is Lacking of Alleged Plot," *Washington Post*, October 4, 1996.

5. See Pete Carey, "'Dark Alliance' Series Takes on a Life of its Own," *San Jose Mercury News*, October 13, 1996.

6. "CIA Admits to Using Nicaraguan Rebels With Drug Ties; Report Says Agency Knowingly Worked with Suspected Narcotics Traffickers," *Los Angeles Times*, July 18, 1998, Orange County ed.: A3.

7. Michael Isikoff, "U.S. Probes Narcotics Unit Funded by CIA," *Washington Post*, November 20, 1993: A1.

whether some of these disturbing allegations are true, but many of these authors did exhaustive research and were certainly in a position to know the truth.

One such person is a decorated former DEA undercover agent named Michael Levine, who wrote in his book, *The Big White Lie: The CIA and the Cocaine/Crack Epidemic*, that the War on Drugs is an illusion. According to Levine, over and over again major drug traffickers against whom the DEA was trying to build a case were regarded by the CIA as "assets," which caused the DEA investigations to be terminated. All of this was done, of course, in the name of "national security."[8] Similarly, Celerino "Cele" Castillo, who wrote *Powderburns: Cocaine, Contras, and the Drug War*, was a supervisory agent for the DEA in El Salvador and Honduras who personally notified highly placed officials in our government that large shipments of cocaine were being smuggled into the United States by mercenary pilots he himself had hired to assist the Contras in Nicaragua. But no action was taken.[9] Gary Webb expanded his newspaper series into a book called *Dark Alliance: The CIA, the Contras, and the Crack Cocaine Explosion*, which chronicles many disturbing allegations of the complicity of United States Government agents with drug trafficking in Central America.[10] In *Cocaine Politics, Drugs, Armies, and the CIA in Central America*, authors Peter Dale Scott and Jonathan Marshall cite extensive evidence that the term "Drug War" really means a covert war financed by the sale of drugs, especially with the support of our own agents.[11] *Hep-cats, Narcs, and Pipe Dreams: A History of America's Romance with Illegal Drugs* states that before World War II, France actively encouraged the cultivation of opium poppies in the Golden Triangle (the intersection of Laos, Burma, and Thailand), and continued to do so in order to finance the Indochina war. By the mid-1950s, the author states that French military intelligence was "up to its neck in drug trafficking." The same book examines U.S. involvement in the

---

8. Michael Levine and Laura Kavanau-Levine, *The Big White Lie: The CIA and the Cocaine/Crack Epidemic* (New York: Thunder's Mouth Press, 1993).

9. Celerino Castillo and Dave Harmon, *Powderburns: Cocaine, Contras and the Drug War* (New York: Mosaic Press, 1994); see also Robert L. Jackson, "Ex-DEA Agent Ties Contras to U.S. Drug Flights," *Los Angeles Times*, September 24, 1996, Orange County ed.; and "Ex-Agent: North Knew of Drug Flights," *Orange County Register*, June 17, 1994.

10. Gary Webb, *Dark Alliance: The CIA, the Contras, and the Crack Cocaine Explosion* (New York: Seven Stories Press, 1998).

11. Peter Dale Scott and Jonathan Marshall, *Cocaine Politics: Drugs, Armies, and the CIA in Central America* (Berkeley and Los Angeles: University of California Press, 1991).

Medellin drug cartel in Colombia, Manuel Noriega's drug trafficking in Panama, the Contras' and Sandinistas' drug and gun-running activities in Nicaragua, and even cocaine trading in Cuba as a way to keep the anti-Castro warriors happy.[12] Even more disturbing are rampant allegations that the CIA itself used an isolated airstrip in Mena, Arkansas, during the 1980s for some of these illegal drug transactions and gun shipments.[13]

In public discussions since April 1992 about why our nation's drug laws have failed and what we can do about it, the most troubling question I have been asked is how a government in which its own people have lost faith can be expected to reform its drug policy. My response is that it is *our* government, and if it is not working, or if it is untruthful or irresponsible, we have no one to blame but ourselves. It is certainly true that one reason for people's distrust of government is a direct result of the War on Drugs. When we talk about the costs of our current drug policy, we must not leave out the cynicism that has resulted from the popular belief that agents of our own government have been lying down in the gutter with the drug-trafficking dogs we are supposedly fighting against.

Government Policy: Don't Discuss It!

Not criminalizing drugs doesn't mean we approve of it, anymore than not criminalizing tobacco means that we approve of cigarette smoking or not criminalizing alcohol means we approve of it. Just because something isn't criminal doesn't mean it is right. And yet that's the way this debate has been cast. If you are against criminalization, you are encouraging use.
Judge Nancy Gertner, United States District Court, Boston, Massachusetts[14]

As we have seen, our country's drug policy has three prongs: massive prisons, the demonization of drug users, and a refusal to discuss alternatives. Having addressed the first two in some depth, we now turn our attention to the third.

---

12. Jill Jonnes, *Hep-Cats, Narcs, and Pipe Dreams: A History of America's Romance with Illegal Drugs* (New York: Scribner, 1996).

13. Susan Schmidt, "CIA Probed in Alleged Arms Shipments," *Washington Post*, August 7, 1996: A6.

14. Judge Nancy Gertner, U.S. District Court, Boston, Massachusetts, unpublished speech at a January 29, 1998, Voluntary Committee of Lawyers, Inc. forum in Boston entitled "Is the Drug War Forever?" See <http://www.november.org>

People who favor our current drug policy often raise an emotional cry that any deviation in course from the War on Drugs would send the "wrong message" to our children. They lump together all possible alternatives to our drug policy under the heading of the "legalization of drugs," and uniformly refuse to debate or even discuss them.

People who employ these tactics are often radicals who devoutly and self-righteously treat as heresy any questions about our current drug policy—and they often intentionally distort or misconstrue any arguments for change. If they are private citizens, that is one thing; but if they are government officials, they are doing their country a major disservice.

In many ways these tactics are identical to those frequently used by criminal defense attorneys who lack a viable defense to the charges faced by their clients. Their method is to put the prosecutor on trial. In the case of drug policy, this tactic makes a lot of sense, because once people understand what is really going on, the position of the drug warriors becomes transparently insupportable. But if these "warriors" are successful in their attacks on dissenters and those who propose an open debate, and are able to deflect criticism with their exaggerations and appeals to the fears and emotions of the voting public, then they will never be forced to acknowledge the truth. Regrettably, these people have been amazingly successful in their tactics, so far.

An additional scare tactic is to raise the specter of widespread drug addiction sweeping the country if we were to make *any* changes in our policy of zero tolerance. It may be true (or then again it may not) that if we were to abandon our prohibitionist policy, drug use would increase temporarily. In my opinion, however, any possible increase would be more than counterbalanced by the enormous benefits we would see in health, crime reduction, tax savings, and international goodwill, to name a few. But test the hypothesis of the naysayers: if illicit drugs were no longer illegal, would you use them? I doubt it. Most people who are going to use these drugs are going to use them whether they are illegal or not, just as most people who are not interested in taking drugs are not going to become interested just because some of the laws have changed. I personally am simply not interested, and I think that is a representative answer. I have never used any illicit drug and I never intend to do so. If our religious leaders blessed them and give them away for free, I still wouldn't be interested. I suspect that most people feel the same way. In addition, it is a near certainty that most of the potential problem substance abusers in our society are using these drugs already. If they are not deterred by our prohibitionist laws, then where is the harm in dispensing those substances under strict regulation? I once saw a survey that asked if people would take up drug use if it became legal. An overwhelming majority said they would not. But when asked if they thought their neighbors would take up drugs, a substantial number said they thought that their neighbors just might. The results of this survey may help explain why the scare tactics of the prohibitionists are so effective: we know that we ourselves are pure, but we're not so sure about everyone else. This may be part of human nature; if so, it is a part that needs working on. Because when we look at the facts about drugs and our current policy, it becomes clear that scare tactics like the one predicting a massive wave of new drug addictions simply have no basis in fact.

The government official most closely associated with our drug policy is the director of the Office of National Drug Control Policy, our "Drug Czar." As this book goes to press, the Drug Czar under President Clinton is Barry R. McCaffrey, a retired army general. General McCaffrey routinely uses all of these scare tactics to forestall open discussion of U.S. drug policy. I wrote an "open letter" to General McCaffrey that was published in the Orange County Register on August 12, 1996.[15] In this letter I stated my firm conviction that the War on Drugs had clearly failed, that we were certainly not in a better position then than we had been five years before, and that our country desperately needed a person in authority who would "not be afraid to take a fresh and objective look at our most basic assumptions and recommend changes based upon the evidence." I quoted the RAND Corporation study about how much more effective drug treatment was than drug prosecution, even for heavy drug users, as well as a number of other facts about the hopelessness of our present situation with regard to prisons, loss of civil rights protections, and violence and corruption here and around the world. I invited his attention to the Drug Policy Resolution, which had been signed by thousands of Americans from all walks of life, including former Secretary of State George Shultz, Nobel Prize winner Milton Friedman, and Baltimore Mayor Kurt Schmoke.[16] I told

---

15. James P. Gray, "An Open Letter to the Nation's Drug Czar," *Orange County Register,* August 12, 1996: Metro 6.

16. See Appendix A.

him that we were not asking him to support any particular approach to the drug problem, only to join us in a non-partisan and nonpolitical search for the truth. Nowhere in the article did I advocate any particular approach to the drug problem other than education, nor did I even hint at favoring the legalization of drugs—which in fact I do not favor.

General McCaffrey's response to my open letter was published on September 29, 1996.[17] He began his response under the subheading, "Public Policy: Legalization would send the wrong message to children." Then, after agreeing with me that education and the honest exchange of information are critical, he used the second half of his reply to say things such as, "The notion that the way to solve the problem is to legalize specific drugs, such as marijuana for 'medical' purposes, is profoundly wrong." Where did this assertion come from? Why did McCaffrey immediately jump to the conclusion that he was arguing with a proponent of the legalization of anything? Why did he not instead address the particular harms I had listed as some of the costs of our current drug policy?

The answer is that in this way he closed off further discussion. In his *prepared* testimony before a committee of the U.S. House of Representatives, General McCaffrey continued the tactics of misrepresentation and exaggeration, saying that those pushing for drug legalization "want drugs made widely available, in chewing gums and sodas, over the Internet and at the corner store, even though this would be tantamount to putting drugs in the hands of children."[18] In fact, of course, no one favors any such thing. Clearly this is not "education and the honest exchange of information" but emotional fear-mongering designed to scare people and prohibit a full and open discussion.

On the subject of politicians not trusting the American people to make their own decisions, by 1999 seven states had voted to allow the medical use of marijuana within their borders. These states are California and Arizona in 1996, Alaska, Arizona (again), Nevada, Oregon, and Washington in 1998, and Maine in 1999. Even though the U.S. Office of Drug Control Policy used federal tax money strenuously to oppose these ballot measures, and argued yet again that, for example,

---

17. Barry R. McCaffrey, "The Drug War: Two Views," *Orange County Register,* September 29, 1996: Commentary 5.

18. Associated Press, "Drug Czar Takes Hard Line On Legalization Measures," *Los Angeles Daily Journal,* June 17, 1999: 4.

"the Nevada pro-pot amendment is a lead-in to drug legalization,"[19] the propositions passed by substantial margins in each state.

One of the most desperate and transparent attempts to prohibit discussion or change of our failed drug policy occurred during the November 1998 election, when Congress actually barred the District of Columbia from spending any money to count the votes on Initiative 59, a medical marijuana measure. Exit polls showed that the measure was being approved by a vote of 69 to 31 percent.[20] All over the country, newspapers wrote editorials denouncing Congress's act, saying such things as, "It is hard to imagine that in the history of American elections—or of American democracy—there is precedent for stifling the legally expressed will of the people by denying the money necessary to count their ballots."[21] But such things happen because of our close-minded adherence to a policy that has failed miserably—and we allow them to happen.

Not surprisingly, on September 17, 1999, a federal judge upheld our democratic system and ordered the votes on Initiative 59 to be counted and the results released. On September 20, the government of the District of Columbia released the results: the medical marijuana measure had passed by a 69-to-31-percent margin.

The prohibition of open discussion also means that drug prohibitionists do not have to appear publicly in debates. Conduct your own inquiry. Talk to someone who has attempted to organize a public *discussion*, as opposed to a speech, about drug policy, and you will find that public officials favoring the continuation of our drug policies will almost never attend. This has happened to me on many occasions. For example, at the meeting of the World Affairs Council in Orange County, General McCaffrey was invited to participate in a debate on drug policy. He responded that he did not have time to be involved in a debate—but he did have time to give a speech.[22]

The same thing happened when Dr. Lee Brown, the Drug Czar under President Bush, spoke at a drug policy forum at the Harvard Law

---

19. Barry McCaffrey, "Seeing through the Haze of Medical Marijuana," *Las Vegas Review-Journal*, October 18, 1998.

20. Peter Slevin and Caryle Murphy, "Results of D.C. Marijuana Vote Kept Secret Pending Court Action," *Washington Post*, November 4, 1998.

21. Editorial, "Marijuana Madness," *Des Moines Register*, November 9, 1998: 6A.

22. James P. Gray, "Is Our Drug Policy Failing? Don't Ask," *Los Angeles Times*, March 29, 2000, Orange County ed.: B-11.

School. Without taking any questions, he left the hall and went downstairs to talk to the press. Since I was scheduled to speak directly after Dr. Brown, I offered half of my time to him if he would only stay and answer questions from the audience present. He refused.

Some drug prohibitionists are so worried about what would happen if the American people were to have a full and open debate on drug policy that they have actually introduced legislation to prohibit federally sponsored research pertaining to the possible "legalization" of drugs. The Anti-Drug Legalization Act (HR 309), proposed by Representative Gerald Solomon (R-N.Y.) on January 7, 1997, would have prohibited all departments and agencies of the United States Government from conducting or financing, in whole or in part, any study or research involving the legalization of drugs. That most expressly would have included any possible research on the medical use of marijuana.

Fortunately, this attempt to prohibit learning about what we are doing or what we could do better was not passed into law. We have not been so lucky, however, in the United Nations. In 1997, the UN's International Narcotics Control Board (INCB) issued a report that called, in effect, for criminalizing any opposition to the War on Drugs. So far, the nations of the world have not acted on this recommendation; but the spirit behind the report has continued to prevent a genuine international debate about drug policy. In addition, the INCB has been actively claiming that a 1988 Convention Against Illicit Traffic in Narcotic Drugs and Psychotropic Substances requires all nations to enact laws that prohibit inciting or inducing people "by any means" to "use narcotic drugs or psychotropic substances illicitly." Officials of the INCB define offenders of this international convention as anyone who "shows illicit use in a favourable light," or who recommends "a change in the drug law." The report goes on to criticize "reputable medical journals" for "favouring the 'medical' use of cannabis," because "such information ... tends to generate an overall climate of acceptance that is favourable to" what is now an illicit drug. It even goes on to criticize the marketing of hemp products like clothing and rope, even though they are not psychoactive at all, because they contribute "to the overall promotion of illicit drugs."[23]

---

23. Phillip O. Coffin, "A Duty to Censor: U.N. Officials Want to Crack Down on Drug War Protesters," *Reason* (August/September 1998): 54–55.

For a public official of the United States to suggest that we even study these critical issues is cause to question his or her motives. When Surgeon General Jocelyn Elders, in response to a question asked after a speech she had given, simply suggested that the legalization of drugs at least be studied in order to determine whether it would lessen drug-related crime, there was an immediate outcry for her resignation. The problem has become so acute that after a presentation to an ABA forum for supreme court and appellate court justices from all over the country, the chief supreme court justice of a southern state wrote to me that he sees the failure of the War on Drugs every day from the bench, but that if he discussed this publicly he would spend all of his time defending his views.

The bottom line is that the drug prohibitionists have been so successful in scaring people away from a discussion of our drug policy that the very people who have the most knowledge and experience on the subject—police officers, clergy, legislators, lawyers, and judges, feel too intimidated to open their mouths.

PART III

Options

Surprisingly enough, whether we should change our current policy of drug prohibition actually comes down to only one question: would the benefits in increased health and civil liberties and in decreased crime, violence, corruption, incarceration, and costs of administration be outweighed by any possible temporary, or even long-term, increase in drug usage under a new policy?

As we have already seen, every drug policy has some benefits and some drawbacks. We must remember that Alcohol Prohibition did not do away with alcohol or alcohol abuse, it simply changed the distribution system and the legal control. And although the repeal of Alcohol Prohibition brought much of the violence and corruption, and many of the problems of alcohol impurities to an end, it also brought with it some new problems. So an enlightened and caring society should act as managers of this complex problem, take an honest view of the true costs of Drug Prohibition, and seek a drug policy that would maximize the benefits and minimize the harms.

Without question, each of our available options would reduce to a greater or lesser degree the current black market control of the drug trade, and would also materially reduce the harms set forth in Part II, which have been inflicted on us as an inevitable result of our drug prohibitionist policy. We have the ability to run the drug dealers out of business by taking away their illegal, obscene, and untaxed profits. But it must be understood that unless we literally remove all restrictions to access to all drugs by a program of complete legalization, we will never completely get rid of the illicit sale of drugs. And since neither I nor anyone I know of favors, for example, allowing access of these drugs to children, we will always have some restrictions, and therefore be forced to deal to some degree with the presence of the black market.

Bearing that in mind, we should open our thinking to an analysis of each available option, or combination of options, and try to come up with a policy that will best meet our needs.

6

Increased Zero Tolerance

We spend an inordinate amount of time, money, resources and lives on the drug war and we're not really getting a lot of bang for our buck. I don't think that we're making any headway the way things are going now.

Judge James L. Smith, Superior Court, Santa Ana, California

Certainly one of the drug policy options open to us is to do more of the same. We frequently hear the exhortation, "Let's really *win* the War on Drugs!" But what does that mean? What can we possibly do differently under this failed policy? How many more Colombian coca fields must we fumigate with poisons? How many more prisons must we build? How many more *billions* of dollars must we throw away on strategies that do not work?

Many people have heard the definition of insanity, attributed to President Clinton, as "doing the same thing over and over again, and expecting different results." Why does that definition of insanity not apply to our drug policy? For the past several decades politicians have waved their arms and insisted repeatedly that we need to *really get tough* on drug dealers and *put them away for good*. And that is exactly the course we have been blindly following—for decades. Yet no one can say with any credibility that we are in better shape today than we were five or ten or twenty years ago—far from it. Nevertheless, further increasing our policy of "zero tolerance" is an option, and it should be fully considered and discussed.

One option would be to pass the bill presented in 1996 by Congressman Gerald Solomon from upstate New York that would punish any group that even *advocates* changing our approach to drug policy. This bill would have taken away the tax-exempt status of any organization that simply favors the "legalization of drugs." This bill, just like the bill Solomon proposed to prohibit federal research on the subject of drug legalization, never made it out of committee, but it did represent a big helping of the "get tough" attitude.

Another bill meant to extend zero tolerance was the so-called "Drug-Free Century Act," which was introduced into Congress in January 1999. This was a multifaceted, 146-page bill that would have made it easier for federal law enforcement agencies to seize assets from persons suspected of drug offenses, and would have reduced the amount of powder cocaine necessary to trigger ten-year and five-year mandatory minimum sentences from 5,000 grams to 500 grams, and 500 grams to 50 grams, respectively. It also would have required a driver's license suspension for any person convicted of "any criminal offense relating to drugs," would have implemented "innovative voluntary random drug testing programs" and systems of closed circuit cameras at schools to detect drug offenses, and would have prohibited the expenditure of any federal monies, "directly or indirectly," on any programs of needle exchanges. In other words, this bill would have done a great deal more of what has already been shown not to work.

Exasperated citizens and some of our leaders have also suggested that we sentence drug dealers to death, as they do in China and Iran. Former House Speaker Newt Gingrich, for example, while campaigning for former Senator Dole in 1996, told a crowd of 3,000 people that drug dealers should be executed.[1] It is unlikely, however, that capital punishment for drug dealers would make any difference whatsoever. Look at our history. Over the last four decades, we have passed a long line of "get tough" mandatory minimum sentences. Each time the problem has only gotten worse. Everybody wants to send the major dealers, or "drug lords," to prison, but we always end up with the couriers, or "mules." Why? It is not at all for lack of effort. Former U.S. District Judge Robert C. Bonner, director of the DEA during the entire administration of President Bush, is a friend of mine from my days in the U.S.

---

1. Associated Press, "Gingrich Wants Drug Dealers Executed," *San Francisco Examiner*, August 18, 1996: A2.

Attorney's Office. I know him to be an intelligent, hard-working, and dedicated public servant. For four years he used his powerful position to do everything humanly possible under our laws to beat back this problem, put the big dealers in prison, and get illicit drugs off the streets. Except for his efforts to expand drug education, however, his efforts failed. He and everyone like him have been soundly defeated because of the profits to be made from dealing drugs. Judge Bonner's efforts helped prove once again that no matter what we do, we cannot repeal the law of supply and demand.

In addition to longer and longer mandatory prison sentences, which are the embodiment of our zero tolerance policy, it has also been suggested that we could adopt something called "humiliation sentences." These, for example, are the punishments meted out to people who have been convicted of drinking and driving in the form of special license plates; or to convicted shoplifters who are forced to affix "mea culpa" bumper stickers to their cars or hang signs on their houses spelling out their crimes; or to men who have been convicted of soliciting prostitutes by having their names published in newspapers or on billboards and radio shows.

Humiliation sentences, it has been suggested, could be required as a condition of probation for drug offenders. In fact, in November 1996, a judge in Port St. Lucie, Florida, ordered a woman to put a paid advertisement in her local newspaper saying that she had purchased drugs in front of her children.[2] This approach probably has its roots in colonial towns, where malfeasants were placed in the public stocks, and it was used successfully for offenses like fornication and shoplifting. It could very well have some deterrent effect for middle- and upper-class drug users. But it certainly would not be a fitting or effective punishment for most drug dealers, and it would probably have little deterrent effect for most drug users.

Another approach that has been used and could be expanded is the taking away of a meaningful privilege as a punishment for a drug offense, even though the drug offense is unrelated to the privilege. The most common example is the suspension of a person's driver's license for an unrelated conviction for the possession or use of an illicit drug. Such laws have been in effect for years, but they could be increased. Public

---

2. Jan Hoffman, "Humiliation Sentences: Are They Just, or Just a Shame?" *Orange County Register,* January 19, 1997: News 1, 6–7.

Law 101-516, for example, was enacted by Congress and signed by President Bush on November 5, 1990. It required all states to enact legislation requiring the revocation or suspension of an individual's driving privileges for a conviction of any violation of the Controlled Substance Act, that is, for any drug offense. The states were given the alternative of passing legislation stating that they had considered this approach but rejected it.

The federal government threatened states with the loss of substantial sums of federal highway money if they failed to put this "smoke a joint, lose your license" law on the books. When California still had not passed this legislation by early March 1997, the federal government threatened to withhold $92 million in highway funds unless it was done, or at least unless a "progress report" was submitted.[3] Eventually, California joined seventeen other states that chose to pass the law revoking drivers' licenses, but the other thirty-two states opted out. Since that time, California's law has expired, but its governor, anxious to show how tough he is on drugs, is trying, over considerable opposition, to bring it back.[4]

A similar measure instigated by the U.S. Department of Education suspends or forfeits a student's qualification for financial aid for schooling if the student is convicted of a drug violation, even though there is no such requirement for those convicted of robbery, rape, or manslaughter.[5] These are desperate attempts to enforce an unenforceable law, and the desperation can be measured by the extent to which the sanctions have no connection to the criminal offenses they are supposed to punish. Parents often use such punishments for small children; for adults, punishments unrelated to the actual offenses are seldom effective and often harvest nothing but resentment. Still, strengthening and multiplying such laws is an option for a stepped-up campaign of zero tolerance. There is really no end of possibilities.

---

3. Carl Ingram, "U.S. Softens Threat to Deny Highway Aid," *Los Angeles Times*, March 11, 1997, Orange County ed.: A3. As of June 30, 1999, California had repealed its provision for the suspension of a driver's license for a drug conviction by taking Vehicle Code Section 13202.3(f) off the books, asserting that individual states should have the right to determine when a license should be suspended.

4. Miguel Bustillo, "Davis Fights to Suspend Licenses in Drug Cases," *Los Angeles Times*, May 24, 2000, Orange County ed.: A3, 25.

5. Anjetta McQueen, "Drug Offenders to Lose Federal College Money," *Orange County Register*, October 26, 1999: News 1.

We could get tougher by encouraging all city and county governments to pass and enforce even more rigorous asset forfeiture laws, like
those in the city of Oakland. Its 1997 ordinance allows the seizure of
any vehicle used to transport even small amounts of drugs, even when
the owner is not charged with—or is even acquitted of—the offense, and
even if the owner was not in the car or did not know of the offense. This
is much harsher than the California state law, which is supposed to be
utilized only for large quantities of drugs and precludes seizure if the
owner was unaware of the offense or if the car is the family's only means
of transportation. But in October 2000 the California Supreme Court
declined to review Oakland's law, which had resulted in the seizure and
sale of about three hundred cars, thus encouraging other governments
to pass similar laws and thereby fatten their coffers.[6]

One big thing we could do, and as we saw this has been seriously suggested by some of the more extreme drug warriors, is to use our military forces to patrol our borders in order to fight the domestic war on
drugs, and to go into drug-supplying countries like Colombia and fight
the War on Drugs there. Actually, we have already embarked on this
dangerous path, so far without much of a cry of alarm. Our military has
been stationed on our border with Mexico for years. The young shep-
herd who was shot and killed while target-shooting with an old .22 rifle
was killed by our Marines in their "protection" of our borders from drug
infiltration. In addition, the United States Navy has increasingly been
used to augment the forces of the Coast Guard to try to intercept the
sleek and extra fast "rogue boats" of the drug traffickers, which are suspected of smuggling about a ton of cocaine into our country each day.[7]
Of course, our military and national guard have also been escalating our
military presence in Colombia, Peru, Panama, Bolivia, and Ecuador
since 1990 as "advisors," in order "to supply information" about drug
interdiction to the host countries.[8] Sound familiar?

We have many reasons to be concerned. Just look at what is happening with our military presence in the situation in Colombia. As of

---

6. "Forfeiture," *Los Angeles Daily Journal*, October 19, 2000: 1.

7. Tony Perry, "Navy Adding Muscle to Drug War," *Los Angeles Times*, March 28, 2000,
Orange County ed.: A3, 16.

8. See Richard Keil, "U.S. Military Joins Fight against Drug Trafficking," *Orange County
Register*, June 26, 1996: News 15; Chuck Frederick, "Guard to Fight Drug War, Local Mem-
bers Leave for Panama Duty Today," *Duluth News Tribune*, September 21, 1996: 1C; Charles
Lane, "The Newest War," *Newsweek*, January 6, 1992: 18–23.

July 1999, the Revolutionary Armed Forces of Colombia (FARC) controlled approximately 15,000 square miles of that Latin American country. This area has, as a practical matter, become the "homeland" for this
rebel army of about 18,000 troops. The Colombian army so far still out-
numbers the rebels by about ten to one. But according to General Fer-
nando Tapias, the commander in chief of the army, this rebel force was
financed in 1998 by about *$600 million* in "protection taxes" from their
drug-growing and smuggling operations. This means that the revolutionary forces probably can outspend the country's army.[9]

The situation in Colombia has deteriorated to the extent that at the
end of July 1999, about three hundred FARC guerrillas actually maintained a three-day attack on a police station in the town of Narino,
about one hundred miles northwest of Bogota. The station was
defended by thirty-five officers, of whom at least nine were killed. Prior
to that strike, the rebels had already captured about 450 other police
officers and soldiers in similar attacks.[10]

What is our federal government's response to this hopeless situation? We throw more money into Colombia for this losing and devastating conflict. In 1998, the United States provided about $289 million
to Colombia in "counter-narcotics assistance," and that amount had
doubled in each of the two previous years. Far from improving things,
each year these increasingly large amounts of money simply made the
situation worse. Nevertheless, in July 1999, in an effort to counter the
"explosion" in cocaine production and spreading insecurity, Drug Czar
McCaffrey recommended that we again increase our spending for this
"assistance" to Colombia to $600 million. But even that wasn't good
enough. President Clinton responded by announcing in January 2000
(it was an election year) that we would provide one *billion* dollars over
the next two years to combat narcotics cultivation and trafficking in
Colombia. Not to be outdone, the Republicans introduced their own
(election-year) plan to fund $1.5 billion over the next three years.[11]

---

9. Georgie Anne Geyer, "The Crisis in Colombia: Three Views," *Orange County Register,*
August 2, 1999: Local News 7.

10. Associated Press, "Colombian Rebels Reportedly Kill 17 in Attack on Police," *Los
Angeles Times,* August 2, 1999, Orange County ed.: A4; Jon Lee Anderson, "The Power of
García Marquez," *New Yorker,* September 27, 1999: 56–71.

11. *Washington Post,* "Clinton Backs $1 Billion Plan for Colombia," *Los Angeles Times,* Jan-
uary 8, 2000: A15; Michael Shifter, "First Signs of a Policy Nightmare," *Los Angeles Times,*
July 25, 1999, Orange County ed.: M2.

Additional "persuasion" for the funding of the "good guys" in Colombia may also have come from the sizable political contributions both parties received from the maker of the P-3 radar planes that are used to track the drug smugglers, from a major oil company that has large investments in Colombia, and from the makers of the sixty Blackhawk and Huey 2 helicopters that are being provided to the Colombian army. The helicopters are being sent even though officials in the Clinton administration acknowledge that the Colombian army neither has sufficient hangars nor enough pilots for so many choppers. Finally, for all of these reasons and more, in June 2000 Congress finally agreed on an appropriation of $1.3 billion dollars to fight the War on Drugs in Colombia.[12]

What have been the specific results of all of this increased spending? The left-wing guerrillas have gotten continually stronger, and so have the right-wing private armies that have sprung up to fight the guerrillas. Both sides are considered to have direct ties to drug traffickers. Further, according to our State Department, an average of ten Colombians are killed each day as a result of criminal violence, mostly by right-wing paramilitary groups. The rule of law has become virtually nonexistent. Based on their own statistics, the police in Colombia fail to solve 95 percent of crimes and do not even investigate most of the murders. The situation has become so utterly hopeless that at one time or another in 1999, most of the highways leading into the capital city of Bogata had been cut off, and in November 1999, half of the nation's mayors threatened to resign their positions because their districts had become ungovernable.[13] A large part of the incentive to resign must also have come from the fact that between 1997 and the end of 1999, thirty-four mayors in Columbia had actually been assassinated, and more than a hundred others had been kidnapped.[14] Through it all, Colombia continues to produce more potent coca plants than ever before, to the

---

12. Michael Isikoff and Gregory Vistica, "The Other Drug War," *Newsweek*, April 3, 2000: 38–39; Joseph Contreras and Steven Ambrus, "The $1.3 Billion Question," *Newsweek*, September 4, 2000: 31; Esther Schrader, "Congress Agrees on Funding for Colombia," *Los Angeles Times*, June 23, 2000, Orange County ed.: A1, 9.

13. Benjamin Ryder Howe, "Out of the Jungle," *Atlantic Monthly*, May 2000, 32–38; Robert Dowd, Lt. Col., USAF, Retired, "Colombia Aid Bill Would Escalate a Failed Policy," *Los Angeles Times*, May 15, 2000, Orange County ed.: B13.

14. Scott Wilson, "Elections under Siege," *(Colorado Springs) Gazette*, October 29, 2000: A15.

extent that production has increased by 140 percent in Colombia between 1995 and 2000 alone.[15] Even with our stepped-up efforts at heroin poppy eradication, drug producers have been able to increase their cultivation of heroin faster than our helicopters have been able to eradicate it.[16]

Now the same General McCaffrey says that this rebellion in Colombia, which is "fueled by cocaine and heroin profits," is "having a terrible impact on their neighbors.... There is widespread concern."[17] Concern for what? The concern should be for changing the policy that fuels the drastic situation, which is dragging us further and further into an unwinnable civil war, and which is also starting to destabilize the neighboring countries of Ecuador and Venezuela, where similar killings, kidnappings, and hijackings are beginning to occur.

This is increased zero tolerance in action. Take a failed policy and escalate it. Pretend that the reality of President Clinton's comment about insanity does not apply to drug policy, and don't even think about the fact that if we could somehow de-profitize these drugs, most of Colombia's problems would cease to exist. The justification for U.S. policy has its own perverse logic: any decline in drug use immediately becomes evidence that we should invest more money and resources in the War on Drugs, because such declines show that it is working. Any increase in drug use, on the other hand, proves that we are not doing enough to fight drugs, so we must redouble our efforts and the funding to reach our goals, whatever they may be. Either way, we continue to throw good money after bad in the interest of a failed policy.

The threat posed by U.S. drug policy is much greater than simply the loss of tax dollars or even increased disruption in foreign lands. As of mid-1999, the United States had about 160 military men and women, 30 civilian Department of Defense personnel, and 100 DEA and CIA operatives stationed in Colombia. In August 2000 that num-

15. Editorial, "U.S. Must Heed Colombia Crisis," *Los Angeles Times*, August 19, 1999, Orange County ed.: B8; Senator Paul D. Wellstone (D.-Minn.), "Throwing Money at Colombia Will Only Make Things Worse," *Los Angeles Times*, August 23, 2000, Orange Country ed.: B11.

16. Juanita Darling, "U.S. Is Losing War on Drugs in Colombia," *Los Angeles Times*, August 8, 1999, Orange County ed.: A1, 11–12.

17. Sebastian Rotella, "U.S. Says It Won't Intervene in Colombia Conflict," *Los Angeles Times*, August 28, 1999, Orange County ed.: A23.

ber was increased by 83 U.S. Special Forces "trainers," sent to teach counterinsurgency methods to two Colombian battalions. Some of the others are advisors in other areas, and still others are pilots and crew on reconnaissance airplanes that spy on the rebels. But since there is really no distinction between the rebels and the drug suppliers, all of our personnel are directly involved in some way in fighting Colombia's civil war. Sound familiar?

In late July 1999, a U.S. spy plane crashed in Colombia, killing five American soldiers, including the female pilot, as well as two Colombians. These needless deaths can be added to those of three American pilots who have been killed since 1997 while flying drug-interdiction missions.[18] The U.S. government imposed a news blackout on the July 1999 crash and said that instead of being shot down by guerrilla forces, the spy plane, with all of its highly sophisticated electronics gear and experienced pilot, flew into a mountain.[19] By the time this book is in print more information may be available; but it is also very likely that by then the overall situation in Colombia will have deteriorated even further, and our country will be even more heavily involved.

So how could we further expand our policy of zero tolerance? We have already discussed additional punishments for drug dealers and users, from sentences of humiliation and the loss of privileges unrelated to the offense to imposing the death penalty or using the military in U.S. domestic affairs, as well as increased spending for foreign interdiction and increasing the U.S. military presence in foreign lands. We have already tried most of these things, and they have, without exception, failed dismally—but we can always do more. We could prosecute medical doctors who dare to defy the federal government by prescribing or even recommending the medical use of marijuana. This has already been threatened but, so far, not carried out, except in the case of pregnant women. In Charleston, South Carolina, a public hospital instituted a policy of notifying the police when the blood of mothers giving birth tested positive for cocaine. Some of these women were arrested

---

18. Joshua Hammer and Michael Isikoff, "The Narco-Guerrilla War," *Newsweek*, August 9, 1999: 42–43; Juanita Darling and Ruth Morris, "Crash Points to Military Role of U.S. in Colombia," *Los Angeles Times*, July 28, 1999, Orange County ed.: A1, 10; Juanita Darling, "U.S. Training Colombia's 2nd Drug Battalion," *Los Angeles Times*, August 6, 2000, Orange County ed.: A1, 9.

19. Robert Novak, "Pilot's Death Reveals New Turn in Drug War," *Orange County Register*, August 9, 1999: Local News 7.

and jailed shortly after their babies were born.[20] Even putting aside the privacy rights of these women, what the hospital did not focus on in trying to protect newborn infants from danger is that enforcing the policy increases the likelihood that women in labor, if they have been using cocaine, will avoid hospitals and have their babies at home, or even seek an abortion.

Some people have also seriously proposed that our government add poison to batches of seized drugs, and then announce with great fanfare that the drugs have been released back into our communities, reasoning that this diabolical approach would serve as a powerful deterrent to drug users.

U.S. drug policy is already responsible for restrictions on cash transactions of $10,000 or more, and is also using our banks more and more as informants to the federal government about "suspicious activities" in private financial transactions.[21] These intrusions could also be increased. The Office of National Drug Control Policy has already been previewing national television shows in order to award financial "credits" to programs that weave "anti-drug themes into their shows." Until this practice became public knowledge, the television networks allowed it without complaint. After all, the policy released them from an obligation to run public service advertisements, which don't pay nearly as well as corporate-sponsored private ads.[22] Some people regard this form of institutionalized government censorship as a truly frightening proposition and directly subversive of our freedoms and our way of life, but its continuation would certainly be one way of stepping up our current efforts in the War on Drugs.

In addition to its efforts at censorship, the Office of National Drug Control Policy electronically and surreptitiously placed "cookies" in the computer programs of individuals who had logged on to the government's anti-drug advertisements on the internet. These software devices monitored the internet habits of these people and made this

20. Richard A. Serrano, "Prosecution of Pot-Prescribing Doctors Urged," *Los Angeles Times*, December 27, 1996: A3; David G. Savage, "Justin Wright Hospital, Police Checking of Patients for Drugs," *Los Angeles Times*, October 5, 2000, Orange County ed.: A5.

21. Edmund Sanders, "Federal Law Turns Banks into Informants," *Los Angeles Times*, December 24, 1999, Orange County ed.: A1, 17.

22. Elizabeth Jensen and Paul Brownfield, "Federal Officials Sought to Preview Scripts, ABC Says," *Los Angeles Times*, January 16, 2000, Orange County ed.: A8; Associated Press, "Rules Eased on Anti-Drug TV Deals," *Los Angeles Daily Journal*, January 20, 2000: 5.

information available to the government. When this program became public knowledge, however, the White House acknowledged that it "might" be a violation of federal privacy guidelines and ordered that it be terminated. But this government program could be renewed and even expanded if we increase our Zero Tolerance approach.[23]

If we want other frightening options, consider that the United States has persuaded Colombia to develop a powerful fungus known as *Fusarium oxysporum*, which could be released on hundreds of thousands of acres now being used to grow heroin poppies and coca plants. This fungus is unmatched in killing these plants, but its effects on humans and groundwater is still unknown. Its ability to mutate and kill plants other than poppies and coca is also unknown, but it is related to major plant pathogens of wheat and corn. In our fanatical crusade to stem the flow of illegal drugs into the United States, however, we would do well to remember the harmful effects on humans of Agent Orange, the defoliant used in Vietnam, as well as the Irish potato blight, Dutch elm disease, and the chestnut blight, each of which was caused by the introduction of an exotic fungus.[24]

We could also increase the use of the civil justice system in our Zero Tolerance programs. One way would be to pass H.R. 1042, the "Drug Dealer Liability Act of 2000," which would allow *anyone* who is harmed, directly or indirectly, by the use of an illicit substance, to bring a civil action against the drug dealer. Parties who could sue would include the user of drugs, as long as "the individual personally discloses to narcotics enforcement authorities all of the information known to the individual regarding all that individual's sources of illegal controlled substances." To people who understand the federal judicial system, this bill is comical. But because frustration with lack of progress is so high, it actually passed in the U.S. House of Representatives on October 10, 2000. Can you imagine—a drug user who drove his car into a tree after using drugs could "narc" on himself and then sue his dealer in federal court, and so could the owner of the tree and other drivers who were delayed in traffic as a result of the crash. If a program isn't working, just pass another law.

---

23. Marc Lacey, "Drug Office Ends Tracking of Web Users," *New York Times*, June 22, 2000: A1.

24. Tad Szulc, "The Ghost of Vietnam Haunts 'Plan Colombia,'" *Los Angeles Times*, August 20, 2000, Orange Country ed.: M2; David D. Porter, M.D., "Biological Warfare in Colombia," *Lost Angeles Times*, September 5, 2000, Orange County ed.: B10.

Another way to increase the use of the civil justice system is to continue to shift the burden of prosecuting small-time drug dealers from the government to other people, such as landlords, who are increasingly being forced to evict "known" drug dealers or face prosecution themselves.[25] In California, landlords are already required—at considerable peril to themselves—to evict a tenant if they have received notice from city prosecutors or city attorneys that the tenant is believed to be dealing drugs.[26] In addition, if any family member or guest of a family member illegally uses, sells, or distributes any illegal drugs in *or near* the tenant's apartment, all the tenants can be evicted—even if they were unaware of the drug offense.[27] Even putting aside the constitutional issues of forcing landlords to take action of this kind, the program simply doesn't work. Just ask the judges who oversee it. One of those is U.S. District Judge Milton I. Shadur in Chicago, who has described attempts to evict public housing tenants for minor drug infractions as a cosmetic, headline-grabbing policy that masks the drug war's failure, and concluded, "Any thought that [evictions are] a meaningful deterrent to the drug trade betrays an abysmal ignorance."[28] And who really benefits when the government causes a family to be evicted because one of their members is believed to be selling drugs? At the very best, this simply moves the drug sales a few blocks away. But at least it lets us feel like we are actually doing something to beat back the problem. Doesn't it?

Other ways to increase zero tolerance include increasing "showcase" areas under the old federal "Weed and Seed" programs. Unfortunately, however, short-lived "cure de jour" federal programs like "Weed and Seed" were no more effective than any of the other failed attempts to stem the drug tide. This particular program involved depressed areas that were hand-selected by the federal government in the early 1990s to receive extra police protection and community assistance, plus federal money for cleanup.[29] And, depending on one's definition of success,

---

25. Editorial, "Due Process Key in Eviction Law," *Los Angeles Times*, March 14, 1999, Orange County ed.: B8.

26. See California Health and Safety Code, Section 11571.1.

27. See *Rucker v. Davis*, 2000 *Los Angeles Daily Journal*, D.A.R. 1661, 9th Cir.; Pamela A. MacLean, "9th Circuit OKs Controversial Eviction Statute," *Los Angeles Daily Journal*, February 15, 2000: 1, 9.

28. Linn Washington, "Drug War Doubters," *Los Angeles Daily Journal*, December 7, 1992: 6.

29. See Gina Shaffer and Agustin Gurza, "Some Fear Weed and Seed Is Just a Temporary Solution," *Orange County Register*, December 14, 1992: A1, 6.

they were successful, so long as we continued to spend the extra money. These few "showcase" areas were cleaned and painted, and because of the extra police presence crime decreased substantially; so the residents were happy. When I was quoted at the time as saying that this was a temporary Band-aid solution involving an exercise in "crime relocation," I incurred the wrath of a local chief of police and the U.S. Attorney. If we had the resources to conduct such programs in every deserving area, that would be one thing. But we did not, we do not, and we will not. And, true to form, the programs always involved a lot of "weeding" (arrests) but very little "seeding" (addressing the educational and economic problems of the area). Today, after great amounts of federal money were spent to make us feel we were doing something positive, all of these showcase communities have, to my knowledge, reverted to their prior condition, while the drug warriors have sailed on to do other good deeds.

In February 1999, Senator Joe Biden (D–Del.) concluded that the drug problem in Mexico was more than that country could handle. He suggested that the United States might be better off simply to purchase all of the drug output of the South American countries and destroy them, as this would probably be cheaper.[30] As far as his argument went, the senator was probably correct. But given the laws of supply and demand, can you imagine how quickly more of these drugs would be planted and harvested if Uncle Sam was the buyer? Even if such a plan were pursued, the drug-producers would undoubtedly sell inferior "leftovers" to the U.S. government and continue to sell the high-quality stuff on the illegal market for even greater total profits. But at least Senator Biden was willing to suggest an alternative to our current policy, and for that he should be commended.

One thing is clear. We continue to reduce our civil liberties in an effort to rid ourselves of this critical problem, and in doing so we risk becoming more like Saudi Arabia and Singapore. We have been eroding our civil liberties ever since we began our policy of Drug Prohibition, and without any benefit whatsoever. But it is completely consistent with a policy of increased zero tolerance to intrude to even greater degrees into people's personal lives with searches, wiretaps, police questionings, asset forfeitures, and other deprivations of liberty.

---

30. Associated Press, "Mexican Drug Cartels Have Grown, DEA Chief Testifies," *Los Angeles Daily Journal*, February 25, 1999: 4.

1

Education

While these issues are being debated among judges, legislators and other policymakers, it would be quite useful to bring the debate to a more broad-based discourse. Although one sees an occasional article about decriminalization of drugs, and there has been relatively extensive publicity about the California marijuana initiative, the arguments and insights contained in the materials included with your July 30 letter are rarely mentioned in the popular press. I believe that the notion of decriminalization may be more popular than our politicians believe, and the only way to get that point across would be to broaden the debate.

Judge Robert W. Gettleman, United States District Court, Chicago, Illinois

veryone is in favor of "drug education"—parents, politicians, law enforcement officials, newspaper editors, and the general public. And in fact, every proposed drug policy option that I have ever heard of contains a major provision for drug education. But what actually is drug education, and how can it be used most effectively?

The first thing to remember is that the problem of drug use and abuse is multifaceted, and that nothing, including a good program of education, is going to enable us to get drug-related problems out of our lives. Education can be a powerful tool, but it will never be a cure-all. The massive public education campaign in this country on the dangers of cigarettes has led to many thousands of people kicking the habit, but others continue to smoke, and as long as tobacco grows on the earth, there will be people who will smoke it.

It is the same with other dangerous and sometimes addicting drugs. Education will almost never sway a chronic, confirmed addict, whether her drug of choice is heroin, cocaine, nicotine, or alcohol.[1] Once she has abstained for awhile and has seen what her life can be like without the drug, education begins to have a chance. But education can and does have a positive effect on casual users or people who are not yet using. Drug education has been quite successful in reducing the use of drugs by casual users, but unless it is combined with concentrated drug treatment programs it has rarely been successful for chronic users.

I remember one time in the mid-1960s when I was purchasing something at the UCLA student store; a young lady in line ahead of me was buying a pack of cigarettes. She noticed, apparently for the first time, the warning label on the cigarettes, and asked the cashier what it was. When the cashier explained, the young lady asked if they had any cigarettes without the warning label. When the cashier said no, she bought them anyway.

Education has its limits. But it is certainly one of our most important tools. Its goal should be to impress upon people, both young and not so young, that drug use is risky, harmful, and unattractive. There are several traditional approaches to accomplish this goal. One, the "cognitive model" of drug use and abuse, assumes that people will make rational and informed decisions either not to use drugs or to use them in moderation, if only they are given true information about drugs. Another approach, "affective education," goes beyond the cognitive model and concentrates on personal and social development, stressing decision making, effective communication, and assertiveness. Affective education attempts to teach the skills needed to resist peer pressure and the glamorization of drug use by the media and popular culture. A third approach is "social learning theory" and is based on the concept that people learn behaviors through modeling, reinforcement by peers and environment, and by community standards and practices. The idea behind social learning theory is that once these factors are discovered, behavior can be guided and changed by applying them in a positive manner.[2]

---

1. Robert L. Jackson, "Chronic Addicts Seen at Core of U.S. Drug Abuse," *Los Angeles Times*, July 21, 1994, Orange County ed.: A16.

2. See Department of Justice, Office of Juvenile Justice and Delinquency Prevention, *Federal Register* 64, no. 122 (June 25, 1999): 34504–9; G. J. Botvin, S. Sckinke, and M. Orlandi, eds., *Drug Abuse Prevention with MultiEthnic Youth* (Thousand Oaks, Calif.: Sage Publications, 1995); and A. Bandura, *Social Learning Theory* (Englewood Cliffs, N.J.: Prentice Hall, 1977).

Of course these traditional approaches to drug education require that accurate information be honestly provided to and discussed with the people to be educated. Unfortunately, current drug policy in many ways prevents this. One obstacle is the Drug-Free Schools and Communities Act,[3] which prohibits the use of federal funds for programs that do not provide a clean and consistent message that the illegal use of alcohol and other drugs is wrong and harmful. Only the message of total abstention or "zero tolerance" is allowed in federally funded schools, which tends to inhibit honest and forthright discussion about drugs. This "one size fits all" approach to education is unrealistic and closed-minded, and simply does not get through to today's youths. Why not, instead, model drug education in schools on the anti-smoking campaign, which has been a real success story? Between 1970 and 1992, the per capita consumption of tobacco in the United States was reduced from ten pounds to five pounds per year, and the percentage of people over eighteen who smoked was reduced from 42.3 percent in 1965, to 32.2 percent in 1983, to 25.4 percent in 1990.[4] This was accomplished not by making tobacco illegal, but by making truthful information available to people and by changing social tolerance of second-hand smoke. There is no reason why similar results cannot be achieved by treating illegal drugs in a similar fashion.

There is no question that tobacco is a killer. About 400,000 people in the United States die each year from smoking.[5] Former U.S. Surgeon General C. Everett Koop once pointed out that that was equivalent to two fully loaded jumbo passenger jets crashing each day and killing everyone aboard. Smoking is also considered directly responsible for thousands of tobacco-induced abortions,[6] and second-hand smoke is also a substantial health risk even to nonsmokers.[7] If any popular substance should be prohibited, shouldn't it be tobacco?

Why isn't tobacco illegal? For three reasons. First, the use of tobacco is deeply imbedded in our country's heritage and lifestyle, and people

---

3. See 20 U.S.C. Section 7116.

4. National Center for Health Statistics (1992).

5. Sheryl Stolberg, "Mortality Study Finds Tobacco Is No. 1 Culprit," *Los Angeles Times*, November 10, 1993, Orange County ed.: A1.

6. Joseph R. DiFranza, M.D. and Robert A. Lew, Ph.D., "Effect of Maternal Cigarette Smoking on Pregnancy Complications and Sudden Infant Death Syndrome," *The Journal of Family Practice* 40, no. 4 (April 1995): 385.

7. Dan Morain, "Report Lists Effects of Smoke on Californians," *Los Angeles Times*, February 25, 1997, Orange County ed.: A3.

would protest this governmental intrusion into their lives as an attempt to take away their rights and freedoms. Second, given the history and failure of Alcohol Prohibition, the public would not support such a thing because they realize that it wouldn't work. Third, the tobacco companies are extremely powerful and well financed, and probably have the political strength to defeat any attempt at prohibition.[8] And so, instead of outlawing tobacco, we treat the use of tobacco products as serious health and social problems and focus on education and treatment programs to reduce the harm that the use of tobacco causes. And since the educational information about tobacco use is for the most part true and accurate, the programs have produced favorable results.

As many people have pointed out, tobacco is not the only harmful substance that we allow to be sold and consumed under FDA and other government agency guidelines. There is alcohol, of course, and also high-fat, high-cholesterol foods like potato chips, cheeseburgers, doughnuts, and french fries. The list is really quite long, when you think about it. What about chainsaws, automobiles, epoxy glue, weed killers and pesticides that we use on our lawns and in our gardens? Instead of outlawing these products, we use intelligence and education in our attempts to reduce the harms associated with their presence in our communities. It could be argued, for that matter, that a debilitating, mind-numbing addiction to television is one of the major afflictions of American society, but we are not about to make it illegal. If we somehow did, however, you can be assured that the black market would quickly find a way around the prohibition.

Unfortunately, the methods now most often used in schools to teach about the harms of illicit drugs are quite different from the ones we use for tobacco and other dangerous products. They frequently use scare tactics and untruthful information about drugs, especially marijuana, even though we have seen time and time again that this is often counterproductive. Children are often told that marijuana is highly addictive and that long-term marijuana users often develop a chemical dependence that makes withdrawal difficult or impossible without professional help. These children find out soon enough that this message

---

8. There is strong evidence that the tobacco and alcohol companies have supported the traditional educational programs in order to reinforce the distinction in the minds of politicians and the general public between illicit drugs, on the one hand, and the "legal" drugs of tobacco and alcohol, on the other. (See Steven B. Duke and Albert C. Gross, "Smoking Out A Drug Policy," *Orange County Register,* July 24, 1994: Commentary 1.)

is untrue, which serves to discredit the messengers. When we spread untruths about marijuana, our children learn not to believe us even when we tell them the truth about such drugs as methamphetamines and cocaine.

In fact, less than 1 percent of all marijuana users in this country use it on a daily basis, and most of them use it only occasionally.[9] We encounter the same problem with the so-called "stepping stone" or "gateway" theory, which holds that smoking marijuana leads to harder drugs. Since marijuana is far and away the most popular illicit drug in the United States today, most everyone who uses harder drugs such as cocaine, LSD, or heroin has probably at one time or another also used marijuana. However, *most* marijuana users never go on to use any of these other drugs, a fact that is often withheld from young people.[10] If we want to apply the gateway theory consistently, we should point out that most people, before they try marijuana, have already used tobacco. Our children, even our younger children, are not stupid. They can think; they can observe; they can reason; and, above all, they are practical. And in today's increasingly fast-paced society, children are growing up earlier and becoming more and more savvy all the time. Here is what a class of fifth graders wrote when they were asked to fill in the blanks of the following proverbs:

Better to be safe than ...	explain it to mom.
Strike while the ...	bug is close.
Don't bite the hand that ...	looks dirty.
A miss is as good as a ...	mister.
You can't teach an old dog ...	math.
A penny saved is ...	not much.
Children should be seen and not ...	spanked or grounded.
If at first you don't succeed ...	get new batteries.
You get out of something what you ...	see pictured on the box.

Drug education for our children, even our young children, must be thoughtful, verifiable, reasonable, and practical—or it will fail.

---

9. See Lynn Zimmer, Ph.D., and John P. Morgan, M.D., *Marijuana Myths, Marijuana Facts: A Review of the Scientific Evidence* (New York: Lindesmith Center, 1997) 26–30.

10. Ibid. at 32–37. See also Appendix B, *infra*.

Take, for example, the "Just Say No" approach, which began simply as a comment made to the media by Nancy Reagan. This is the "poster child" slogan for total abstinence and zero tolerance. This message may be sufficient for a minority, and total abstinence does work for the lucky few, but it irrefutably and categorically does not work for everyone.

Most of our pre-adolescent children and many of our older children do abstain totally from mind-altering drugs. But beginning at adolescence, many children begin to experiment with all kinds of risk-taking activities, including drug use. Sometimes "Just Say No" becomes "Just Say Maybe" or "Just Say Sometimes." Unfortunately, there are even occasions on which it becomes "Just Say Yes." Children see all kinds of drugs used every day. They see how their parents react to their teenage daughter's emotional response when the boy of her dreams asks someone else to the prom: they give her a Valium to calm her down. They see their parents come home from work and have a couple of stiff drinks. If they have trouble paying attention in school, they themselves may be prescribed Ritalin. It is even increasingly common for children to be given Prozac or Zoloft for "depression." Even caffeine, considered a relatively harmless drug by our culture, is pushed on children as young as three or four, in soft drinks that are aggressively marketed to young people. In fact, many children have become addicted to it. Our children are confused about the difference between "good drugs" and "bad drugs," and it's no wonder. Add to this confusion the hypocrisy, which certainly does not escape our children's attention, when many of our public officials are caught taking illegal drugs or admit to having used them in the past. The former mayor of Washington, D.C., Marion Barry, was captured on videotape snorting cocaine. Governor Gary Johnson of New Mexico publicly acknowledged his prior use of both marijuana and cocaine. President Clinton acknowledged having used marijuana in his youth but denied inhaling, a denial that immediately became a huge and lasting joke in the media. Vice President Gore, who is on record as opposing the medical use of marijuana, is believed to have smoked marijuana on numerous occasions when he was a cub reporter in the early 1970s,[11] and there is testimony that Texas Governor George W. Bush, Gore's opponent in the 2000 presidential election, used cocaine himself, a charge he deflects with statements about the past being past. Of course Governor Bush's alleged cocaine use did not stop him from sign-

---

11. "Comment: Gore's Greatest Bong Hits," *New Yorker*, February 7, 2000: 31–32.

ing a 1997 bill mandating a minimum 180-day jail sentence for first-time offenders convicted of possessing a gram of cocaine or more.[12] The list of elected political leaders who have used drugs goes on and on. Our children might legitimately ask if anyone really believes that it would have helped any of these national leaders to have been arrested and put in jail for their youthful drug use. Is it any wonder that our young people, and people all over the world, simply do not believe us or take us seriously?

Of course, tens of thousands of people who are not elected politicians are currently serving lengthy prison sentences for drug convictions. In Texas, 60 percent of the prison population is serving time on drug charges. Our children might well ask whether drug use is really such a heinous crime, whether marijuana or even moderate cocaine use is really so harmful, or whether it is a personal matter, so that even former drug users can be elected to office—even to the presidency!—without ill effect.

Over the years, police departments all over the country have been forced to recognize the practical harm they were causing themselves by attempting to enforce "zero tolerance" in their hiring practices. Because that policy had the unintended consequence of making large numbers of otherwise excellent recruits ineligible, many police departments have changed their requirements to accept applicants who have acknowledged prior drug use. Under the coercion of polygraph testing, for example, fully 65 percent of the recently hired recruits in the Denver police department acknowledged some past drug use—and not just marijuana. One recruit accepted into the police academy stated that he had used drugs on approximately 150 occasions, including crack cocaine, LSD, mescaline, PCP, methamphetamines, Darvon, and Valium.[13] Even the police have realized that their recruits should be assessed on their overall merit and not disqualified just because they used drugs in the past.

It is a great—and completely unnecessary—irony that when we preach zero tolerance, we forfeit the ability to communicate with large numbers of children precisely at the time when they are at the most

---

12. William F. Buckley, Jr., "The Long Arm of Cocaine," *Orange County Register,* September 2, 1999: Local News 9.

13. Jesse Katz, "Past Drug Use, Future Cops," *Los Angeles Times,* June 18, 2000, Orange County ed.: A1, 12–13.

vulnerable and needy stage of their decision-making lives. This is not only stupid and shortsighted, but it can have very negative consequences.[14] Instead of simply teaching our children to follow directions and promoting unrealistic behavior with tee-shirt slogans like "I believe in a drug-free America," we should be facing actual problems and circumstances with a realistic educational approach. By definition, zero tolerance does not do that. Therefore, programs that advocate zero tolerance make zero sense. Instead of the meaningless "Just Say No," an effective program would be based on individual responsibility and "Just Say *Know.*"

We have made a great mistake in following the mindless rationale that we do not dare to try a different approach to drug education because "it would send the wrong message to our children." Doesn't it make much more sense for parents to sit down with their children, have a frank and open discussion about the dangers of drugs and discourage their children from using drugs in the strongest possible terms, but add the message that if the children ever find themselves in a situation in which they feel their safety is in jeopardy due to their or their companions' use of alcohol or other drugs, instead of taking a risk they should call the parents for a ride home, and the ride will be provided—with no questions asked? Is it better, or more effective, to tell children that they are "bad," that they have disappointed or betrayed you—with the inevitable result that they will hide the truth from you in the future? Doesn't it make more sense to give our children the message that their safety is the most important thing?

How exactly should we, as parents, talk to our children about drugs? Marsha Rosenbaum of the Lindesmith Center in San Francisco wrote and then published a letter on this subject to her son Johnny, who was then a freshman in high school. After telling him the truth about various drugs, discussing their dangers, and explaining and why she felt that he would be smart to abstain from them completely, she closed her letter as follows:

> Despite my advice to abstain, you may one day choose to experiment. I will say again that this is not a good idea, but if you do, I urge you to learn as much as you can, and use common sense. There are many excellent books and references, including the Internet, that give you credible information

---

14. See Tibor Machan, "Zero Tolerance Adds Up to Little Sense," *Orange County Register,* March 15, 1998: Commentary 4.

about drugs. You can, of course, always talk to me. If I don't know the answers, I will try to help you find them.

If you are offered drugs, be cautious. Watch how people behave, but understand that everyone responds differently—even to the same substance. If you do decide to experiment, be sure you are surrounded by people you can count upon. Plan your transportation and under no circumstances drive or get into a car with anyone else who has been using alcohol or other drugs. Call us or any of our close friends any time, day or night, and we will pick you up—no questions asked and no consequences.

And please, Johnny, use moderation. It is impossible to know what is contained in illegal drugs because they are not regulated. The majority of fatal overdoses occur because young people do not know the strength of the drugs they consume, or how they combine with other drugs. Please do not participate in drinking contests, which have killed too many young people. Whereas marijuana by itself is not fatal, too much can cause you to become disoriented and sometimes paranoid. And of course, smoking can hurt your lungs, later in life and now.

Johnny, as your father and I have always told you about a range of activities (including sex), think about the consequences of your actions before you act. Drugs are no different. Be skeptical, and most of all, be safe.

Love, Mom[15]

Dr. Ronald K. Siegel, a professor of pharmacology at UCLA, wrote in his book *Intoxication: Life in Pursuit of Artificial Paradise* that it is in the nature of all mammals, including human beings, to use mind-altering drugs in times of stress. He gave the example of water buffaloes in Vietnam, which are large but very tranquil beasts. When subjected to the stress of B-52 raids during the Vietnam War, they immediately headed for the local coca leaf plants and start chewing on them. When the raids subsided, they went back to their prior activities.[16]

So it is a fact of life that all mammals are inclined to take drugs on some occasions. Our children are the same way. Sometimes this causes harm, sometimes not. For centuries South American peasants have chewed on the coca leaf for relief from fatigue, hunger, thirst, cold, and other miseries.[17] *Even in the American embassies* in Quito, Ecuador, and

---

15. Marsha Rosenbaum, "A Mother's Advice About Drugs," *San Francisco Chronicle*, September 7, 1998: A23.

16. Ronald K. Siegel, Ph.D., *Intoxication: Life in Pursuit of Artificial Paradise* (New York: E. P. Dutton, 1989) 129–30.

17. See Jacob Sullum, "Snow Job: The Demonization of Cocaine," *National Review*, September 27, 1999: 30–32; and Peter T. White, "Coca: An Ancient Indian Herb Turned Deadly," *National Geographic*, January 1989: 2–47.

La Paz, Bolivia, coca tea has been served for years to visitors as a remedy for altitude sickness. Many Jewish children begin drinking wine at an early age during religious ceremonies, and French children learn to drink wine regularly at meals from an early age. These people traditionally have fewer problems with alcoholism than people who began drinking alcohol at a much later age. Certainly total abstinence would be best from a health and social standpoint, but total abstinence is unrealistic. No matter what we do, some people are going to take, and in some instances be harmed by taking, mind-altering drugs.

I happen to be a member of a group called the World Affairs Council of Orange County, which puts on public interest forums on international topics of interest. This group's slogan is, "America's greatest security is a well-informed public," and the group prides itself on presenting as many sides of an issue as possible. The same slogan could and should be used with regard to our nation's drug policy.

Another slogan might be, "In a democracy, we get the government we deserve." When I was in the Peace Corps in Costa Rica from 1966 to 1968, there was an article in the national newspaper about a recent election in Ecuador. The manufacturers of a commercial foot powder had decided to take advantage of the upcoming elections by taking out ads that said, "Vote for Stop-Itch, Vote for Stop-Itch." Well, Stop-Itch won the election as a write-in candidate.

Just as there is no easy path to good government in a democracy, there is no easy path to effective drug education. Our best hope is for parents to take an active interest in their children, assist them with honest information, and help them to develop the confidence, security, and strength of character to resist outside pressure, whether from their peers, the advertising industry, or popular culture generally. Teach them that only they have sovereignty over their own bodies, and that if they abuse them, their bodies will not forget. Although there are some things that only hard experience will teach, such an approach would surely help children to make rational and informed decisions. The simplistic but politically popular educational policy of zero tolerance (which sometimes encourages children to turn in their parents for drug violations and often results in silly outcomes like banning the use of dummy air rifles in high school ROTC classes),[18] teaches children that it is all right

---

18. "Has Zero Tolerance Gone Too Far?" *Los Angeles Times*, June 24, 2000, Orange County ed.: B13.

for adults to be arbitrary in the name of "consistency," and keeps them from facing the hard decisions in life. One-size wisdom has proved time and time again to be not only ineffective but also, sometimes, lethally unjust. Moreover, children can see that schools often back down from their seemingly arbitrary positions the minute Daddy shows up with a lawyer, which is certainly not a good lesson for us to impart. Edmund Burke said, "Example is the school of mankind, and they will learn from no other." Our approach to drug education bears him out. The truth about the dangers of drugs is reason enough to give our children pause; there is no reason to stoop to sensationalism, arbitrariness, or false-hood. Instead we must encourage educators to be open and honest with everyone, including our children, and allow free and open discussion. And it is critically important to drive home the point that just because we do not advocate a "zero tolerance" approach to decision making does not mean that we do not hold people accountable for their actions, or that we accept excuses for a lack of performance. But confining our-selves in a box by prescribing a punishment before we know the offense and the circumstances results in arbitrariness, and that is what our chil-dren rightly find unreasonable.

In pursuing a more realistic and effective drug education policy, we must also acknowledge that drug use depends not only on the pharma-cological properties of the drugs themselves but also on the "set," or psychological state of the user at the time of usage, and upon the "set-ting," including such things as social conditions, geography, and even the weather.[19] This is reality, and we will never make progress by fak-ing that reality. Examples of the importance of the set and the setting in combating drug abuse can be seen in what happened at the end of the war in Vietnam. When Saigon fell in 1975, our Department of Defense knew that thousands of returning GIs were addicted to nar-cotic drugs. These soldiers were young, far from home, often for the first time, scared, had time on their hands, had spending money, and narcotic drugs were freely and cheaply available. So they took them and in many cases became addicted to them. Defense Department per-sonnel were rightfully worried. They handed out contracts for drug treatment by the hundreds so that addicted servicemen would have somewhere to go when they got home. Then they waited for the onslaught.

---

19. See Norman Zinberg, *Drug, Set and Setting* (New Haven: Yale University Press, 1984).

But it never really came. A large percentage of the soldiers left their addictions behind them. As soon as they were back in safe and familiar surroundings, most of them reverted to their prior, non-addicted lifestyle. Once the psychological state and the social conditions of the users changed, they were no longer "hooked."

The phenomenon of set and setting was anecdotally explained by Malcolm X in his *Autobiography*.[20] Under the spiritual direction of the Muslim religion, hard-line heroin addicts from Harlem and elsewhere who were robbers, con men, and philanderers changed almost overnight into clean-cut and well-disciplined followers of Islam. Not only were they nonviolent and law-abiding, but they also gave up alcohol and other drugs and would not have sexual relations outside of wedlock. How does Malcolm X explain this transformation? Their conversion to the new faith gave these violent men a reason to change, something to believe in that gave their lives meaning. In other words, the men's conversion changed the set and the setting.

For the same story, but in reverse, talk to almost any parole officer. Large numbers of drug users and addicts are released from prisons each day throughout this country. While in prison these people had access to drugs, but since drugs are much more expensive in prison, few if any of these inmates were still physically addicted at the time of their release. And yet, as soon as they re-entered their "home turf," where they saw the same buildings, people, and lifestyle, they frequently became addicted to their drugs again—without even taking them. Why does this happen? Set and setting: psychological state and social conditions of the user.

How can this situation be overcome? Education and treatment. Give the addict a reason to get out of bed in the morning other than his fifteen-minute high on drugs. Work with her before she leaves prison (or, better yet, before she is sent there in the first place); help teach her about health considerations and job and parenting skills so that she is equipped to do something other than fail when she re-enters society. As we will see in the next chapter on rehabilitation and treatment, these efforts can be enormously successful and gratifying. But they do not have the public's attention or wholehearted backing, and so they are not politically popular. The question of drug education is complicated

---

20. Malcolm X and Alex Haley, *Autobiography of Malcolm X* (New York: Ballantine Books, 1964).

because human beings are complicated. Problems of drug abuse are not solved by slogans, tricks, or gimmicks. Like anything else, positive results come from understanding, hard work, and perseverance. Sure, gimmicks can be fun. But most of the time they are ineffective, and only create the illusion that we are accomplishing something. Does anyone seriously believe that stenciling the words "Just Say No to Drugs" on a strainer in restroom urinals actually accomplishes anything? We must remember the lesson learned by the school board that furnished fourth graders with pencils that said, "It's not cool to do drugs." The children quickly saw that when you sharpened the pencils they soon read, "cool to do drugs," and eventually, "do drugs." This does not mean that we should not be creative in our public service reminders, such as the memorable holiday enforcement message on a highway in Phoenix that said, "Drive Hammered—Get Nailed." But slogans and gimmicks will never substitute for intelligent policy.[21]

We must also insist on truthful and accurate reporting from both our government and our media. In August 1996, a federal agency reported that 32 out of 4,500 teenagers surveyed responded that they used heroin at some time during the previous year. The same survey the prior year had found that only 14 teenagers had acknowledged the use of heroin. So how did the government and the media report the result? Teenage heroin use—no, the generalization is better—teenage drug use has *doubled* in America. Everyone joined in the posturing. Senator Bob Dole, who was running for president at the time, ran television commercials based on this survey accusing President Clinton of being "soft on drugs." President Clinton, not to be outdone, announced that the government would provide an extra $112 million to various Latin American countries to help them fight drugs. Thus the eighteen self-reported additional teenage heroin users translated into fifty-three UH-1H helicopters for Mexico alone.[22]

The British are way ahead of us in this area. They are sophisticated enough to understand that effective drug education must encourage young people to develop their own views about drugs and make informed decisions about their own and other people's drug use. They

---

21. For valuable insights on raising children in a world full of temptations to try drugs, see Julian Cohen and James Kay, *Taking Drugs Seriously: A Parent's Guide to Young People's Drug Use* (London and San Francisco: Thorsons, 1994).

22. Peter King, "Dispatch From the Drug War," *Los Angeles Times*, September 25, 1996, Orange County ed.: A3.

begin by not tying national funding to any particular type of educational approach, which leaves more room for innovation and new techniques. One of the innovations that has been developed in Britain is the Healthwise Program in Liverpool, which recognizes that prevention must focus on specific risks rather than unattainable goals, regardless of how politically useful those goals might be. Healthwise provides information about specific drugs and their effects, and explains what people experience when they take them. Since scrupulous honesty is the basis for the program, Healthwise staff even acknowledge some positive drug experiences along with the dangerous ones. This program's realism has made it more effective than approaches used in the United States. It recognizes that drugs will always be with us and that there will always be some demand for them. So it provides full and accurate information and prepares as many people as possible to make responsible choices about their use—and to be prepared to be held accountable for the choices they make.[23]

Before we move on, let me pass along the message set forth in the book *Wonderland Avenue*, by Danny Sugerman,[24] who was and is the agent for Jim Morrison's rock group "The Doors." Sugerman describes in detail the glamor and excess of the life that he and his friends led under the influence of drugs. It was a life of nightclubbing where handfuls of colorful pills were passed out like candy and chased down with large quantities of alcohol. Sugerman and his friends, like so many rock stars and their fans in the drug culture of the 1960s and '70s, were truly living the "fast life," and, I confess, he tells an interesting story. Eventually, however, Sugerman found out that his kidneys were giving out and that he was dying. Fortunately, he went into a treatment program at the urging of his brother, who is a doctor, and so far has been able to continue with his recovery, even learning the meaning of a "natural high" along the way. I mention this story because in the Afterword to the book, Sugerman provides the reader an update on the lives of the friends whose story he has just told. Sixteen of the twenty-

---

23. See Rodney Skager, "Do the Sensible British Have a Better Approach to Drug Education?" *Prevention File* (summer 1999): 18–20. For further information, write to Healthwise Program, 1st Floor, Cavern Walks, 8 Mathew St., Liverpool L2 6RE, United Kingdom; telephone 011 44 151 227 4415. E-mail <admin@healthwise.org.uk>; web site: <www.healthwise.org.uk>.

24. Danny Sugerman, *Wonderland Avenue, Tales of Glamour and Excess* (New York: Plume/Penguin Group, 1989).

nine characters were dead by the time the book went to press.[25] Of the thirteen who were still alive, two were in jail; one had confessed to a large misappropriation of funds; one was "living" in a wheelchair, blind and unable to speak, with her left side paralyzed by an overdose; and one was making his third try at a recovery program. As one of the reviews of the book put it, "One of the scariest arguments yet against using drugs." I agree, and I believe that this is a part of drug education that will be effective without falsehoods, slogans, or gimmickry— because these drugs are dangerous, and that is the truth.

I close this chapter with the words of Cal Thomas, the conservative syndicated columnist and co-author with Dr. Edward Dobson, a member of the Moral Majority and follower of Jerry Falwell, of "Blinded By Might: Can the Religious Right Save America?":

> [Alcohol] Prohibition was an effort by Christians, mostly women, to combat alcoholism and drunkenness. Zealous leaders believed they could reform America by enacting laws outlawing alcoholic beverages, but the movement was a spectacular failure. It effectively subsidized organized crime and created a bigger monster than the one it had fought. Good people properly diagnosed a social ill, but they used the wrong methods to correct it. The lesson: by and large, the Christian mission should be to change hearts, not laws.[26]

History has shown us that we can pass all the laws in the world. But as long as there is a demand for drugs, the demand will be met. Our criminal laws will always be trumped by the law of supply and demand, and addiction cannot be eliminated by fiat. Fortunately, even people like conservative Christian Cal Thomas are beginning to understand that open, truthful, and realistic education, instead of shallow gimmicks and punitive laws, is what is needed to change the hearts, minds, and actions of our people.

---

25. Along this line, Sugerman said, "Jim Morrison, as far as I know, is still dead."
26. Cal Thomas, "Not of This World," *Newsweek*, March 29, 1999: 60.

Drug Treatment

If the resources now spent on criminalization of drugs were devoted instead to education and treatment, the cost and danger of drug use would be greatly reduced. More funds would be available for schools, hospitals, libraries, and courts. The money spent on police practices that fail to reduce consumption could be directed to traditional areas of law enforcement that have been pre-empted by this futile war effort.
Senior Judge John L. Kane, Jr., United States District Court, Denver, Colorado

On June 13, 1994, the RAND Corporation released a study that found that drug treatment is seven times more cost-effective than domestic law enforcement in addressing drug abuse, eleven times more cost-effective than our attempts to interdict illicit drugs as they come across our borders, and twenty-three times more cost-effective than our drug eradication and crop substitution programs overseas.[1] When this respected "think tank" found that every dollar spent on drug treatment resulted in seven dollars of overall savings, whereas the same tax dollar spent on law enforcement alone resulted in only ninety-nine cents in savings, many newspapers editorialized that money for domestic drug enforcement and incarceration should be reduced by at least one-quarter, and money spent for drug treatment should be correspondingly increased.[2]

---

1. Carolyn Skorneck, "Treatment Is Cheapest Way to Cut Cocaine Use in Nation, Report Says," *Orange County Register,* June 14, 1994; Chronicle Wire Services, "A Cheaper Way to Fight Cocaine," *San Francisco Chronicle,* June 14, 1994: A7.

2. Editorial, "How to Be Effective against Cocaine," *Los Angeles Times,* June 16, 1994, Orange County ed.: B6.

A similar study funded by the state of California and conducted by the University of Chicago's National Opinion Research Center reached virtually the same conclusions in August 1994. The study found that the use of crack cocaine, powder cocaine, and amphetamines declined by almost one-half after treatment; that heroin use declined by more than one-fifth; and that alcohol use declined by almost one-third. After this study was released, Alan Leshner, director of the National Institute on Drug Abuse, stated that "Most people don't believe treatment works, and they're wrong. That's why a study like this is so important." Similarly, Andrew Mecca, director of the California Department of Alcohol and Drug Programs, called the results "slam dunk evidence," and estimated that the $209 million spent by California in drug treatment between October 1991 and September 1992 had resulted in savings to the taxpayers of $1.5 billion.[3]

Anecdotal corroboration of these studies has come from an unlikely source. For years, former California State Assemblyman Pat Nolan, an archconservative from Glendale, consistently spoke and voted in favor of longer and longer periods of incarceration for all drug offenses. However, after serving a two-year prison sentence for political corruption, he announced publicly that he had changed his mind once he had seen the results of that policy with his own eyes. Nolan saw large numbers of people in prison who simply should not have been there. He summarized his conclusions this way: "We should reserve our prison space for people we are afraid of, instead of people we are mad at."

Many people in the law enforcement community also understand that many more of our scarce resources must be spent on drug treatment—and often will say so privately. One who has said so publicly, for years, is San Francisco Sheriff Michael Hennessey. Recognizing that we have a limited amount of money to be spent in this area, Sheriff Hennessey stated:

> Taxpayers should be concerned about how law enforcement officials are spending their tax dollars to break the cycle of crime and substance abuse. How are inmates to rid themselves of their addiction? Substance abuse is a vicious addiction, notoriously difficult to shed. But treatment does work, and it does reduce crime. If we really care about reducing crime and drug use,

---

3. Sheryl Stolberg, "Drug Treatment Efforts Called Cost-Effective," *Los Angeles Times*, August 29, 1994, Orange County ed.: A1, 14.

let's not waste resources performing costly drug tests—at $9 a pop—on 1.7 million prisoners. That money would be far better spent on approaches proven to reduce crime committed by addicts.[4]

There is an old story about two men who were walking along a river when they saw a person in the water being dragged along by the current. No sooner had they rescued that person than they saw another, and another in the same danger. They dragged person after person out of the water, until finally one of the two men turned to leave. "Where do you think you're going?" asked the second man. "I'm going upstream to stop these people from falling into the river in the first place."

In Sheriff Hennessey's San Francisco, they are implementing programs that serve as alternatives to incarceration, such as drug treatment, job training, and counseling. In doing this, they are going "up river" to help people before they are swept further away by the current of drug addiction. The result is that they have had a decline in the number of incarcerations from 2,136 in 1993 to 703 in 1998. And violent crime has been reduced by 33 percent in San Francisco since 1995.[5]

All over the country, much lip service is given both by our various governments and by the news media to the term "drug treatment," although the term is rarely defined or explained. Drug treatment and prevention have been shown to have a major effect in keeping people from drowning in the river of drug abuse, but what exactly is drug treatment? In actuality, treatment can mean many fundamentally different things. The one thing that sets it apart from the policy of zero tolerance, however, is that drug treatment addresses the use of drugs as social and public health problems, leaving the criminal justice system to concentrate on holding people accountable for their conduct.

Needle exchange programs, methadone or other drug substitution programs, and drug maintenance programs all fall under the heading of medicalized drug treatment. We will address them here under the heading of "medicalization." There are some other non-medicalized, or rehabilitation, programs that we will also discuss. And, since the emphasis is beginning to move away from automatic, zero-tolerance incarceration

---

4. Michael Hennessey, "Just Say No to Prison Drug Testing," *San Francisco Chronicle*, February 6, 1998; see also Michael Hennessey, "Our National Jail Scandal: Re-Engineering the Industry of Incarceration," *American Jails* (The Magazine of the American Jail Association), July/August 1993: 11–16.

5. Ray Delgado, "Drop in S.F. Crime Attributed to Drug Treatment, Counseling," *Los Angeles Daily Journal*, October 27, 1999: 9.

and toward recovery and future law-abiding and medically safe conduct, our nation's "drug courts" will also be discussed as an example of a rehabilitation drug treatment program.

Rehabilitation

The articles were enlightening and reinforced the conclusion I reached some time ago—we are losing the so-called war on drugs at a terrible cost of lives and resources. I am particularly upset at the sentences we are required to impose under the guidelines and mandatory minimums.

I fully agree with the harm reduction strategy suggested and the decriminalization of marijuana and other "soft" drugs.

Senior Judge Marvin H. Shoob, United States District Court, Atlanta, Georgia

Whether or not a person will be successful in a drug treatment program is a highly individual matter. It depends both on the individual and his or her motivation and on the program itself. Given the much higher expense of incarcerating someone for a year, both in financial and human terms, and given that rehabilitation is seven times more cost-effective in treating drug addiction and abuse, what do we have to lose? Particularly when almost half of our nation's 1.8 million people behind bars have serious drug problems, and when less than ten percent of these prisoners are involved in any material kind of drug treatment program.[6] We have already seen that experimentation with different types of clinics was abandoned after the passage of the Harrison Act in 1914. But there is no reason why we can't pick up where we left off and once again start adopting treatment programs and policies that work.

There are many reasons for hope. One model for a successful rehabilitation program is operated by the Delancey Street Foundation, which is based in San Francisco and has facilities in three other cities. In its first twenty-five years of existence, more than 10,000 felons, drug abusers, and prostitutes went through this live-in program, teaching themselves job skills, discipline, responsibility, and social skills in order to become healthy and productive citizens.

The foundation owns and operates—solely through its residents— various businesses, including a moving company, a catering operation, and an advertising specialties company. These businesses net more than

---

6. Mathea Falco, "Treatment Breaks the Crime Cycle; Jail Doesn't," *Los Angeles Times*, March 6, 1995, Orange County ed.: B9. Ms. Falco is president of "Drug Strategies," a nonprofit group in Washington that released "Keeping Score," a report on federal drug spending.

$3 million per year. To stay in the program, the participants are required to cut their hair, wear business attire for dinner, learn at least three marketable job skills, and earn a high school equivalency diploma. Use or possession of any mind-altering drugs, including alcohol, or even the threat of violence, is automatic grounds for dismissal. Upon acceptance into the program, participants must commit to stay for a minimum of two years. Then, after getting a job on the outside and continuing to live at the facility for a three-month transition period, participants are encouraged to maintain contact by volunteering with the foundation. Since its inception, *80 percent* of the participants have kept that commitment.[7]

This enormously successful program is still run by its founder, a diminutive woman named Mimi Silbert. A psychologist and criminologist, she is the only professional on the staff. Here is how Ms. Silbert describes her philosophy:

> We're trying to prove that the "losers" in our society can, in fact, be helped, and also that they, in turn, can help. Essentially they make up an underclass. A third of our population was homeless. The average resident is four or five generations into poverty and two or three generations into prison. They've been hard-core dope fiends. They're unskilled and functionally illiterate. They've had horrible violence done to them, and they've been violent.
>
> Most people would rather see them locked up for the rest of their lives, but our point is the opposite—that they can be taught to help themselves. They can learn to be responsible and self-reliant. And we believe that helping these same people is a critical part of turning around all the rest of society.[8]

Nationally, of the approximately 800,000 prison inmates who have drug and alcohol abuse problems, only one in six receives any kind of drug treatment at all, and most of this consists of sporadic education and counseling that provide little lasting benefit. In the state of California, there are only about four hundred drug treatment positions available throughout the entire prison system for the 120,000 prison inmates. More than half of those positions are at the Donovan State Prison in San Diego County.

---

7. Hank Whittemore, "Hitting Bottom Can Be The Beginning," *Parade Magazine*, March 15, 1992: 4–6; Anne Colby, "Working to Kick Criminal Habits," *Los Angeles Times*, June 3, 1995, Orange County ed: B15.

8. Whittemore, "Hitting Bottom," *supra* at 5.

Donovan is unusual in that it contracted with a private company in 1990 to provide a strict and comprehensive drug treatment program for 220 of its inmates at a total cost of $1.5 million per year. The program emphasizes basic life skills, such as anger management, job skills, parenting, overall health considerations, general responsibility for conduct, and an honest appraisal of the risks and benefits of using drugs. The success of this program is best expressed by Captain Michael Teischner, who for four years was the supervisor of the prison's drug treatment program. When he began this assignment, Teischner was a skeptic who did not think drug treatment programs worked. His experience at Donovan has made him a believer. "The only problem with drug and alcohol treatment," he says now, "is that the exploding prison population can't get enough of it."

The reason for Teischner's transformation is simple: statistics show the program works. A 1997 federal study showed that only *16 percent* of the inmates who had completed Donovan's drug treatment program were arrested within one year of their release from prison, as opposed to 65 percent of Donovan inmates who did not participate in the program. Unfortunately, the California state prison system has provided intensive drug treatment for only about 3,000 of its estimated 120,000 inmates with substance abuse problems.[9]

The routine at Donovan is rigorous, and no inmate gets his sentence or workload reduced for participating. Nor are these hardened, substance-abusing criminals isolated from the rest of the prison population, so access to smuggled drugs is an everyday temptation. The California Department of Corrections has calculated that if 2,100 additional inmates were to be treated in programs such as Donovan's over a seven-year period at the same relative cost, taxpayers would recoup the entire cost of the program and save an additional $4.7 million per year in prison costs alone.[10] The U.S. Justice Department has reached similar conclusions, saying, "In addition to keeping people drug-free and out of prison, these programs are cost-effective—a powerful argument in favor of implementation. . . . [The] savings in crime-related and drug-use associated costs pay for the treatment in about 2 to 3 years. It is an

9. Editorial, "Attacking the Drug/Crime Link," *Los Angeles Times*, January 7, 1999, Orange County ed.: B8; see also Lewis Yablonsky, Ph.D., "Link between Drugs and Crime," *Los Angeles Times*, January 16, 1999, Orange County ed.: B9.

10. Dan Weikel, "Prison Drug Rehab That Pays Off," *Los Angeles Times*, April 25, 1997, Orange County ed.: A1, 18.

inescapable conclusion that treatment lowers crime and health costs as well as related social and criminal justice costs."[11]

An equally successful program is the Key program in Delaware, which combines twelve to fifteen months of drug treatment and job training in prison with six months of aftercare once the person has been released. Of those offenders who did not go through the program at all, 70 percent were arrested for another criminal offense within eighteen months of their release, compared to 52 percent of the offenders who went through the prison but not the aftercare portion, 35 percent of those who went through only the aftercare portion, and 29 percent of those who went through both portions.[12]

Another type of drug rehabilitation program beginning to be used effectively around the country is the drug court. The first such program was established in Miami in 1989, when U.S. Attorney General Janet Reno was the head prosecutor. It was seen as such a hopeful model that Congress passed Title V of the Violent Crime Control and Law Enforcement Act of 1994, authorizing the attorney general to grant federal monies to the states in order to establish their own programs.

Most of these drug court programs are offered only to nonviolent first offenders charged with drug or property offenses. These offenders are given the opportunity of going into a treatment program instead of going to jail; but it is intended that the requirements are to be rigorously enforced. Instead of being given only one chance and being sent back to prison if they fail to stay clean, offenders are frequently given short stints in jail, encouraged to do better, and placed back in treatment. In order to qualify for the federal money, the programs must include mandatory periodic drug testing; counseling; criminal justice sanctions in the event of noncompliance or failure to show satisfactory progress; and aftercare services, such as relapse prevention, health care, education, vocational training, job placement, housing placement, child care, and other family support services.[13]

---

11. Douglas S. Lipton, "Prison-Based Therapeutic Communities: Their Success With Drug-Abusing Offenders," *National Institute of Justice Journal* 230 (February 1996): 12–20, at 17.

12. Elliott Currie, *Crime and Punishment in America* (New York: Metropolitan Books, 1998): 166–67.

13. See Yumi L. Wilson, "Court Gives Hope To Drug Abusers," *San Francisco Chronicle*, December 6, 1993: A17, 21; "Law, Health Officials Seek to Establish Drug Court," *Los Angeles Times*, August 29, 1994, Orange County ed.: B1, 4.

The problem with drug court programs is that they are labor-intensive for judges, probation officers, health officers, attorneys, and staff. Most last for about twelve months, and about one-third of the participants graduate. As of the end of 1998, there were about three hundred drug court programs around the country and, given the fact that so many offenders coming through the criminal justice system have substance abuse problems, many of these programs are beginning to include multiple offenders and even some cases involving some level of violence.

Studies released on November 10, 1998, by Physician Leadership on National Drug Policy, a bipartisan group of doctors and public health leaders, including former members of the Clinton, Bush, and Reagan administrations, show that forcing drug users who commit nonviolent crimes into rehabilitation programs significantly reduces drug use and re-arrest rates. Since programs like these cost about $3,000 per year and are successful, and since it costs taxpayers about $25,000 per year to keep one person incarcerated, this group concluded that drug courts will help save tens of millions of taxpayer dollars per year, reduce the prison population by 250,000 over the next five years, and reduce crime.[14]

Before leaving the subject of drug courts, however, a note of caution. In many ways, drug courts represent a highly positive revolution in the criminal justice system, for they treat criminal defendants as real human beings with real problems. But there is a risk in the use of drug courts, in that they can be used to perpetuate the failed War on Drugs against drug users. This would be a major mistake. Drug courts should be used only for *problem* drug users whose *conduct* brings them into the system.

If a person commits an assault, a forgery, a theft, or drives under the influence of cocaine or some other illicit drug, and he has a drug problem of any kind, charge him with that and send him to drug court. Through drug court he can serve an appropriate time in jail, make restitution to the victim(s), and be coerced into drug treatment. But it is counterproductive to bring people into the criminal justice system simply for their choice of drugs, and, as we have seen, the collateral harms to society of trying to prohibit these drugs are enormous. The

14. Associated Press, "Experts: Drug Courts Working," *USA Today*, November 11, 1998: 21A.

problem users will find their way into the court system anyway; the non–problem users are best addressed by education and medical care.[15]

Dollar savings provide plenty of reasons to implement drug treatment programs for all people who want them, whether they are in or out of prison. But the savings to society are actually much greater. Studies done in Germany show that youthful offenders who were sent to prison had much higher rates of recidivism than those who were given alternative sentences. The basic reason was that removing these people from society had a large negative impact on their employment rates when they were eventually released—even though they were given job training while confined. In addition, other studies showed that the recidivism rates (i.e., rates of re-offending) increased by 7 percent above average for those who were incarcerated, but *decreased* by 13 percent for those who received alternative sentencing. Finally, the studies found that while about 40 percent of the offenders were unemployed at the time of their offenses before incarceration, within three months of release their unemployment rate had increased to 60 percent.[16]

So not only is the direct financial benefit seven times greater with drug treatment, as reported by the RAND Corporation survey, there are additional benefits that accrue to society from using drug treatment rather than imprisonment. Not only do these benefits translate into increased physical and medical safety for drug-addicted people, they also directly result in increased physical and medical safety for us all. It is a fundamental truth that "hurt people hurt people." So even if we care nothing for the safety and well-being of drug addicts, we must make drug treatment available to those people who are hurting, or we will have a good chance of being hurt ourselves. When taxpayers actually understand the benefits they will receive from a change of policy,

---

15. Another note of caution: another movement that many people are attempting to use to overturn Drug Prohibition is so-called "jury nullification." This movement advocates that all juries be instructed by the trial judge that if they do not agree with any particular law in a case, they can choose not to enforce it. In my view, this is a genuinely destructive doctrine. Our country was founded upon the premise that we are a government of laws, not of men. If anyone, including a judge or a juror, can ignore or negate our laws because they do not agree with them, we will run the direct risk of falling into anarchy. We must have reasonable laws, but we must enforce those laws. The best way to get rid of a bad law is not to ignore it but to enforce it—very loudly. This will cause the bad law to be repealed or changed.

16. U.S. Department of Justice, Office of Justice Programs, "Alternative Sanctions in Germany: An Overview of Germany's Sentencing Practices," *National Institute of Justice, Research Preview*, February 1996.

they will be calling their government representatives and demanding immediate implementation of drug treatment programs all across the country.

Medicalization
Needle Exchange Programs

Drug use, legal and illegal, is principally a health problem which is best dealt with not by driving it underground with prohibition tactics, but by having it out in the open to allow for treatment and education. . . . It is difficult to understand why illegal drug addiction should be treated differently from alcoholism or nicotine addiction: all are basically public health problems.[17]
Chief Judge Juan R. Torruella, United States Court of Appeals, Hato Rey, Puerto Rico

Probably the most straightforward medicalization programs are "needle exchange." These programs have evolved around the world in direct response to the spread of dangerous and often fatal contagious diseases such as hepatitis C, tuberculosis, and HIV/AIDS. This is a truly serious health threat. AIDS is the leading cause of death among twenty-five- to forty-four-year-olds in our country, and the largest group afflicted with this disease is drug users who use needles, their sexual partners, and their offspring.[18] Studies show that almost 50 percent of all minorities who contract AIDS do so from dirty needles used in injecting illicit drugs. The same studies show that injection drug use and sexual contact with injection drug users account for a full 71 percent of AIDS cases for adult and adolescent women.[19] Tragically, if the woman with AIDS is pregnant, the fetus is also exposed to this deadly disease.

Undoubtedly the seamiest side of all drug use is found in the "shooting galleries" of the slums of large cities, such as New York. As a 1992 four-part series in the *Los Angeles Times* described it, here "in a dank, burned-out building, addicts engage in microbiological roulette, sharing contaminated needles. Here, America's drug war meets failure and

---

17. Chief Judge Juan R. Torruella, U.S. Court of Appeals for the First Circuit, "One Judge's Attempt at a Rational Discussion of the So-Called 'War on Drugs,'" unpublished lecture at Colby College, Waterville, Maine, April 26, 1996, at 14.

18. Peter Lurie, M.D., MPH, "When Science and Politics Collide: The Federal Response to Needle-Exchange Programs," *Bulletin of the New York Academy of Medicine* 72, no. 2 (winter 1995): 380–96.

19. The White House, National Drug Control Strategy (February 1994) 11.

AIDS is spread."[20] In these places, many injection drug users are serviced with the same hypodermic needle because, unbelievably enough, it is frequently harder for these people to find a clean needle than it is to find drugs. As of 1992, *about 35 percent* of the estimated 1 million injection drug users in the United States were HIV positive, and they had passed on this deadly virus to 50,000 to 75,000 non-injectors, mostly through unprotected sexual relations. As we will see when we look at decriminalization programs in Holland, needle exchange has reduced that country's rate of HIV infection through contaminated needles to about four percent.

Needle exchange programs allow a person to exchange a dirty needle for a clean one—without charge and without questions. It is that simple. There is no drug treatment component, and no providing of drugs or drug substitutes. Most of these programs do furnish information, if it is requested, about how to inject the drugs in a less dangerous way, and about how to seek medical treatment for drug addiction and other medical conditions. The programs also provide the important collateral benefit of bringing the drug-injecting users closer to the medical professionals that can help them.

In 1992 Congress passed a bill commissioning a study by the National Academy of Sciences, a federally chartered but independent research organization, into whether needle exchange programs actually are effective, and whether they increase drug use. In September 1995 the National Academy published its conclusions, finding that needle exchange programs greatly reduce the spread of the AIDS virus and do not increase illicit drug usage. A program in New Haven, Connecticut, for example, reduced the rate of HIV infection by about one-third, while a needle exchange program in Tacoma, Washington, caused an eightfold decrease in hepatitis among injection drug users.[21]

The National Academy was not alone in reaching these conclusions. In October 1993 twelve researchers at the University of California published a 700-page report prepared for the National Centers for Disease Control and Prevention. This report similarly concluded that needle exchange programs are effective in reducing contagious diseases and do

---

20. Barry Bearak, "Headquarters for Heroin and HIV," *Los Angeles Times*, September 27, 1992, Orange County ed.: A1, 18–20.

21. Warren E. Leary, "Report Endorses Needle Exchanges as AIDS Strategy," *New York Times*, September 20, 1995: A1.

not increase illicit drug usage.[22] The Centers for Disease Control endorsed the study and recommended that the federal government fully support needle exchange programs. In 1994 the Institute of Medicine of the National Academy of Sciences also recommended federal support for needle exchange programs. The National Commission on AIDS, the Office of Technology Assessment, the General Accounting Office, and the American Medical Association have all agreed.[23] Researchers from the University of California at San Francisco discovered in 1993 that the percentage of injection drug users who shared needles dropped from 66 percent to 35 percent as a result of a needle exchange program in that city. A UCSF health policy analyst and lead author of the study said, "The bottom line is that syringe exchange reduces needle sharing and doesn't lead to increased substance abuse."[24]

Once again, public health officials and political leaders in European countries are far ahead of the United States in recognizing that needle exchange programs appreciably reduce the incidence of serious contagious diseases among addicted people. The British have set up hundreds of needle exchanges around their country, and needle exchange vending machines can be found in dozens of European cities. In Amsterdam, needle exchange cites are located in police stations, which makes a lot of sense in that police stations are clean, safe, well-lit and open twenty-four hours a day.[25]

In the face of overwhelming evidence of the obvious benefits of needle exchange programs, and in spite of the fact that new syringes cost less than ten cents apiece, the U.S. government not only persists in refusing to fund any needle exchange programs, federal laws continue to prohibit the importation or transportation of drug paraphernalia, such as syringes, in interstate commerce. Only at the end of February 1997 did the U.S. Secretary of Health and Human Services bow to the weight of the evidence and acknowledge that needle exchange programs

---

22. Lurie, *supra* at 385; Paul Recer, "Study Finds Needle Exchanges Don't Promote Illegal Drugs," *Orange County Register,* September 20, 1995: News 12; Sheryl Stolberg, "Needle Exchange Cuts Risks, Study Finds," *Los Angeles Times,* January 12, 1994, Orange County ed.: A3, 18.

23. Joanne Jacobs, "Drug War Sticks a Needle in the AIDS Battle," *Orange County Register,* March 5, 1997: Metro 9.

24. Stolberg, *supra* at A3.

25. Ethan Nadelmann, "Europe's Drug Prescription," *Rolling Stone,* January 26, 1995: 38–39.

slow the spread of AIDS. Even then, however, the secretary would not recommend lifting the federal ban on funding these programs or advocate the repeal of any of the federal prohibitionist laws.[26]

The policy of the United States government appears to be the same now as it was in June 1992, when the office of the Drug Czar published a report entitled "Needle Exchange Programs: Are They Effective?" This report concluded that "there is no getting around the fact that distributing needles facilitates drug use and undercuts the credibility of society's message that using drugs is illegal and morally wrong."[27] One commentator responded, "The real message sent by the federal ban is this: Go ahead and die. If you shoot up drugs, or have sex with someone who shoots up, or are born to a mother who had sex with someone who shoots up, your life is not worth saving."[28]

The Honorable Kristine M. Gebbie, RN, MN, who was the "AIDS Czar" under President Clinton, understood the importance of needle exchange in reducing the spread of AIDS. She wrote to me, in fact, on September 16, 1993:

> You are correct in recognizing the synergistic relationship between drug policies and the demonstrable spread of the AIDS epidemic into a wider world beyond the traditional high risk groups who have borne the brunt of the disease to date.
>
> My staff, along with others within the Departments of Health and Human Services and Justice, as well as staff members of key members of Congress, have been looking for some time at the spread of AIDS through needle sharing. As you know, changes in such programs can only come through strong government leadership supported by even stronger community commitment to change.

Unfortunately, Ms. Gebbie's position did not carry very much political influence. And when the strong government leadership did not materialize, she resigned.

Most of the states in this country have followed the lead of the federal government. As of August 1996, a report published in the *American Journal of Public Health* found that forty-six states and the District of Columbia still had laws restricting the possession or distribution of "drug paraphernalia." Many of these states also have laws requiring a

---

26. Jacobs, *supra.*
27. Lurie, *supra* at 382–83.
28. Jacobs, *supra.*

person to have a medical prescription in order legally to obtain a syringe. Obviously these laws subject people involved in needle exchange programs to possible criminal prosecution. Of the eleven prosecutions discovered by the report, however, nine resulted in acquittals either because the jury simply nullified the "offense" or because the jury accepted the defense of "necessity." In spite of the federal and state governments' prohibitions, the courageous and public-spirited people in charge of needle exchange programs have continued to operate them.[29]

If you are still not convinced that we should openly implement and promote needle exchange programs, go and visit one yourself. You will see that they are about helping real people with real problems, and you will change your mind. And take your children with you, because they will see firsthand that this life is not something they want for themselves.

Drug Substitution Programs

I have been of the opinion for quite some time that the Government's war on drugs has not worked. Most of our criminal docket is made up of drug cases. Every time a dealer is caught and convicted, there are many others waiting to take over the work. I am also of the opinion that the sentencing guidelines have not worked, especially as to drug cases. I do not know what the answer is, but I do believe we should come up with another approach to this perplexing problem.

Judge James C. Turk, United States District Court, Roanoke, Virginia

Drug substitution programs, as the name suggests, substitute the use of one drug for another one. The most widely known programs of this type involve methadone, which is generally substituted for heroin, and these programs have been existence since the early 1960s. Other programs substitute morphine for heroin. One of the first drug substitution programs took place in Shreveport, Louisiana, under the direction of Dr. Willis P. Butler, and was one of the morphine substitution programs forced to close down after Congress passed the Harrison Act in 1914 and the Supreme Court ruled in *Webb v. United States* in 1919 that it was not a legitimate medical practice for doctors to prescribe narcotic drugs for the prevention of narcotics withdrawal.

In the United States today, the only active drug substitution programs involve methadone, which somehow has been exempted from our pro-

---

29. Scott Burris, J.D.; David Finucane, J.D.; Heather Gallagher, J.D.; and Joseph Grace, J.D., "The Legal Strategies Used in Operating Syringe Exchange Programs in the United States," *American Journal of Public Health* (August 1996): 1161.

hibitionist laws. Methadone, an addictive narcotic in its own right, takes away much of the craving for heroin in many addicts. Some drug users have described the effects of methadone with an analogy of a person who is looking forward to a feast but is given half a turkey sandwich. It is food, but it does not satisfy what the body and mind were anticipating. In effect, methadone is to heroin as a nicotine skin patch is to a cigarette. And like any other program, it is highly individualized: quite successful for some people, modestly successful for others, and almost completely unsuccessful for many more.

Methadone is a synthetic opiate that takes away both the sense of euphoria and the symptoms of withdrawal that heroin produces. The benefits for the user, and for society, are clear. The users who are taking methadone instead of heroin are able to function quite normally, which makes them quite indistinguishable from non-drug users. The drug is usually taken orally, so the problems related with injections are not an issue, and it is longer-acting than heroin, so a dosage can be taken once every twenty-four to thirty-six hours, instead of multiple times per day. This usually allows the user to be treated on an outpatient basis. Studies show that within one year of beginning treatment, 70 percent of the users no longer used heroin, and after three years the use of heroin had decreased by about 85 percent.[30]

Although researchers in the United States pioneered the use of methadone for programs of drug substitution, many other countries have now gone far beyond us. All U.S. methadone programs are strictly regulated at the federal level by both the FDA and the DEA. This strict control evolved from the history of the use of the drug. When methadone was new, it was often oversold to the public as a virtual panacea. Programs were established too quickly, without sufficient knowledge and training, and without following prudent guidelines. Many treatment facilities falsely believed that addicted people would need to use methadone for only a few months before being free of their addiction. And many providers either gave dosages that were too small, so their patients continued to use heroin on the side, or gave too much, which enabled patients to sell the surplus on the black market. The federal government overreacted to these problems, to the degree that today these agencies are micromanaging methadone clinics. In addition, some state

---

30. The Committee on Drugs and the Law, "A Wiser Course: Ending Drug Prohibition," *The Record of the Association of the Bar of the City of New York* 49, no. 5 (June 1994): 521, 562–63.

and local agencies have ladled on additional requirements over and above the federal ones. We now have strict federal requirements for such things as staff/patient ratio, admission criteria, treatment requirements, the security of the premises and the dosage levels to be given, as well as the time to be allowed for treatment. These requirements often withdraw the methadone treatment before patients are ready, and medical doctors are prohibited by administrators from prescribing methadone outside of designated treatment cites.

And then there are the hassles that face the patients themselves. Everyone knows that for a program to reach its true potential, it must be user friendly. But in the United States methadone patients are required to come to the maintenance facility to receive their dosages, instead of being able to procure them at their local pharmacies. Even people who are regularly employed and who have been in the program for twenty years must still travel to the site to get their dose. Further, at the beginning of their involvement in methadone treatment and for quite a while thereafter, all patients are required by federal regulations to come to the actual clinic every day and swallow their dose on site. Patients are also required to take urine tests for as long as they are in the program. For people who have discovered the benefit of being able to live a normal life free of heroin addiction, putting up with the hassles dictated by the federal government is worth it. But many of those just starting out do not see the benefit of exchanging the hassles of the street for the hassles of the bureaucracy, and they slip away.[31]

So methadone programs have a high success rate for addicted people who are motivated to start and who actually stay with the programs for at least three months. But programs are only effective if the appropriate people will use them. It is estimated that there are more than 500,000 people in our country who are addicted to heroin, but only about 115,000 of these people are involved in a drug substitution program. That is just a little better than a ratio of two to ten. In Amsterdam, where they utilize more user-friendly programs, the ratio is six to ten. In all of Western Europe, Australia, New Zealand, and Hong

31. See Edward Senay, M.D. and David C. Lewis, M.D., "The History and Current Status of Drug Substitution for Narcotic Addiction in the United States," (forthcoming); and Ethan Nadelmann and Jennifer McNeely, "Doing Methadone Right," *The Public Interest* 123 (spring 1996): 83.

Kong (before it was turned back to the Chinese), affirmative steps have been taken to attract heroin addicts to methadone treatment clinics. In Amsterdam, Frankfurt, and Barcelona, they utilize methadone buses as roving clinics so they can reach a larger proportion of the addicted population. Where our government severely restricts the number of medical doctors who can prescribe methadone, these countries have literally thousands of doctors who are directly involved in methadone maintenance. Belgium and Germany actually have very few clinics, as such, and instead utilize general medical practitioners as their principal source of methadone distribution. In addition, of course, our bureaucratic restrictions are needlessly expensive. In the United States, only about 7 percent of the program costs are actually spent on the methadone itself.[32]

Fortunately, other countries have learned the important lesson that each case is different. Each person has individual problems and needs. Breaking bad habits, much less addictions, is hard work, and backsliding is an inevitable part of recovery for most people. As Mark Twain said, "Giving up smoking is easy; I've done it lots of times." The same is true for heroin, and the less onerous we make the path to treatment, the more successful our treatment programs are likely to be.

The Institute of Medicine reported in 1995 that our current drug substitution policy "puts too much emphasis on protecting society *from* methadone, and not enough on protecting society from the epidemics of addiction, violence, and infectious diseases that methadone can help reduce."[33] Any reasoned and unemotional analysis will disclose that it is far more favorable for society, as well as for drug-addicted people themselves, to be on a program of methadone maintenance than on a program of street heroin, with all of the crime and medical dangers that accompany it. We can learn a lesson from our own history and from the histories of numerous other countries, and follow the recommendations of the Institute of Medicine by easing up on the restrictions and barriers we have placed in the path of the providers of methadone maintenance and the drug-addicted people they are intended to serve. By doing this, we will greatly increase the effectiveness of our drug-substitution programs.

---

32. Nadelmann and McNeely, *supra* at 90.
33. Ibid. at 84.

Drug Maintenance Programs

In Topeka, Kansas I handle a good number of drug offenses and am convinced we are losing the war on drugs. My reactions are certainly in agreement with the recommendations made in the published reports, and I would start with a greatly changed view on the penalties for marijuana use. The Swiss plan has much to recommend it on the use of methadone and other drugs to reduce hard drug use and HIV infections.

It is my hope that the political courage will be found in America to work on the drug problem before we have a majority of Americans in prison. We have great need of a public health war on the growing problem.

Judge Richard D. Rogers, United States District Court, Topeka, Kansas

Drug maintenance programs provide drug-addicted people with their drug of choice through a prescription and under the care and supervision of a medical doctor. The rationale of the program is that if these people are going to obtain their drugs anyway, it is much less dangerous for them, and safer and less expensive for society, to make the drugs available under controlled and medically supervised programs that will keep the users as healthy as possible until the time comes that they will seek drug treatment.

As we have seen, however, since the case of *Webb v. United States* in 1919, drug maintenance programs have been illegal in the United States. In England, however, in 1926, a royal commission under the chairmanship of Sir Humphrey Rolleston, President of the Royal College of Physicians, concluded that drug addiction was a medical problem and successfully kept the police from interfering in doctor-patient relationships—the lobbying of U.S. Commissioner Anslinger notwithstanding (see Appendix B). As a result, doctors in England were able for decades to work quietly with these addicts, often prescribing them opiates and mostly keeping them out of trouble. Under this "non-system," drug abuse was simply not a significant problem.

Then came the "flower generation" of the 1960s and the corresponding increase in drug abuse, mostly by working-class youth. At that point, the British people found to their shock that the number of addicts in England had literally doubled in five years. Unfortunately, they failed to take into account that the numbers had increased from only about 700 to about 1400 nationwide. (During the same period, the United States had probably 20,000 addicts on the island of Manhattan alone.) But many of these new addicts had long hair, were not gainfully employed, and were something of an eyesore. So the British passed legislation that required an addict to be treated only at a treatment center and with a doctor who was specially licensed to prescribe heroin and cocaine on a continuing basis. "Non-addicts" could still receive prescriptions from other doctors without restriction, as before.

But the damage was done. For whatever reason, the British decided to follow the lead of the United States in setting up drug treatment centers, and we convinced them that emphasizing total abstinence was the way to go. So they established a system in which addicts would be given a drug substitute such as methadone on a decreasing dosage, which was designed to wean them off drugs as quickly as possible. At that point, drug-addicted people began to deal with the criminal underworld for their drugs. Prices of drugs skyrocketed, crime and violence increased, and so did the number of people in prison and the number of deaths from drug overdoses. In short, the British experience began to parallel our own.[34]

Fortunately, though, far from the political spotlight, some places in England continued to administer the same drug maintenance programs that had been so successful for decades. One of these was in the port city of Liverpool. In 1982 a psychiatrist who was certified to prescribe heroin and cocaine, Dr. John Marks, arrived fresh from school at this Liverpool clinic. He thought the idea of prescribing these dangerous drugs to addicts was silly, but he decided to go along with the program in order to prove its administrators wrong. Once this was accomplished, he planned to shut the program down and institute a psychiatric program that would succeed.

At the Liverpool clinic, a team made up of a doctor, social worker, and registered nurse would interview narcotics addicts in the neighborhoods and encourage them to seek treatment. To those who were not interested in treatment at that time, they would offer their drug maintenance program, if the potential client satisfied three criteria—that the person actually was an addict (which was not too hard to prove), that the addict did not want to enter into treatment at that time, and that

---

34. For a discussion of the origins of the English experience, see Mike Gray (no relation), *Drug Crazy: How We Got Into This Mess and How We Can Get Out* (New York: Random House, 1998) 153–70; Arnold S. Trebach, *The Heroin Solution* (New Haven: Yale University Press, 1982) 85–117; and Colin Brewer, "Recent Developments in Maintenance Prescribing and Monitoring in the United Kingdom," *Bulletin of the New York Academy of Medicine* 72, no. 2 (winter 1995), 359.

the addict would be crime-free in the future. If people satisfied these criteria, they were placed in the program, which meant that once their drug usage was stabilized in a hospital setting they would be given a prescription for their drug of choice, be it heroin, cocaine, or even crack cocaine. They could then take the prescription to a local pharmacy and have it filled for free. As long as these patients appeared regularly at meetings to show that they continued to be healthy and crime-free, they could live their lives as they chose. But if they were even arrested for a criminal offense, they would be dropped from the program.[35]

The longer Dr. Marks observed the results of this program, the more favorably impressed he became. None of his injection drug users had contracted the AIDS virus. Most of them were healthy and had jobs. The local police told him that crime had been materially reduced in the local neighborhood. In fact, the police had conducted a study of one hundred of the drug addicts in the clinic, and had found a 94 percent reduction in theft, burglary, and property crimes. They also found that there were fewer drug users in the neighborhoods surrounding the clinics, because the patients no longer needed to sell drugs in order to support their habits. And since their former suppliers had lost good clients, they had moved elsewhere. The program actually seemed to be preventing the spread of addiction. In short, Dr. Marks saw that this program actually worked, and so he continued it.[36]

---

35. Personal interview with Dr. John Marks, Drug Policy Foundation convention in Washington, D.C., November 18, 1993.

36. Mike Gray, *supra*. This program was not a new idea, even in the United States. It was proposed in a book written in 1966 by Saul Jeffee entitled *Narcotics—An American Plan* (New York: Paul S. Eriksson, 1966). As the author stated in the preface: "The American Plan is a proposal that involves free ambulatory maintenance of addicts by the administration of drugs in government-operated Community House clinics. With the treatment of both the motivated and the non-motivated addict, under responsible supervision, we as a people can begin to destroy the economic factors which have created and sustained the illegal but highly profitable trafficking in narcotics in the United States" (xiii). The introduction to this book was written by a man named Will Oursler, who had previously collaborated on a book with U.S. Commissioner of Narcotics Harry J. Anslinger. Significantly, Oursler wrote, "The Commissioner was at that time and almost certainly still is opposed to the concept of government-run clinics for treating and maintaining addicts. . . . Yet it appears indisputable that some kind of new action is called for, *that the old techniques of control via penal codes, prison terms and similar punishments have not worked*, even when associated with related programs of medical treatment. A new, all-embracing and unified procedure is called for.

"The clinic Community House concept is startling in many aspects. It is a daring new idea; if enacted into law *it will present a total break with the unsuccessful past*" (vii–ix, emphasis added).

This drug maintenance program was so different, and so successful, that it caught the attention of the television show *60 Minutes*, which featured it on December 27, 1992. In this broadcast, Ed Bradley talked extensively to Dr. Marks and focused on the story of Julia Scott, who had been a heroin addict for ten years. Before she joined the program, Ms. Scott had worked as a prostitute to support her habit. But once she began at the clinic, she stopped her prostitution right away. She did return to prostitution just once, and "was almost physically sick just to see these girls doing what I used to do." During her three years in the maintenance program, she led a normal life. She was employed as a waitress, paid her taxes, and took good care of her three-year-old daughter.

During the broadcast, Ed Bradley made the following comment:

> In the '70s, the British weren't content with minimizing the harm of drug abuse. They adopted the American policy of trying to stamp it out altogether. Prescription drugs were no longer widely available, and addicts who couldn't kick the habit had to find illegal sources. The result? By the end of the '80s, drug addiction in Britain had tripled. In Liverpool, there was so much heroin around it was known as smack city. And then came a greater threat.
>
> More than anything else, it's been the threat of AIDS that has persuaded the British to return to their old policy of maintaining addicts on their drug of choice. In New York, it's estimated that more than half of those who inject drugs have contracted the AIDS virus through swapping contaminated needles. Here in Liverpool, the comparable number—the number of known addicts infected—is less than 1 percent.[37]

Dr. Marks summarized his view of the situation slightly differently:

> If they're drug takers determined to continue their drug use, treating them is an expensive waste of time. And really the choice that I'm being offered and society is being offered is drugs from the clinic or drugs from the Mafia. . . . [Giving them drugs] doesn't get them off drugs. It doesn't prolong their addiction either. But it stops them offending; it keeps them healthy and it keeps them alive.[38]

On April 1, 1995, the Drug Maintenance Program run by Dr. Marks in Liverpool was shut down by the local government health care authority, which gave the contract for psychiatric services to a different company. To no one's surprise, this new company's philosophy was much more in line with the official policy of the United States, which was to

---

37. Transcript, CBS News, "60 Minutes," vol. XXV, December 27, 1992: 24.
38. Ibid. at 21–22.

wean heroin addicts onto methadone and then promptly into abstinence. Most of the approximately 450 addicts who had been at the Liverpool clinic left the program and went back to the streets, to desperation, to crime, and to prison. Within two years, said Dr. Marks,
twenty-five of his former patients, including Julia Scott, were dead.[39]

What caused the termination of this demonstratively effective program? In the view of Dr. Marks, it was the publicity from *60 Minutes*
that resulted in the cancellation of his contract. In his view, the success
of the clinic—a 90 percent drop in the local crime rate, no cases at all
of AIDS, the elimination of homelessness and taking people off welfare
rolls and into productive jobs—flew directly in the face of American
Drug War policy. Dr. Marks said he had been warned by friends in the
British Home Office that officials at the U.S. Embassy were exerting
tremendous pressure to shut him down.[40] At the end of the day, they
were successful.

But even if Dr. Marks was right about the cause of the shutdown, the
U.S. Embassy's efforts were too late. The word was out.

Switzerland, like every other country in the world, has a drug problem. But the Swiss are fortunate in that they have no ghettos. For this
reason their drug addicts are more visible. The Swiss government has
tried to treat people humanely and to remove the unsightliness of hard-
using addicts from public places.

The first attempt by the Swiss in this direction was a disaster. No
matter how often police chased drug addicts out of public areas, they
always ended up somewhere. So the Swiss authorities in Zurich decided
in 1987 to be practical and allow these people to congregate undisturbed in a particular park, which was located behind the central railroad station. The place became known formally as Platzspitz, or "Needle Park." This live-and-let-live approach worked quite well for a while.
The local police kept a close watch on the so-called house dealers and
arrested them if they allowed their clients to become a nuisance in the
neighborhood, or if they sold poor-quality or adulterated products. In
time, however, the Zurich authorities ran into the "Netherlands problem," which was that eventually knowledge of the park became so widespread that drug addicts from far and wide journeyed to Zurich so that
they could be left alone with their drugs. According to Professor

---

39. Mike Gray, *supra*, at 162.
40. Testimony of Mike Gray presented to The Los Angeles Citizens' Commission on U.S.
Drug Policy, University of Southern California, May 23, 1999.

Ambros Uchtenhagen, M.D., who directed the experiment, over 80 percent of the people who were using drugs in Needle Park came from outside Zurich—indeed, many came from outside the country. These people eventually overran the park and the place became truly disgusting, so the experiment was terminated.[41]

Many drug prohibitionists cite Needle Park as a failed experiment in drug "legalization," but this is simply not true. The authorities supplied no drugs, only clean needles in order to limit the spread of disease. The program did not affect the total number of drug addicts one way or the other; it simply gave them a place to be and tried to keep them out of sight. The problem was that when so many drug users migrated to Needle Park it became an unsightly and sometimes repulsive place. But when the experiment was closed down, the same problems remained. The same number of people continued to use drugs, probably with the same unsightly results; but they were not concentrated in one place. As author Mike Gray described it, "The debacle in Platzspitz was nothing more than an unsuccessful attempt at street cleaning."[42]

To its credit, the Swiss government did not stop trying to address the drug problem—and the next experiment was much more successful. The Swiss established fixerraume ("injection rooms") in several large cities for addicted people to use as safe and hygienic environments in which to inject their drugs. Studies showed that these sites were effective in reducing drug overdoses and in reducing the spreading of the AIDS virus. Local officials in Frankfurt, Germany, noted the Swiss success and soon opened their own Gesundheitsraum ("health room"). As Horst Burghardt, who supervised the Gesundheitsraum when it began, said, "If you sit in a garden or behind a truck, you have neither light nor clean water, and you can't find your veins because they contract in the cold. That's when overdoses happen."[43]

As of the end of 1998, Frankfurt was operating a total of four Gesundheitsraumen. The results? "The people who come here are in much better physical and psychological shape than they were before. Current drug policy doesn't reach the homeless junkies, but here you have a complete network of help," said Wolfgang Barth, who runs one of the new centers. With such positive results, German Chancellor

---

41. Richard Karel, "New Swiss Program Will Distribute Hard Drugs to Addicts," *The Drug Policy Letter* 21 (November/December 1993): 10.

42. Mike Gray, *supra*, at 163.

43. Nadelmann, *supra* at 39.

Gerhard Schroeder encouraged legislation to make the Frankfurt model legally possible nationwide.[44]

The Swiss are practical people, and when they learned about the success of the Liverpool clinic run by Dr. Marks, they were seriously interested. Their health officials studied the project, interviewed the British doctors who were directing it, and went on to establish the largest and most scientific heroin maintenance program ever attempted. Using Marks's program as a model, the Swiss began in January 1994 with their own drug maintenance program experiments in eight cities. As recounted by the Swiss Federal Office of Public Health:

> From January 2nd 1994 to January 1st 1995 ... actually 232 patients [were] treated in heroin prescription programmes, 37 in morphine prescription programmes and 51 patients in i.v. methadone prescription programmes. An additional study with 16 patients took place in order to test the side effects of morphine prescription. The feasibility of the heroin prescriptions has been demonstrated in the course of 1994 with *no major incidents.* For the morphine condition, side effects were observed. Both i.v. morphine and i.v. methadone were less acceptable to drug addicts than heroin and for both substances there were lower recruitment rates. Since October 1994 an adaptation of the trials is planned according to a decision of the Federal Government. (Emphasis added.)
>
> The number of drug addicts in Switzerland who are consuming regularly i.v. substances is estimated to be about 25,000 to 30,000 [the population of Switzerland is about 7 million]. In spite of a wide spread network of institutions for therapy and substitution programmes with oral methadone (1993: 15,000 patients in treatment) a group of socially disintegrated and severely addicted patients could not be addressed by the existing treatment system. For this group of addicts all other treatment efforts had failed so far. The trials for the medical prescription of narcotics were supposed to approach this subgroup of addicts.[45]

This was the official government evaluation of its drug maintenance programs after the first year with these "socially disintegrated and severely addicted patients": No major incidents! According to the Swiss government itself, the programs were successful. The federal govern-

---

44. Ian Traynor, "Frankfurt Lets Addicts Get a Fix without Fear," *Chicago Sun-Times,* November 2, 1998: 34.

45. Swiss Federal Office of Public Health, "Status Report on the Medical Prescription of Narcotics," January 1995. See also Margret Rihs-Middel, "Medical Prescription of Narcotics in Switzerland," *European Journal on Criminal Policy and Research: Innovations in Criminal Justice Research* 2, no. 4 (1994); and Donald MacPherson of the Social Planning Department of Vancouver, Canada, "Comprehensive Systems of Care for Drug Users in Switzerland and Frankfurt, Germany," unpublished article, June 1999.

ment was planning to "adapt," or increase, the trials after only ten months of operation, because they were working so well. The Swiss also found, consistent with the results here in the United States, that many addicted people do not find methadone to be as acceptable as heroin, so they do not use it. Therefore, to their credit, the Swiss officials pursued an additional program, and it worked.

Having found at the end of 1994 that when addicts took their drugs in controlled, safe, and hygienic conditions, the drugs caused few health problems, there was no black market diversion of drugs, and the health of the addicted people improved demonstrably, the Swiss government did indeed expand the experiment. By July 10, 1997, when the final research report was released, the program had been expanded to eighteen treatment centers in fifteen cities and served 1,146 drug addicts.

The Swiss regulation required that applicants to the programs had to be at least twenty years old, had to be drug-addicted for at least two years, had to have made several unsuccessful attempts at other drug treatment, and had to show demonstrable health or social damage as a result of their drug addiction. The program required that addicts pay about $10 per day for their prescriptions, although the cost was waived for those who could not pay it.

This final report of the Swiss government should have made headlines around the world. It showed that individual health and social circumstances improved dramatically, usually in a very short time. Of the 350 addicts who left the program, half started treatment in another therapy, and of those, *eighty-three gave up heroin and switched to abstinence therapy;* the government report noted that the "probability of this switch to abstinence therapy grows as the duration of individual treatment increases." Stable employment among the addicted people increased from 14 percent to 32 percent; and unemployment decreased from 44 percent to 20 percent. One-third of all of the addicted people who had depended on care institutions became able to function independently. Criminal activities decreased dramatically, from 59 percent of those in the program to only 10 percent. The total amount spent on medical and social care and crime control decreased from ninety-six Swiss francs to fifty-one Swiss francs per day.[46] These were not people who had a minor

---

46. Ambros Uchtenhagen, Felix Gurzwiller, and Anja Dobler-Mikola, "Programme for a Medical Prescription of Narcotics: Final Report of the Research Representatives," July 10, 1997. (This report is available from the Swiss Federal Office of Public Health in Berne, and from the Addiction Research Institute in Zurich.)

problem with drugs; these were hard-core, chronically addicted people, the kind of people who in the United States are clogging our prisons. No major negative incidents, increased employment, a drop in crime, a significant number choosing to go into abstinence therapy—even declining costs! This kind of program is exactly what we need and profess to be looking for. So where are the headlines?

With results like these, why are we not implementing pilot programs throughout our country to maintain addicted people in a healthy manner and help put them in a position to hold jobs, raise their families, and pay their taxes until they are ready for abstinence therapy? Does anyone truly believe that this would be sending the "wrong message" to our children? Does anyone think that Swiss parents love and want to protect their children any less than parents in the United States do? What do we think will happen, that our children begin taking heroin so that someday they too can have a prescription for that dangerous drug filled at a pharmacy? That is like arguing that with modern advancements in artificial limbs our children will want to cut off their hands so they can have new, state-of-the-art prosthetic devices.

For obvious reasons, law enforcement and health officials declared this state-distributed drug maintenance program an outright success.[47] And the Swiss people, once they were given the opportunity to observe the results of the program, voted overwhelmingly, in a nationwide referendum, to continue it. On September 28, 1997, 1.3 million Swiss citizens, or 70.6 percent of voters, opposed an initiative entitled "Youth Without Drugs" that would have ended their country's drug maintenance programs. The Swiss cabinet and most of the Parliament also opposed the initiative, saying that their drug maintenance programs had helped to reduce crime and at the same time improved the lives of their drug-addicted people.[48] In October 1998, the Swiss Parliament voted overwhelmingly to make their experimental program permanent.[49]

---

47. See Clare Nullis, "Swiss Heroin Program Cuts Crime," *Philadelphia Inquirer,* July 11, 1997: A20; Associated Press, "Swiss Call Heroin Giveaway Program a Success," *Chicago Tribune,* Southwest ed., July 11, 1997: 19; and "Swiss Say Drug Program a Success," *Houston Chronicle,* July 11, 1997: A27.

48. Associated Press, "Swiss Vote Overwhelmingly to Keep Drug for Addicts," *Orange County Register,* September 29, 1997: News 3.

49. Associated Press, "Controlled Heroin Distribution Given the Nod," *The Australian,* October 10, 1998.

Noting the Swiss success, twenty of the thirty police chiefs of the major cities in Germany also voiced their support of (carefully delineated) heroin maintenance programs,[50] and German Minister of Health Andrea Fischer, noting the Swiss success, announced that state-controlled distribution of pharmaceutical heroin to addicts in Hamburg and Frankfurt would soon be initiated.[51]

A simple review of the costs involved shows that everyone wins when an assortment of drug programs are utilized. The drug-addicted person's health and quality of life improve. To state the obvious, "dead junkies can't get clean," but those who can be brought closer to medical professionals have a reasonable chance to stay alive and healthy, and also hold jobs, pay their taxes, and support their children. Crime and the costs of crime come down. Even putting aside human considerations and applying a strictly economic calculus, the costs to taxpayers are substantially reduced. Compare the average annual cost of these drug treatment programs to the average annual cost of imprisonment:

Regular Outpatient	$1,800
Intensive Outpatient	$2,500
Methadone Maintenance	$3,900
Short-term residential	$4,400
Long-term residential	$6,800
Incarceration	$25,900[52]

I have lost count of the number of times I and my fellow trial judges have heard these words from a drug-addicted person about to be sentenced for yet another burglary: "I know that I have a drug problem, so three months ago I went to a health clinic and asked for drug treatment. They told me that they understood and agreed, but that I should fill out some paperwork and come back in six months; because they said they didn't have the money." I am well aware that there are plenty of offenders who, at the time of sentencing, will tell the judge whatever they think he or she wants to hear. But in some cases these stories simply have to be true.

---

50. "Heroin vom Staat," *Der Spiegel*, May 1997: 41–45.

51. Associated Press, "Heroin to Be Distributed First in Hamburg and Frankfurt," *Siegener* (Germany), November 15, 1998.

52. Medical News and Perspectives, "Physician Leadership on National Drug Policy Finds Addiction Treatment Works," *Journal of the American Medical Association* 279, no. 15 (April 15, 1998): 1149.

What a colossal waste of resources! How much does it cost society when a burglar has to support a $300 per day heroin habit? Since a burglar normally sells his stolen property to a "fence" for about 10 percent of its value, he needs to steal about $3,000 *per day* because we "can't afford" to spend $3,900 *per year* for a methadone program. But then, we spend an average of $25,900 per year to incarcerate him without blinking an eye.

I often get letters from relatives of prison inmates that tell me the same things. Here is a representative example (I have changed the name of the inmate):

> About a month ago, I read the article in the *Orange County Register* concerning the lack of Drug Rehab facilities in Orange County. I think it's a good idea because there are a lot of weak willed souls locked up with hard core criminals.
>
> Now to get to the reason I'm writing. My son John is presently located at the Waco [Prison] facility. Granted I'm not saying he's innocent of any of the crimes he's been arrested for, but the whole thing is, the only person he ever hurt, besides me, was himself. He never manufactured or sold drugs, he was always under the influence or arrested with such a small amount he could never be considered a dealer, and the total amount of money ever found on him was $15.00 of $20.00 at the most. Hardly an amount that could be of questionable interest. . . .
>
> With all the times John has appeared in court and seen his probation officer, never once was the subject of rehab mentioned. John is the sort of person rehab would have helped, he's the type of person that needs help, but not to be locked out of life for 16 months. As the sentencing Judge put it: "We've given you too many chances, with 30 days, and 90 days locked up, but *no help.*" Every time I tried to find out about Rehab, I was shut out, because since John is 29 years old, he is an adult. Not even close.
>
> He was getting his life turned around at the time of his last arrest, meaning he'd finally got a job he really enjoyed and he was working full time and getting his bills paid. Plus his boss at his last job said he would hire him back because he was such a good worker. Hopefully by the time John gets out the guy is still the boss there.
>
> I'm not expecting you to do anything, but if you were interested [here is my son's address].
>
> Thanks for listening.
>
> (Signed by) John's Mom

While we spend only 20 percent of our multi-billion-dollar yearly federal drug budget on drug treatment programs, we continue to allow our politicians to spend the vast majority of it on incarceration.[53] As one newspaper editorialized:

> California's jails are filling up. We can't build them fast enough. Most county facilities are filled with drug users. Users, but few dealers. Far too many go to jail drug dependent and come out state dependent or worse, dependent on crime. . . .
>
> Keeping addicts clean is a matter of survival—ours, not theirs.
>
> One immediate benefit of effective treatment is that we're less likely to find an addict ransacking our homes or robbing us as we withdraw cash from ATMs. But there's some real, countable savings as well.
>
> The Legislative Analyst's office estimates avoided costs to society at about $1.5 billion for every $200 million worth of treatment. The lion's share of projected savings comes from a decrease in criminal activity and subsequent avoided costs to the justice system. Law enforcement, courts, incarceration— all could post substantial savings if the majority of addicts can be kept off drugs and alcohol.
>
> In other words, it's cheaper to treat 'em off the streets than keep 'em off.[54]

Although we must bear in mind that drug addiction is a chronic condition, that recovering addicts are prone to relapse,[55] and that strict but "user-friendly" drug treatment programs are not going to make drug addiction disappear, we could take a gigantic leap in the right direction by creating well-run drug treatment programs that address the real and human problems of addiction—instead of creating and enforcing ever larger numbers of bureaucratic rules and regulations *that do not solve the problem.* Then we could return to using the criminal justice system for the purpose for which it was designed and intended, i.e., holding people accountable for their actions that harm others.

---

53. Lauran Neergaard, Associated Press, "Treatment Best Cure for Addicts, Study Says," *Pasadena Star News,* March 18, 1998. See also Associated Press, "Experts: Drug Courts Working," *USA Today,* November 1, 1998: 21A.

54. Editorial, "An Impact that Works," *Pasadena Star News,* July 25, 1999: A20.

55. For more policy recommendations from a group of leading physicians, visit the website of the Physician Leadership on National Drug Policy at <www.caas.brown.edu./plndp>.

9

De-profitization of Drugs

ne major pitfall in the discussion of our current drug policy and alternative options is that people do not define their terms. It is, regrettably, very common for one person not to know what another person is talking about, which naturally leads to a great deal of miscommunication and misunderstanding. If everyone would take care to define their terms, we would make a lot more progress. In this chapter I will discuss several options available to "de-profitize" what are now illicit drugs, taking care to define and explain my terms and to show how these alternatives are working in other countries.

Legalization

There is just so much money to be made that the slim chance of being caught is always worth the risk. Believe me, after 20 years as a prosecutor and judge, I can assure you that we only catch the stupid ones.[1]
Magistrate Judge Ronald Rose, United States District Court, Santa Ana, California

The "legalization of drugs" is an oft-heard phrase. People who favor maintaining the status quo routinely and misleadingly characterize everyone who favors some form of change as "drug legalizers." It is almost never spelled out what that actually means, but the term connotes—and is designed to connote—that the drug "legalizer" doesn't feel

---

1. Matt Lait, "Make Drugs Legal, U.S. Judge Says," *Los Angeles Times*, April 25, 1992, Orange County ed.: A25.

that dangerous drugs are "any big deal," and further doesn't care if someone sells cocaine to your twelve-year-old child on the corner outside his school. The U.S. Congress may have had this mental image of the "legalization of drugs" when it said in the Anti-Drug Abuse Act in 1988, "The Congress finds that legalization of illegal drugs, on the federal or state level, is an unconscionable surrender in a war in which, for the future of our country and the lives of our children, there can be no substitute for total victory."[2]

This reflection was followed by the proclamation that "It is the declared policy of the United States to create a Drug-Free America by 1995."[3]

But it is very important that people define what they mean by "legalization"; otherwise misunderstandings inevitably arise and impede the progress that could be made in this discussion if people would only define their terms.

Under the definition of "legalization," the price of a product (in this case, drugs that are currently illegal), would be set by the free market, without any restrictions on advertising, brand names, or price. Picture a situation in which a person goes to his local supermarket for groceries. He puts into his cart some frozen lemonade, chocolate chip cookies, aspirin, grapes—and a six-pack of cocaine. A friend has recommended the "Big Kick" brand of cocaine and the store is having a special sale: six hits for the price of four. In this scenario, all of the products in this man's cart are sold in a "legalized" or "free" market.

Under such a program, the FDA would ensure the cleanliness and purity of all of these products, and see to it that they were labeled accurately for their contents and strength. This is how the FDA regulates the sale of aspirin, a fully "legalized" drug in this country. If the manufacturer or vendor were to misrepresent the cocaine or violate the health conditions of its sale, users could sue the manufacturer or vendor in civil court, just as they can for any other product.

The obvious defect in this policy is that cocaine and other dangerous drugs would be "pushed" on people through advertising, and otherwise made glamorous and much too easily available. People who believe in the "legalization" of drugs as I have defined it are what I would call "free marketers."

---

2. Public Law No. 100–690, Section 5011 (1988).
3. Ibid. at section 5252 B.

There are not very many free marketers around, of course, though drug warriors like Barry McCaffrey like to pretend that this is what is meant when people speak of legalizing drugs. Most people who advocate the legalization of drugs actually mean something quite different. Often they are talking about programs involving rehabilitation and treatment, medicalization, decriminalization, regulated distribution, or something else, or a combination of one or more of these various options.

That was probably the intent of Abigail Van Buren when she responded, in her "Dear Abby" column, to a letter from a Mr. Pottratz, an attorney in Minnesota:

> Just as bootleggers were forced out of business in 1933 when Prohibition was repealed, making the sale of liquor legal (thus eliminating racketeering), the legalization of drugs would put drug dealers out of business. It also would guarantee government-approved quality, and the tax on drugs would provide an ongoing source of revenue for drug-education programs. An added plus: There would be far less crowding in our prisons due to drug-related crimes. It's something to consider.[4]

It was also probably the intent of Edward Ellison, the former head of Scotland Yard's Anti-Drug Squad, who said:

> As a former drugs squad chief, I've seen too many youngsters die. I'm determined my children don't get hooked—which is why I want all drugs legalized.
> Seven years of my life was spent in Scotland Yard's anti-drugs squad, four as its head. I saw the misery that drug abuse can cause. I saw first-hand the squalor, the wrecked lives, the deaths. And I saw, and arrested when I could, the people who do so well out of drugs: the dealers, the importers, the organizers. I saw the immense profits they were making out of human misery, the money laundering, the crime syndicates they financed. We have attempted prohibition. All that happened was that courts became clogged with thousands of cases of small, individual users, and a generation of young people came to think of the police as their enemies. There were no resources left to fight other crime. I say legalize drugs because I want to see less drug abuse, not more. And I say legalize drugs because I want to see the criminals put out of business.[5]

Since the repeal of Alcohol Prohibition, most states have made the sale of liquor available under programs of regulated distribution. It is

---

4. "Dear Abby" (Abigail Van Buren), "Attorney Makes His Case for Legalization of Drugs," *Orange County Register,* May 3, 1994: Accent 5.
5. Edward Ellison, *London Daily Mail,* March 10, 1998.

likely that Ms. Van Buren and Mr. Ellison were recommending a similar program for other mind-altering and dangerous drugs—or maybe they had another option in mind. Some of the many other well-known and concerned people who have called for the "legalization of drugs" without defining what they meant by the term are former U.S. Secretary of State George Shultz,[6] former Colombian Attorney General Gustavo de Greiff,[7] author and syndicated columnist William F. Buckley, Jr.,[8] New Mexico Governor Gary Johnson, and U.S. District Court Judge Robert W. Sweet of the southern district of New York.[9] In fact, as we saw earlier, the term "legalization" of drugs is not really accurate. The more precise term would be the "re-legalization" of drugs, because before the passage of the Harrison Narcotic Act in 1914, and a couple of state and local statutes prior to it, there were no illegal drugs in the United States.

One of the few scholars, to my knowledge, who would take us back to those times is Thomas S. Szasz, a true libertarian free marketer who favors "free trade in drugs for the same reason the Founding Fathers favored free trade in ideas: in a free society it is none of the government's business what ideas a man puts into his mind; likewise, it should be none of its business what drug he puts into his body." Szasz is such an extreme free marketer that he equates government prohibition of drug sales with government prohibition of roadside sales of corn or tomatoes, and even sees government intervention in this matter as equivalent to state laws about the practice of various religions: he finds it unconstitutional and unjustifiable. But not even Mr. Szasz advocates removing age restrictions from drug sales. "Kids," he remarks. "Merrill Lynch can't sell stocks and bonds to children. A real estate agent can't sell houses to children. We are not talking about children. Children do not have any rights. They don't have a right to freedom of religion; they have to follow their parents. We are talking about adults."[10]

---

6. Stanley Meisler, "Interest in Prestigious Circles," *Los Angeles Times*, November 20, 1989, Orange County ed.: A3, 18: "We need at least to consider and examine forms of controlled legalization of drugs."

7. James Brooke, "A Captain in the Drug War Wants to Call It Off," *New York Times*, July 8, 1994.

8. William F. Buckley, Jr., "Awash in Drugs, U.S. Wars on Itself, Only Legalization Can Stop the Futile Battle," *Orange County Register*, October 25, 1989.

9. *New York Times*, "U.S. Judge Urges Legalization of All Drugs," *Orange County Register*, December 13, 1989: A7.

10. Milton Friedman and Thomas S. Szasz, *On Liberty and Drugs* (Washington, D.C.: Drug Policy Foundation Press, 1992), 122, 159, 160.

Even Nobel Prize-winning economist Milton Friedman, whose piv-otal work *Free to Choose, A Personal Statement*,[11] which he wrote along with his wife Rose, underscores the crucial link between the free enter-prise system and a free society, would not "legalize" drugs in the free-market manner in which I defined it above. He would "legalize drugs by subjecting them to exactly the same rules that alcohol and ciga-rettes are subjected to now. . . . Television advertising is forbidden today for alcohol . . . for hard liquor. And I say treat this the same way as you would treat alcohol. So, presumably such ads would be forbidden for this."[12]

There is no reason why we cannot adopt one option for one sub-stance and another option for others. For example, why not legalize hemp? Nothing could be easier than to accomplish this simple goal, with a regulation that would read, "Any cannabis sativa plant that has a THC content of .3 percent or less is legal to cultivate, possess, and sell in the United States of America." These plants could then be raised and harvested without any more state interference than exists for rais-ing cotton or soybeans. The same would be true for the products man-ufactured from the seeds and fibers of the plant. Right now, farmers in Canada and England are legally raising hemp for commercial purposes. Why can't we? A THC amount of .3 percent or less would have no use at all for marijuana smokers. If the THC content were above that limit, those plants would be governed by whatever the laws and regulations were in place for marijuana. By adopting this approach, we could reclaim an entire profitable industry.

To give a sense of the potential magnitude of the commercial mar-ket we are talking about, farmers can get the same amount of paper pulp from one acre of hemp as they can from four acres of trees; and it takes twenty years to grow the trees, but only one season to grow the hemp. This means that in addition to again using hemp in the making of rope, paper, cloth, and sails for boats, newer products could be produced on the open market as well. As stated in *U.S. News & World Report*, "Modern-day hemp products include cosmetics, carpets, salad oil, and snacks, as well as construction materials and biodegradable auto parts. Hemp fibers are used in the trunk and door panels of the

---

11. Milton and Rose Friedman, *Free to Choose: A Personal Statement* (New York: Avon Books, 1981).

12. Friedman and Szasz, *supra* at 76–77.

German-manufactured 5 and 7 series BMW, and Ford is studying their potential for use in radiator grills."[13] U.S. farmers are attempting to get the federal government to allow them to compete once again in this historic and potentially lucrative market. Where is the harm in allowing this to be done?

I am reminded of the joke about the man who, as a part of his therapy, was shown a number of inkblots and was asked by his therapist to describe what he saw. To each one he answered that he saw "a man and a woman having sex." Finally the therapist told the man that he was obsessed with sex, to which the man replied, "Me? You're the one with all of the dirty pictures!"

There is a similar dynamic at work in the War on Drugs. No matter what substance is being addressed, drug warriors see only a picture of prohibition and prison. Given that a person could not get any more reaction from smoking .3 percent cannabis sativa than she could get from smoking this page you are reading, isn't it time we start considering each of these substances separately, based on their potential harm to the user and the society at large? Some people argue that legalizing hemp would make the detection of marijuana more difficult because it could be grown within the hemp field. But it is unlikely that marijuana growers would attempt this, because the hemp plants would quickly germinate with their marijuana, which would lower the THC content of the marijuana plants. Even so, there are solutions to that potential problem—if people are really afraid it could become a problem. For one thing, we could require farmers to register their hemp crops, which would actually make detection easier. And there are field kits that can quickly measure the THC content of the plants. In fact growing and manufacturing hemp presents almost no potential risks at all, and it has enormous beneficial potential as an industry. So let's consider legalizing hemp and allowing it to be raised and sold on the open market.

Hypodermic needles are another item that we could consider legalizing for adults, perhaps in combination with the type of needle-exchange program discussed earlier. Studies have shown that needle-exchange programs do not increase the use of drugs. Moreover, deposit

---

13. Elise Ackerman, "The Latest Buzz on Hemp, U.S. Farmers Want the Ban on Cultivating the Plant Lifted," *U.S. News & World Report*, March 15, 1999: 50. See also Craig Turner, "New Hemp Isn't Meant for Smoking," *Los Angeles Times*, May 16, 1994, Orange County ed.: A1, 10; and Dan McGraw, "Hemp Is High Fashion," *U.S. News & World Report*, January 20, 1997: 54, 56.

and refund programs for the recycling of bottles and cans have successfully removed tons of those items from our communities—maybe a tax on needles would encourage their recycling. Freely available clean needles would, as we have seen, decrease the transmission of the AIDS virus, hepatitis B, hepatitis C, and other infectious diseases, and would also decrease the chances that we or our children will accidentally stick ourselves by stepping on a contaminated needle lying in the street, a park, or a vacant lot.

But opposition to proposals like these is ferocious, and so far it has prevailed, in spite of massive evidence that our current policies are complete and utter failures, flawed at their very core. As Walter Wink, a Quaker and a professor of biblical interpretation at Auburn Theological Seminary in New York City, said, "The drug war is over, and we lost. We merely repeated the mistake of Prohibition. The harder we tried to stamp out this evil, the more lucrative we made it, and the more it spread. Our forcible resistance to evil simply augments it. An evil cannot be eradicated by making it more profitable."[14]

With the exceptions of hemp, hypodermic needles, and medical marijuana, I think it is unlikely that most currently illegal drugs will ever be "re-legalized" in this country. My purpose is not to advocate legalization or any particular option, however, but to encourage a free and open discussion of our options. Let us turn now to another one of these—decriminalization.

Decriminalization

Whether or to what degree drugs should be decriminalized in the United States is one of the central issues of our times. What is highly disturbing to me is the lack of national debate on the subject and the intransigence of practically all decision-makers to open the subject to examination. What is presently held as true is the belief that the war on drugs is winnable if only we tried harder. Few people are willing to test the proposition in a public arena.
Judge Phyllis W. Beck, Superior Court, Bala Cynwyd, Pennsylvania

In 1976, the Dutch adopted a formal policy of pragmatic nonenforcement for violations involving the possession or sale of up to thirty grams of marijuana, which is enough for about sixty marijuana cigarettes. In

---

14. Walter Wink, "Getting Off Drugs: The Legalization Option," *Friends Journal*, February 1996: 13.

1995, due to international political pressure, that amount was reduced to five grams, or enough for about ten cigarettes. Being realists, the Dutch understood that a ban on marijuana was futile, and since people were going to use it anyway, it was better to have the transactions out in the open rather than in the shadows, and to govern behavior instead. In an attempt to steer a middle course between the futility of Drug Prohibition and the unknown perils of drug legalization, Holland thus began its program of *gedogen* (tolerance) and "decriminalization" of drugs.

Under this program, the possession, use, and sale of street drugs are still illegal. But as long as people stay within certain well-known guidelines, and do not otherwise commit any crimes, the police will "look the other way" and not enforce the drug laws. Coffee houses have been established in Dutch cities where patrons can get coffee, tea, and sandwiches, as well as marijuana and hashish. Alcohol and harder drugs are not sold; there is no advertising; sales to minors under seventeen are prohibited; and the sellers at the coffee houses are not allowed to make a nuisance of themselves by hawking passersby on the streets. If those rules are followed, the sellers and the patrons are left alone.[15]

Hard drugs are treated in a similar manner. Dutch policy attempts to lessen the problems that accompany drug use instead of decreasing drug use itself. Even though the police have strong powers against hard drugs, as of 1985 the Ministry of Justice instructed them not to use those powers. The government was persuaded that enforcement would simply turn a health problem into a crime problem. One senior policeman explained the reasoning behind this approach: "If we kept chasing grass or hashish, the dealers would go underground, and that would be dangerous."[16] And so, in Holland, sellers and users of hard drugs have also been tolerated, as long they do not violate any other laws, do not make a general nuisance of themselves, and quantities stay within widely recognized public guidelines.

The nonenforcement of the drug laws for small-scale transactions, however, tells only a part of the story about the Dutch approach. The

---

15. See Ed. Leuw and I. Haen Marshall, eds., *Between Prohibition and Legalization: The Dutch Experiment in Drug Policy* (Amsterdam and New York: Kugler Publications, 1996); "Holland's Drugs Policy: War by Other Means," *The Economist*, February 10, 1990: 50; Stephen Chapman, "Drug-Tolerant Netherlands Not Suffering," *Colorado Springs Gazette Telegraph*, November 10, 1995: B11; and William F. Buckley, Jr., "In the 'Coffee Shops' of Amsterdam," *Orange County Register*, June 17, 1996: Metro 5.

16. "Holland's Drugs Policy: War by Other Means," *supra.*

Dutch are really quite intolerant of drug abuse, but they oppose it not in itself but because of the harm it does. "Harm reduction" is pursued both by aggressively utilizing medical programs, such as drug treatment and needle exchange, and educational programs, rather than criminal crackdowns. With these programs the Dutch government is trying to keep the drug users alive and healthy until they seek their own cure, which is the equivalent of saying that if you must play football, at least wear pads and a helmet. At the same time, Dutch parents are saying to their children that even though drugs are available through their peers or other sources, this does not mean that it is right, or smart, to use them.

At a 1999 conference of police chiefs at Stanford University, the chief of police of a mid-sized city in New England echoed the Dutch message when he said, "I burned out being a narc, and I grew up when I became a father. I would not arrest my child for drug possession or usage—and would not want anyone else to either. We are doing it wrong. Putting them in jail is the worst thing we can do. That punishment is not banishment from the tribe, which is to say that they will come back. And when they do, they will come out worse. Instead, take the kids to their parents. The parents care if their kids are doing drugs."

Harry Belafonte, honorary chair of the Citizens' Commission on U.S. Drug Policy, which took testimony at the University of Southern California in May 1999, reached similar conclusions based on his own experiences and observations:

> Having grown up in Harlem during the Great Depression, I knew that the real roots of drug abuse and addiction had more to do with poverty, alienation and despair than crimes of malice. Most of the violence associated with drugs stems from our policies of prohibition—just as the notorious gangsters of my youth derived their wealth through bootlegging alcohol. Together we must find a more compassionate and effective drug control policy. As President Jimmy Carter said in 1977, "Penalties against possession of a drug should not be more damaging to an individual than the use of the drug itself."[17]

The Dutch have carefully constructed a program that tries not to do more damage than the use of the drugs themselves, and the results show

---

17. Institute for Policy Studies, "The War on Drugs: Addicted to Failure—Recommendations of the Citizens' Commission on U.S. Drug Policy," May 2000, at 3. For a copy, write to I.P.S at 733 15th Street NW, Suite 1020, Washington, DC 20005, or <www.ips-dc.org>.

that their approach is working. Holland has a lower per capita marijuana usage ratio than we do in the United States, for both teenagers
and adults. In fact, use of marijuana by teenagers in Holland is
roughly half of what it is in the United States.[18] As Eddy Engelsman,
the former Dutch Drug Czar, put it, "We succeeded in making pot
boring."[19]

Even more importantly, in Holland between 1979 and 1994, "for the
generation under 22 years of age, the percentage using hard drugs
went down from 15 percent to 2.5 percent," according to Dirk H. van
der Woude of the Municipal Health Service. "And the average *age* of
hard-drug users has gone up from 26.8 years in 1981 to 34.2 years in
1993."[20] This means that younger people are not becoming addicted
to these drugs, which results in an average increase in age each year
for narcotic drug addicts. Similarly, in 1987, only 1.7 percent of adults
in Amsterdam said that they had taken cocaine during the past year,
while about 6 percent of the adults in New York said that they had used
cocaine in the past six months. And finally, although cocaine users are
frequently psychotic, Holland has no cocaine-related crime and no
cocaine-related deaths.[21]

And importantly, even though powder cocaine is available in Holland for people who want it, there is no crack cocaine particularly to be
found. Why? Not because it is difficult to manufacture. In fact, any user
knows that powder cocaine can be turned into crack by adding baking
soda and water and cooking it in a microwave oven. But crack cocaine

---

18. Compare the study by J. P. Sandwijk, P.D.A Cohen, S. Musterd, and M.P.S Lange-
meijer, "Licit and Illicit Drug Use in Amsterdam II, Report of a Household Survey in 1994
on the Prevalence of Drug Use among the Population of 12 Years and Over" (Amsterdam:
Department of Human Geography, University of Amsterdam, 1995), with the study of the
National High School Drug Use Survey conducted by the Institute for Social Research, University of Michigan, on behalf of the National Institute on Drug Abuse, for 1996. About 2.3%
of Amsterdam's twelve- to fifteen-year-olds and 10.9% of its sixteen- to nineteen-year-olds
had used marijuana in the previous thirty days, compared to 11.3% of fourteen-year-olds,
20.4% of sixteen-year-olds and 21.9% of eighteen-year-olds in the United States. See also a
comparison of a SAMHSA, Office of Applied Studies, Washington D.C., study and a study
by the University of Amsterdam, which shows that drug usage in the Netherlands is two to
ten times lower in all relevant categories than in the United States. Visit "Common Sense for
Drug Policy" at <www.DrugSense.org>.
19. Ethan Nadelmann, "Europe's Drug Prescription," *Rolling Stone*, January 26, 1995: 38.
20. Georgie Anne Geyer, "The Dutch Can Teach Us about Drug Programs," *Orange
County Register*, July 11, 1994: Metro 7.
21. "Holland's Drugs Policy: War by Other Means," *supra*.

is much riskier than powder, and users know that, too. So as long as they can afford to purchase powder cocaine, they have no interest in crack. This strongly supports the conclusion that the United States brought the "crack epidemic" on itself as a result of its prohibitionist policy on powder cocaine. In other words, this was not really a "drug" problem, it was a "drug prohibition" problem.

For all of its successes, the Dutch have also had some problems with their approach. For example, the people who sell the small amounts of marijuana and other drugs must still obtain their supply from illegal underground dealers, which continues to engender some corruption and violent crime. In addition, since Holland is a small country, fully a third of the people who use and abuse drugs inside its borders are foreigners who come "to have a good time." The Dutch have not yet solved this problem, a variation on Switzerland's Needle Park problem, and they may not be able to solve it on their own. But if other countries adopted the Dutch approach, the problem, obviously, would evaporate, since there would be no need for drug users to crowd into one country or one area. And each country that reformed its policies along Holland's lines would reap the same internal benefits of a drop in drug-related crime and a drop in drug use itself. And indeed, some other European countries are moving in that direction, although international reaction to Holland's domestic drug policy has been mixed. The majority of German states are gravitating toward the Dutch harm-reduction and normalizing approach with both marijuana and the harder drugs. Holland has taken some political heat, however, from France and Sweden—not to mention the United States—since Holland's liberal approach runs contrary to several international conventions and also results in a greater flow of drugs into neighboring countries.[22] But the pragmatic Dutch have no intention of formally withdrawing from these conventions that outlaw the sale and use of these drugs; they simply ignore them. The fact that their drug use rates are lower than ours, that their drug addicts are living longer and healthier lives than ours, that fewer young people are using drugs, and that Holland has no cocaine-related crime or deaths all combine to justify the continuation of their practical, realistic, and effective harm-reduction approach. We would do well to learn from their experience.

---

22. Leuw and Marshall, eds., *supra* at x–xi.

Regulated Distribution

I have viewed and experienced our federal drug laws in action since their serious inception about 1973. The war on drugs is lost for the same reasons that national prohibition of alcohol consumption failed in the '20s and early '30s.

Education, legalization with governmental control and not prohibition can solve our drug problem.

Senior Judge Edward J. McManus, United States District Court, Cedar Rapids, Iowa

Let us look a bit more closely at alcohol. Today most U.S. states allow the sale of this dangerous and sometimes addictive drug through a program of regulated distribution. This means that the sale of this mind-altering drug is controlled through regulations and restrictions. In effect, regulated distribution constitutes a recognition that, just as we cannot effectively eliminate air or water pollution by "banning" sewage or automobiles, we can best reduce and control the harms associated with alcohol by a program of public management and control. It is further based on the realization that *it is much easier to control, regulate, and police a legal market than an illegal one.* While abuses and harms will still occur, at least there are some controls in place. There are no controls at all on illegal drugs under our policy of "zero tolerance"—except those implemented by drug dealers. But by regulating alcohol in the market-place, we have virtually eliminated the problems of alcohol impurities in drinks like "bathtub gin," and there is no trafficker-related crime or corruption. No one hands out free samples of alcohol on high school campuses, both because it is effectively policed and because there is no money in it. So how could we implement a program for the regulated distribution of some presently illicit drugs?

One possibility would be to allow the purchase of heroin, cocaine, and marijuana *by adults* at state-licensed package stores. Dosage units of drugs that are now sold on the streets for about $10 would be sold for about $2.50 at these package stores, which would eliminate the profitability of illegal sales at one simple stroke. Higher-strength doses would cost more money. The dosages would be "plain-wrapped," with the dosage amount and strength clearly marked, and the package wrapper would contain appropriate warnings. The drugs would *never* be advertised, and would *never* go on sale at a reduced price. Along with the dose, the package would contain a sterile disposable needle (when appropriate), as well as educational material about the dangers of using drugs and the addresses and telephone numbers of organizations that could assist the user in getting off drugs.

The FDA would monitor and ensure the quality of the drugs, just as it now does our foods and prescription medicines. However, the sale, transfer, or furnishing in any manner any quantity of these drugs to a minor would be severely punished. Laws dealing with driving a motor vehicle under the influence, public drunkenness, assaults while under the influence, and so on, would not be changed.

The unlicensed sale of heroin, cocaine, or marijuana would remain a violation of law. Importantly, however, if the practice continued to any material degree, the price at the government package store would be lowered in order to reduce further the financial incentive to make such illegal sales. Using this ultimate control of setting the price, society would have the clear means of putting virtually every drug dealer in the country out of business.

Of the approximate purchase price of $2.50, about $.75 would go to the grower/packager, who would be on a low-bid contract with the government; and about $.75 would go to the retailer, who would also be on a low-bid contract with the government. The remaining $1 would take the form of a tax, which would be used expressly and solely for education about and treatment of drug abuse.[23]

The only thing we cannot say for certain, under such a policy, is whether the use of currently illegal drugs would increase or decrease in the short run, or increase or decrease in the long run. Studies and experiments in England, Switzerland, Holland, and elsewhere suggest that drug use would decrease in the long run, but we cannot predict the same result with any certainty. We would have to attempt this reform in order to find out.

Many things would affect the outcome. But we can say that implementing a program of this kind for adult use of these drugs would not necessarily result in an increase in their use. It is currently estimated that about 20 million people in the United States use marijuana to some degree; but only half a million use heroin. Both of these drugs are widely

---

23. This proposed program is taken directly from the notes I wrote and distributed at the news conference I held behind the courthouse in Santa Ana, California, on April 8, 1992, which were published in James P. Gray, "We Cannot Win the War against Drugs: A Legal Brief for Decriminalizing Use of Heroin, Cocaine, and Marijuana," *Orange County Register,* April 10, 1992: B13, and James P. Gray, "Proposed Plan for Regulated Distribution of Heroin, Cocaine and Marijuana," *The State Pen,* the Newsletter of the California Chapter of the American Correctional Health Services Association 13, no. 3 (fall 1993): 1, 7, 10. For a discussion of similar suggestions, see Dirk Chase Eldredge, *Ending the War on Drugs* (Bridgehampton, New York: Bridge Works Publishing, 1998): 166–73.

and readily available from drug dealers, and the disparity in the number of users of the two drugs reflects personal preference rather than availability, or even price. But if 20 million people demanded heroin, the illegal market would surely supply it, just as the enormous demand for alcohol was met during Alcohol Prohibition.

Remember too that heroin and cocaine were legal in this country before 1914 but were not widely used. And 100-proof alcohol is widely and legally available now to adults, but it is far less popular than 86-proof. And, finally, many people began using drugs because they were enticed into it by drug dealers. Taking the profit motive out of these drugs would virtually eliminate that dynamic. Drugs would literally be de-profitized.

There is no denying that a program of regulated distribution could result in some increased drug use, and I believe, at least in the short run, that it would. The law clearly makes a statement about what is unacceptable in our society, and there is no question that many people abstain from certain forms of conduct because they are illegal. But there would also be incentives for decreased drug use. Just as increased awareness and education have led many people to move away from or at least reduce their use of alcohol and tobacco, we could reasonably expect to see the same thing with other drugs. And more money would be available, thanks to the drug tax, for education and treatment of drug abusers, which would certainly reduce overall usage. The ban on advertising is a crucial feature of this plan, and since the government, not private companies, would control and regulate the sale of these drugs, no one could legitimately complain about First Amendment free speech issues. Not only would the glamour of these drugs be substantially reduced by removing their "forbidden" status and black market influences, there would be no brand names, billboards, or media ads at all—not even any posters on the walls at the package stores. Just mundane, plain-wrapped packages stamped with the name and strength of the product. How boring. The financial incentives to "push" any of these drugs would be virtually eliminated.

With the exception of possible increased usage, *every* other result of this program would be beneficial. Crime would be materially reduced. Even if someone still had to steal in order to pay for his drug habit, he would steal three-quarters less than under our current system. Even allowing for possible increased usage, burglaries would still be reduced, and there would be much more room in the criminal justice system to investigate, prosecute and incarcerate those offenders. Funding for gangs and terrorist groups here and all around the world would be substantially reduced, while funding for education about and treatment of drug abuse would be substantially increased. Treatment of drug abuse, moreover, would be less encumbered because the drug-addicted people would not be automatically regarded as criminals. No new taxes would be needed for jail or courthouse construction. Prison overcrowding due to drug possession and use would be a thing of the past. In fact, it is likely that we would be able to close some existing prisons. And our police departments and courts would once again be available to address society's other pressing needs. In short, the program of regulated distribution I have described would cost the taxpayers nothing, but would actually reduce expenses and at the same time raise appreciable amounts of money for drug treatment and educational programs.

Such a program would take the profit out of the drug business, which would substantially decrease the potential for corruption of public servants here and abroad. The pressures created by the War on Drugs for ever more desperate measures—the utilization of the military in domestic affairs, continually increasing criminal penalties, increased restrictions on the individual rights of our people, and so on—would be virtually eliminated. The work ethic for our youth and many of our older people could be revitalized. Lower-income areas could be reclaimed from drug sellers. Farmers in the world's developing countries would switch from illicit drugs to more economically productive crops. Our country's balance of payments problems would be significantly reduced. The spread of HIV and hepatitis from contaminated needles would be significantly reduced. Appreciably fewer overdoses from impure or unknown strengths of drugs would occur.

Whether this program would be expanded to drugs other than heroin, cocaine, and marijuana would be left for the future. There is evidence that marijuana is actually the drug of choice for many users of harder drugs, and therefore there is reason to hope that many of these would revert back "down the ladder" to marijuana if it were no longer illegal. It is also possible that under this program users of synthetic drugs like PCP, methamphetamines, and LSD would revert to the organic drugs so that there would be less need to increase the number of drugs sold at package stores. Of course, if the black market for synthetic drugs continued to prosper, expansion of the program could be considered.

Would we put the police, courts, and prisons out of business? Of course not. We will certainly always need the criminal justice system, regardless of our drug policy; but we could once again emphasize the areas in which that system works most effectively: *holding people accountable for their conduct.*

One of the first things that I realized as a judge of the municipal court in Orange County, California, was that the prosecution of defendants charged with driving motor vehicles while under the influence of alcohol ("DUI") presented probably the most severe problem area faced by that court. I began to study this area in an attempt to see what could be done other than simply "moving the cases along" through the court system. After about six months of personal interviews, educational seminars on alcohol abuse, and other research, I reached several conclusions about the nature of the problem and how to deal with it. Then, with the assistance and guidance of several others, a majority of judges on our court joined me in initiating a pilot program for the screening and sentencing of "first-time" DUI defendants. The results were gratifying, and the statistics showed that we were successful in keeping about 65 percent of these problem drinkers off alcohol for nine months, which was as long as we were able to keep statistics. Among other things, this experience convinced me that a mind-altering, dangerous, and sometimes addictive drug does not have to be illegal for the criminal justice system to reduce its use by problem users.[24]

The program began on December 17, 1984, and specified that all defendants who either had an alleged blood/alcohol level of 0.15 percent or above or refused to take a blood/alcohol test would be considered "high-risk problem drinkers." That is, in the absence of further information, these defendants were considered likely to become recidivists or repeat offenders. We offered these defendants a fairly severe first-time sentence, which included ten days in jail, a fine, and a suspension of their driver's licenses for six months. Their other option was voluntarily to provide further information to the court as to their alcohol status, in which case a court-sanctioned screening process was immediately available to them. The screening process was designed so that a report was provided to the Court within one hour of the refer-

---

24. This section is condensed from James P. Gray, "Non-Traditional Sanctions," in *Drunk Driving Laws and Enforcement: An Assessment of Effectiveness* (American Bar Association, Criminal Justice Section) February 1986: 143–46.

ral. Then, as a result of the screening process, if a defendant was found not to be a high-risk problem drinker after all, he or she was offered the same, less severe sentence offered to defendants with lower blood/alcohol level, which was typically a ninety-day restriction of their driver's license, plus a fine and completion of a first-offender educational program.

To defendants still considered high-risk problem drinkers after the screening process who were willing to show by future conduct that they merited extra consideration, we still offered the less severe probationary sentence, but with several conditions. These strictly enforced conditions were that the defendants completely abstain from ingesting any alcohol for as long as they were on probation, attend meetings of Alcoholics Anonymous, have a medical doctor interpret their blood test in order to see if they had alcohol-related medical conditions, alcohol counseling, report back to the court with proof of enrollment, and complete the program, among other things. Basically, we instituted a "drug court." And it worked.

As judges in the criminal justice system, we are in a unique position to give problem alcohol and other drug users some "motivation" to start them on the way to the realization that they have a problem. Jail is not a cure for the problem, but the threat of jail can go a long way toward helping defendants take the critical step of stopping their drug use so that they can begin to see the damage they are doing to their lives and to the lives of those around them. Jail must, however, be more than a threat: it must be utilized fully as the punishment it was meant to be for all of those who choose not to engage in any self-evaluation, or who substitute excuses for actual performance.

Of course the hope is that once users enroll in a drug-abuse program, the coercion represented by jail will be replaced by legitimate self-concern. Instead of the threat represented by a person in a black robe, they may be moved to reform their behavior when a person in a white smock tells them that their liver is failing because of alcohol or their heart and lungs have been damaged. Maybe a defendant will get the message when an AA meeting shows her by example and by a refusal to accept excuses that stability and a satisfying life are once again possible through sobriety. Perhaps it will be the improvement of a defendant's own family, social, or professional life, when forced by the criminal justice system to remove these dangerous drugs from her life that will provide the genuine motivation to begin a meaningful recovery. Or perhaps it will be a drug counselor who will be able by her insight and industry to break through to a particular defendant.

Since beginning my duties as a judge, I have discovered that I have the power, one way or another, to help put a substance abuser on the path to productive sobriety. I have received letters from the wives of abusive alcoholics I have "sentenced" to drug rehab, telling me that since their husbands stopped drinking, the beatings and abuse had stopped, and that these women were hopeful that the marriage could be saved after all. I also have heard favorable stories from employers about the regained productivity of many employees who had been sentenced to our program. I have seen slovenly defendants return to court thirty days later looking clean and presentable. Once I sentenced a man with a large tattoo of a marijuana leaf on his forearm. When he returned thirty days later, I noticed that the tattoo was different, and I asked him about it. He said he did not have enough money to have the tattoo removed, so instead he had the tattoo redesigned as a peacock. I considered that a genuine sign of progress. Professor Mark A. R. Kleiman, an author and professor of policy studies at the UCLA School of Public Policy and Social Research, has written about the benefits of using the criminal justice system in the manner for which it was designed: holding problem drug users accountable for their actions.

> The key to controlling illicit drugs is to focus on the fewer than 4 million hard-drug addicts. This relatively small group accounts for about 80 percent of the total consumption of cocaine, heroin and methamphetamine. They create problems out of any proportion to their numbers. They suffer enormously and cause suffering around themselves.
>
> Of the conventional tools of drug policy, only treatment has much relevance to controlling the problems of this group. A mountain of data shows that treating a hard-core addict, even if with only partial success, creates very large benefits. Although long-term cessation is a highly desirable goal, even imperfectly successful treatment episodes greatly reduce drug consumption and drug-related harm, both while treatment lasts and for some time thereafter. These gains are more than adequate to cover the cost of treatment.
>
> Getting hard-core, hard-drug users into treatment and keeping them there remains a major problem. This is the group least likely to enter treatment voluntarily, most expensive to treat and least likely to succeed by the standard of total abstinence. Many prefer drugs to treatment, as long as they can get the drugs.
>
> The choice, however, need not be left entirely up to the addicts. Sooner or later, most wind up under the jurisdiction of the criminal-justice system.

About three-quarters of all heavy cocaine users, for example, are arrested in the course of a year. The criminal-justice system can become a powerful tool for changing drug-taking behavior.[25]

We know that our criminal justice system can coerce *problem* drug users into meaningful and productive sobriety, or, if necessary, can remove *problem* drug users from society for long periods of time if they are violent or simply do not take their recovery seriously. So why do we persist with our failed drug policy, which imprisons weekend pot smokers? If a person uses or even abuses one of these illicit drugs but is not a "problem" drug user to anyone but him or herself, let us try to educate that person away from this pattern of self-harm, and provide treatment on demand. If users are a harm to other people, they will find their way into the criminal justice system, and judges like me will hold them accountable for their actions, even to the point of removing them from society if need be. This program has worked very effectively in combating alcohol abuse, and it can be just as effective for the abuse of other mind-altering drugs as well. The secret is to focus on people's conduct rather than their drug selections. It works!

---

25. Mark A. R. Kleiman, "Middle Ground," *UCLA Magazine*, December 1998: 10–11. See also Mark A. R. Kleiman, *Against Excess, Drug Policy for Results* (New York: Basic Books, 1992).

10

Federalism,
Not Federalization

Since Milton Friedman made his points some years ago, I have come to this conclusion: Treating drugs like alcohol and tobacco seems the best approach. But how will we ever get the public—and hence the elected officials—to listen and think?
Judge Gilbert S. Merritt, United States Court of Appeals, Nashville, Tennessee

Our country was founded on the concept of federalism. This means that, except for certain matters that are reserved by the U.S. Constitution to the federal government, all states can and should be separate experimental units, doing what they decide is appropriate for them. President Ronald Reagan, who always advocated reducing the size and power of the federal government, explained the concept this way: "The federal government did not create the states; the states created the federal government."

With regard to the drug problem, federalism would mean that each state determined its own drug policies. We do not need to have a one-size-fits-all approach to drug policy. If, for example, Illinois implemented a program that showed promising results, while Virginia tried one that did not work, other states, including Virginia, would logically be inclined to follow the program that was working in Illinois. Iowa might try an approach that worked well for a more agrarian state, but New York and California might need a policy better suited to urban populations.

And in fact this is exactly what happened after the Twenty-First Amendment repealed Alcohol Prohibition. The individual states were left to implement programs that worked best for them, and the power of the federal government was strictly limited to investigating and prosecuting the importation of alcohol into a state "in violation of its laws." Some states adopted the sale of alcohol through government package stores; most went to a mixture of regulated distribution and free market; and some counties within some states elected to remain "dry" and not allow the sale of alcohol within their borders.

The federalist approach is completely consistent with the Tenth Amendment to the Constitution, and also with the *Federalist Papers* of James Madison (Numbers 45 and 46), and Alexander Hamilton (Number 17), all of which state, basically, that the powers delegated to the federal government are few and defined. The rest are reserved for the individual states.

The problem, of course, is that neither people nor governments often relinquish power or control willingly. Over the years the federal government has steadfastly wrested control of drug policy away from the states. But even as late as the mid-1960s, the states were still basically in control. Commenting on the status of drug prosecutions, Nicholas Katzenbach, the assistant attorney general of the United States from 1961 to 1965 and the attorney general under President Lyndon Johnson from 1965 to 1966, said:

> We saw the role of the federal government as assisting the states and giving the principal responsibility to the states, with the federal government assisting in technology and things that could be done on a common base. And one of the major things we dealt with was trying to improve statistics on crime to find out what was really going on. . . .
>
> We did not do a lot on drugs because that was just beginning to be a problem. There was some talk about treatment. I do not think we appreciated at that time the enormous political potential of declaring the War Against Drugs. Now, as I have said, all crime has an emotional appeal and there is a great deal of political appeal in playing the role of the tough enforcer. Successful prosecutors can become governors, senators, even aspiring to the Presidency as Tom Dewey did, and *the War on Drugs is an ideal vehicle for political rhetoric.*[1] (Emphasis added.)

---

1. Nicholas Katzenbach, "A Rational Discussion of Current Drug Laws," *Fordham Urban Law Journal* 25 (April 23, 1998): 801, at 802.

Many influential people inside and outside government have decried the acts of the federal government in continually intruding into what traditionally and constitutionally was the domain of the individual states. They lament the gradual "federalization" of crimes. In fact, this awareness has actually been a part of the vernacular for years. Frequently, when there is a problem that others are trying to make larger, the response is, "Don't make a federal case of it." In this instance, especially, we should follow our own advice and counteract the efforts of our politicians, who have been using it as "an ideal vehicle for political rhetoric" for decades.

U.S. Supreme Court Chief Justice William Rehnquist agrees. On December 31, 1998, in his "Year-End Report on the Federal Judiciary," Chief Justice Rehnquist asked Congress to stop the politically popular practice of enacting federal laws against crimes already handled in state courts, calling this trend not only "taxing the judiciary's resources and affecting its budget needs, but it also threatens to change entirely the nature of our federal system. . . . Federal courts were not created to adjudicate local crimes, no matter how sensational or heinous the crimes may be. State courts do, can and should handle such problems."[2]

Similar sentiments were expressed by a task force sponsored by the American Bar Association and chaired by Edwin Meese III, attorney general under Ronald Reagan, which felt that too many prosecutions at the federal level could result in a dangerous concentration of police power, overtax the federal judicial system, and divert congressional attention from more substantial federal crime issues.[3]

Senior U.S. District Court Judge Whitman Knapp from the southern district of New York accurately summed up this approach back in 1993, when he wrote an op-ed piece that read in part:

> After 20 years on the bench I have concluded that federal drug laws are a disaster. It is time to get the government out of drug enforcement.
>
> As long as we indulged the fantasy that the problem could be solved by making America drug free, it was appropriate that the government assume the burden. But that ambition has been shown to be absurd. . . .

---

2. Chief Justice William H. Rehnquist, *The 1998 Year-End Report of the Federal Judiciary, December 1998;* Associated Press, "Rehnquist Report Assails Glut of Federal Offenses," *Chicago Tribune,* January 1, 1999: sec. 1, 3.

3. Edwin Meese III, "The Dangerous Federalization of Crime," *Wall Street Journal,* February 22, 1999: A19.

The variety, complexity, and importance of these questions make it exceedingly clear that the federal government has no business being involved in any of them. What might be a hopeful solution in New York could be a disaster in Idaho, and only state legislatures and city governments, not Congress, can pass laws tailored to local needs.

What did the nation do when it decided to rid itself of the catastrophes spawned by [Alcohol] Prohibition? It adopted the 21st Amendment, which excluded the [federal] government from any role in regulation of alcoholic beverages and strengthened the powers of the states to deal with such matters.

That is precisely what the Congress should do with respect to drugs. It should repeal all federal laws that prohibit or regulate their distribution or use and devise methods for helping the states to exercise their respective powers in those areas.[4]

Amen to that.

---

4. Whitman Knapp, Senior Judge, U.S. District Court for the southern district of New York, "It Is Time to Dethrone the Drug Czar," *Orange County Register*, May 11, 1993: Metro 7.

PART IV

What We Can Do About It

I found a . . . quote to describe the drug war which I want to share with you in closing: "The war against drugs provides politicians with something to say that offends nobody, requires them to do nothing difficult, allows them to postpone, perhaps indefinitely, the more urgent questions about the state of the nation's schools, housing, employment opportunities for young black men, the condition to which drug addiction speaks as a symptom not a cause. They remain safe in the knowledge that they might as well be denouncing Satan and so they can direct the voices of prerecorded blame at metaphors and apparitions, wars and battles."

The war on drugs becomes a perfect war for people who would rather not fight. A war on which politicians who stand fearlessly on the side of the good, the true, and the beautiful need do nothing else but strike noble poses as protectors of the people and defenders of the public trust.

We can't let that continue. Thank you.

Judge Nancy Gertner, United States District Court, Boston, Massachusetts

S o our drug laws have failed. So our prisons are beyond being full, and our freedoms and civil rights are being severely reduced. So drug sellers here and around the world have become obscenely wealthy; money from the sale of illicit drugs has corrupted large numbers of our public officials and private citizens and is directly responsible for revolutionary

---

Epigraph: Judge Nancy Gertner of the U.S. District Court in Boston, Massachusetts at a January 29, 1998, forum of the Voluntary Committee of Lawyers, Inc. in Boston, entitled "Is the Drug War Forever?" See <http://www.november.org>.

movements and terrorism all over the world; and drug-addicted people are unnecessarily committing crimes and contracting dangerous diseases, which they spread to other non-using people.

So what?

How can I actually do anything to make a difference about this situation? We have seen that there are viable options to our failed drug policy, and that virtually any change would improve our situation, but what can one person do, particularly against such powerful vested interests, both illegal interests and entrenched institutional ones?

Actually, every one of us can work effectively to bring some sanity and reason back into our drug policy. Here is how:

First, we as individuals must intentionally open our minds to realities and to possibilities, remembering that just because we discuss or ask questions about our drug policy, or even if we adopt a different drug policy, does not mean that we condone drug use or abuse.

Next, we must educate ourselves, realizing that we have viable options to our current policies. I once knew a man whose grandmother, when she turned seventy-two, started walking five miles per day. Now she is seventy-seven, he said, and he hasn't the faintest idea where she is. Similarly, and for whatever reasons, our legislators have passed a series of Drug Prohibition laws without even considering alternatives. And now most people haven't the faintest idea where those laws have carried us. We need to consider where we are.

Each one of us can look critically at television reports, newspapers, and magazines. When we become aware of a problem caused by illegal drugs, we can ask ourselves whether there is a drug policy option that could have eliminated or at least reduced that particular problem. Then we can ask if, overall, society would be less harmed by that alternate approach.

Then each one of us can help to educate other people by doing the following:

Make copies of the Resolution contained in Appendix A, sign it, and get your friends, neighbors, coworkers, and acquaintances to do the same.[1] Send one copy to me at the Superior Court in Orange County,

---

1. This Resolution has already been signed by thousands of concerned citizens and groups all over the country, including hundreds of judges and lawyers; state senators and representatives; mayors and other local officials; law enforcement and social services officials; members of the clergy; medical doctors, therapists and counselors; retired foreign service officers of the state department and commissioned officers of the armed forces; members of the media and

California, at 700 Civic Center Drive, Santa Ana, CA 92701, and send others to your elected representatives in Congress and your state representatives as well. These will not be ignored.

Write letters about this subject to the editors of any and all newspapers, magazines, and trade journals you read. When you hear a host or guest or speaker on a radio talk show or at a public discussion make an insupportable statement about the War on Drugs, challenge it. Of course, do not swear or raise your voice, but state simply and rationally that the facts do not support their statement, and call to their attention that there are other options between the two extremes of "zero tolerance," on the one hand, and "legalization," on the other.

Organize a discussion or presentation or speakers' forum about our nation's drug policy. Nearly everyone is involved with some group of people who would be interested in an intelligent discussion on this subject. Service clubs, church groups, bridge clubs, alumni groups—the list is practically endless. All you need to do is do it. Even if you feel like you are "swimming upstream" at first, jump into the water and begin. Most people, once they are equipped with the facts contained in this book, will be able to make such a presentation themselves. But if you are not comfortable with public speaking, invite your local chief of police, district attorney, public defender, probation officer, or sheriff to discuss the subject. But first, give that person a copy of this or a similar book, explain that you have concerns about the issues raised and will be asking questions about them. Or, if you prefer, call a group like the Drug Policy Foundation in Washington D.C., at (202) 537-5005, and ask for the name of a good speaker who lives or works in your area. Regardless of exactly how you go about it, you will make a difference because of your efforts. And I promise that you will feel enormous gratification for having done something truly worthwhile for your country and its people.

Contact your representatives in government and tell them that we want to change our nation's drug policy and adopt programs that work—programs based on the four criteria discussed above: education, prevention and treatment, incentives that encourage people to do what is socially acceptable, and personal accountability.

---

entertainment industry; educators and business leaders of all types; and religious, service, civic, humanitarian, and political groups and organizations, in addition to officials from all over the world, including public prosecutors and law enforcement officials from the Netherlands and elected officials of the Australian and Colombian governments.

So what are the forces that stand in the way of changing our nation's drug policy? What forces prefer to maintain the status quo of prisons, demonization of drug users, and prohibitions on open discussion of alternatives?

The biggest obstacle to change is decades' worth of rhetoric. Vast numbers of Americans have been programmed by this rhetoric to believe that there are no viable alternatives to our current drug policy. Many people oppose change simply because they have not been exposed to or thought about the actual facts of the so-called War on Drugs. It is a universal human characteristic to fear and resist change. But the stakes are so high, both in human misery and in taxpayer dollars, that it behooves us all to put this matter at the top of the political agenda in this country.

In addition to decades of rhetoric and general human inertia and fear of change, we must also confront those with vested economic or psychological interests in maintaining the status quo. These include illegal drug dealers on the one hand, and federal and local governmental agencies, many politicians, many law enforcement organizations, prison guards' unions, prison construction companies, burglar alarm companies, and many others too numerous to mention, on the other hand. Drug dealers, including foreign drug lords, stand to lose tens of billions of dollars in profits each year, and we can be sure that they will be prepared to spend hundreds of millions of dollars to protect their economic interests. If there is to be any real hope of reforming our drug laws, we must be prepared for that. I am reminded of the story about a "dry" county in Nevada. There came a point at which some of the county leaders thought it might be time for a change, so they commissioned a survey to see what local voters thought about becoming a "wet" county. Eighty percent of the voters supported repealing the county's prohibition on alcohol, so the community leaders put the matter on the ballot as a referendum. The 80 percent lead held until about two weeks before the election, when the county received a "Madison Avenue blitz" that seemed to come out of nowhere. Slick, sophisticated advertising bombarded the county showing how the county was much better off staying dry. The 80 percent lead quickly evaporated, and on Election Day the referendum lost in a close vote.

In the aftermath of the defeat, the community leaders began investigating where the money for this advertising blitz had come from. Some thought it must have been the churches. But no, their investigations soon showed that the churches had not been the source. So who had financed this operation? It turned out to be the liquor stores on the county line, which had been selling alcohol to the residents in the dry county for years. They knew they would lose that income if the referendum passed, so they spent the money necessary to keep it.

The drug lords of the world will do at least as much to protect their astronomical profits; so we must be prepared to lobby our elected representatives to resist their money and their power. We may not be able to match the dollars of the drug lords, but if we bring concerted pressure to bear, and refuse to give up, we will eventually prevail.

On the governmental and law enforcement side of things, I am optimistic. My years on the bench have convinced me that the shortsightedness of these people can and will be overcome. With only a few exceptions, I believe that the current drug warriors really do want what is best for our country, and will be willing to put their own self-interest aside. As long as they understand that the public knows that it is the drug policy that has failed, and not the individuals responsible for enforcing it, they will come around.

Even now progress is being made. In the 1998 election, every single ballot measure that proposed some kind of reform in our drug policy— whether it involved limited medical use of marijuana, or the decriminalization of personal, recreational use of marijuana, or putting an end to jail sentences for simple possession of even "hard" drugs—passed, and by comfortable margins.[2] These victories were won even in the face of a concerted federal effort, financed by our tax money, to defeat them. Public awareness of the dismal failure of our War on Drugs is growing, and the voters have, in effect, said that it is time to go over the heads of politicians and rethink the idea that all addicts are criminals. They also have come to realize that using amphetamines or smoking crack is not always just done by dangerous minority men on urban street corners—it is a problem tormenting families of every race and social class.

The next step is to translate this new awareness into pressure for change. More and more public officials, too, are coming forward to challenge the failed logic of the War on Drugs. U.S. Congressman Tom

---

2. In Alaska, medical marijuana passed by a vote of 58 to 42 percent; in Arizona it passed by 57 to 43 percent; in Nevada by 59 to 41 percent; in Oregon by 55 to 45 percent, and in Washington by 59 to 41 percent. In addition, an Oregon measure to re-criminalize marijuana failed by a vote of 67 to 33 percent.

Campbell of California has gone on record in favor of a trial program
of drug maintenance like that of Switzerland,[3] and New Mexico Governor Gary E. Johnson, a Republican and tri-athlete, has stated publicly that "Our present course is not working. Our War on Drugs is a
real failure."[4] It is only a matter of time before we repeal our failed
drug policies. Meanwhile, for each day that they remain in effect, lives
are being ruined and lost, needlessly, and our treasury is being squandered.

With your help, we will be able to implement programs that work,
including:

- *Education*—Our drug education programs must tell people the truth,
  especially young people. We must treat our children like the real
  human beings that they are. Slogans may be okay for our young children, but adolescents and young adults need to have an honest and
  truthful presentation of risks and benefits. Educational programs
  must take into account that, dangerous as they are, these mind-altering
  drugs are here to stay, and all of us in varying ways will receive pressure to use them. But if we do take these drugs, there are risks involved, legally, socially, and physiologically. One way or the other,
  each of us will be held accountable for our actions.
- *Needle Exchange*—Lobby our governmental representatives to institute and support these proven programs. This is a "no-brainer."
  Needle-exchange programs have been proven materially to increase
  the health of the user while not increasing drug use or abuse. Further, they have the collateral benefit, just like the programs for re-
  cyclable bottles and cans, of removing them from our streets, thereby
  reducing the risk that we and our children will contract AIDS or
  other infectious diseases by coming into contact with dangerous
  hypodermic needles that are now thrown away as litter. And do not
  permit anyone to say in your presence that needle exchange programs "send the wrong message" to our children. The message we
  are sending under our current drug policy is, "Go ahead and die. We
  don't care about your health, your life, or even the lives of your sexual partners or your children if you use drugs."
- *Send the Right Message*—Help to end the federal subsidy on tobacco.

---

3. Joanne Jacobs, "Our Drug Policies Are Broken," *Orange County Register,* December 16,
1999: Local News 9.

4. Mike Gray, "Mutiny in New Mexico," *Rolling Stone,* February 3, 2000: 36–37.

- *Hemp*—Lobby our governmental representatives to legalize hemp, that is, marijuana plants with a THC level of .3 percent or lower. This is also a no-brainer. A THC level of .3 makes the plant impotent as a mind-altering drug. But the hemp from the stalk of these plants can re-institute a historically profitable industry. The legalization of hemp will make a major positive impact on our job market and our environment. At a time in which more and more of our old growth forests are being withdrawn from logging operations, we can rejuvenate our industries for paper pulp, plywood, two-by-fours, rope, textiles, nontoxic paints and varnishes, and many other products from fast-growing hemp. Why cut down trees when hemp can do the job just as well?

- *Medical Marijuana*—Lobby our governmental representatives to pass legislation to allow licensed medical doctors to prescribe marijuana to their patients. The most expeditious route would be for the president to reschedule marijuana as a Schedule II rather than a Schedule I drug. If the president lacks the courage to take this simple step, then we must pursue the legislative course. It goes without saying that a doctor who over-prescribes this or any other drug must be held accountable under our current regulations. But the viability of marijuana to relieve the symptoms of cancer, AIDS, and other serious illnesses has been proved, and it is heartless, if not criminal, to deprive suffering patients the relief that this substance can bring.

- *Medication*—Allow our medical doctors, instead of police officers, to determine appropriate medications for various maladies and to relieve pain—and hold the doctors accountable for any possible abuses.

- *The Eight-Percent Early Intervention Program*—Significant studies have shown that 8 percent of all juvenile offenders commit about half of all juvenile offenses. These "eight-percenters" can be detected by screening them to determine if they have three or more of the following four profile factors: 1) significant family problems, such as abuse, neglect, criminal family members, or a lack of parental supervision and control; 2) significant problems at school, such as truancy, failing more than one course, or a recent suspension or expulsion; 3) a pattern of drug or alcohol use; and 4) delinquent peers, chronic runaway, or patterns of stealing. This screening should be done the very first time any juvenile offender is taken into the juvenile justice system. Then we must, if only for our own safety and preservation, provide more services not only to that juvenile offender, but also to that offender's entire family. This program reduces both crime and substance abuse.[5]

- *Community Policing*—Policing programs that get the officers out of their patrol cars and back into the communities they are attempting to serve have been proven to work. Studies have shown not only that violence from the police begets further violence, but also that peaceful involvement from the police begets community cooperation and peaceful conditions. In effect, this is a mentoring program for the entire community. Of course police must still arrest and jail offenders. But just as medical doctors use surgery as a last resort, police should use their powers of arrest in the same fashion.[6]

- *Strictly Administered Probation for Nonviolent Offenders*—Strictly administered probation costs much less money than prison—and it is much more effective. And it can be combined with a strict program of restitution paid by the offender back to the crime victim. Unfortunately our present system punishes the victims of crime three times: first, when the crime is originally perpetrated against them; second, when they are forced to come to court on several occasions to testify; and third, when we force them to reach into their pockets and pay for the incarceration of the offender. Concentrate instead on a strictly applied program of restitution from the offender to the victim, which would be much more effective for the offender, for the victim, and for society itself. This would also allow us to reserve prison space for violent offenders, who simply must be removed from society for as long as possible.

- *Drug Treatment*—Make quality drug treatment programs available on demand for everyone. The Delancey Street treatment programs are a successful model in teaching self-sufficiency to heavily addicted people. Mentoring, caring, hope, and personal accountability are the

---

5. Orange County Probation Department, Michael A. Schumacher, Ph.D., "The '8% Problem': Chronic Juvenile Offender Recidivism," March 1994. For information, contact Program Planning and Research Division, 909 N. Main Street, Santa Ana, California 92701, (714) 569-2140.

6. See, for example, Susan M. Hartnett and Wesley G. Skogan, "Community Policing: Chicago's Experience," *National Institute of Justice Journal* (April 1999): 3–10; Nicholas Pastore, chief of police, New Haven, Connecticut, "Policing in the 21st Century," *Justice Newsletter* (March, 1994): 4–5; Sam Vincent Meddis, "Mean Streets Lighten Up with Community Policing," *USA Today*, July 27, 1993: 6A; and Michael Ryan, "It's All About Dignity and Respect," *Parade Magazine*, January 9, 1994: 12, 14.

keys. As long as we continue to incarcerate nonviolent offenders, their treatment facilities should be low-security institutions. These will cost the taxpayer much less money and achieve much lower recidivism rates. And if the person incarcerated is a single parent, a residential program should be available that would allow the family unit to stay together in appropriate circumstances.

- *Drug Courts*—These take more judicial resources and patience; but they work with addicted people and give them hope. But again, just as with alcohol, the mindaltering drug does not have to be illegal in order to use the criminal justice system effectively to coerce the problem user into treatment. Use drug courts for appropriate nonviolent but problem drug users who find their way into the criminal justice system because of their misdeeds, just as we do now for nonviolent problem alcohol offenders.

- *De-profitize the Drug Market as Best We Can*—Bring the use and possession of these drugs back under the law! Of course these drugs are dangerous, but the money from their sale causes more harm than the drugs themselves. A black market of some kind will always be with us, but it can be severely diminished in size and power. Under our current system there are no controls at all on who can buy these drugs, on their quality or purity, or on quantities sold, except those controls enforced by the criminal drug sellers, who, of course, pay no taxes on the sales. And it is easier for our children to buy cocaine or heroin than it is for them to buy a six-pack of beer. The distribution of alcohol is controlled by the government. The distribution of drugs like cocaine is controlled by the mob. Virtually any system would be better than what we have now.

- *Drug Substitution Programs*—Take the governmental paranoia out of this area. Protect our communities more from the harmful actions of drug-addicted people, and a little less from the potential harms of drugs like methadone.

- *Drug Maintenance Programs*—Until our drug-addicted people will participate in drug treatment programs, maintain them under medical supervision on their drugs in as safe a manner as possible. Remember that "dead addicts can't get clean."

- *Reform Asset Forfeiture Laws*—Allow forfeiture of money and other property involved in drug law violations only after a criminal conviction, with the issue of forfeiture being submitted to the same jury.

We obviously must fund our law enforcement agencies sufficiently for them to protect our people, but this funding must not come from sharing in the "plunder" of drug forfeitures.

- *Reward Prison Wardens for Low Recidivism Rates*—Changing the incentives to recognize and reward prison wardens for reduced rates of recidivism of their inmates would result in every one of them adopting drug treatment programs and other proven programs that would materially improve the lives of the inmates and their families, reduce the overall costs to the taxpayers, and make us all safer.
- *Safe Passage to Seek Medical Care*—Pass laws allowing people to seek medical care for other people who have overdosed, with no questions asked.
- *Revise Our Spending Priorities*—The federal government is spending more on TV commercials than on after-school programs for our children—even though these programs are the most effective way to prevent adolescent drug abuse.
- *Mandatory Minimum Sentences*—Repeal laws that take away discretion from judges in the sentencing of nonviolent criminal offenders. Instead, hold judges accountable by requiring them to specify the reasons for their sentences on the public record. Mandatory minimum sentences have filled our prisons with low-level drug offenders, have unnecessarily ruined thousands of lives, and have discredited the law in the eyes of hundreds of thousands of Americans—and rightfully so.
- *Three-Strike Laws*—Utilize these laws only for serious or violent felonies. Otherwise we will continue to fill up our prisons, at great human and financial expense, with low-level, nonviolent drug offenders.
- *Prison Construction*—Write frequent letters to your elected officials demanding a moratorium on all prison construction until the War on Drugs is repealed.
- *Teach Classes in Addiction Medicine*—Our medical schools should be encouraged to educate our future doctors in the area of addiction medicine.
- *Prescription Drug Abuse*—Focus on the problems of all drug abuse, including prescription drugs and alcohol, instead of only on drugs that happen to be illegal at the time.
- *Alcohol Abuse*—End the glamorization of alcohol through such things as advertising, particularly to our children. Today's sports events,

rock concerts, and even political events often seen like one big beer advertisement. And tighten the restrictions the keep alcohol from being available to children and adolescents.

- *Support and Encourage Research*—There are some exciting studies that show, for example, that a substance called ibogaine reduces the problems of addiction, that a deficiency of manganese results in greater aggression and addiction, and that marijuana reduces the symptoms of several serious illnesses. Other studies are beginning to show that addiction may actually be a brain disease, or may be connected with genes associated with our "biological clocks."[7] Encourage people to keep their minds open, and support the funding of this important research.

- *Help Defend Our Civil Liberties*—Raise the alarm about the loss of protections under the Bill of Rights as a direct result of U.S. drug policy. Ask yourself and others what Thomas Jefferson, Tom Paine, Abraham Lincoln, or Theodore Roosevelt would have done under these circumstances.

- *Send the Right Message*—Prohibit the sale of all alcohol at gasoline stations.

- *Federalism*—Support the "federalism" instead of the "federalization" of drug policy. As we did after the repeal of Alcohol Prohibition, allow each state to address these problems in the manner best suited for its needs, and restrict the federal government to helping each state enforce its chosen laws.

- *International Agreements*—Revise our treaties with other nations to allow each country to adopt programs addressing its domestic drug problems in the way that best meets its needs.

- *Stop the Political Charade*—Put an end to the embarrassing and arrogant political game of certifying various nations around the world according to our perception of their "cooperation" in pursuing our War on Drugs.

Will these programs cost money? Certainly, many of them will. Can we afford them? Of course we can! We have more than enough money; the problem is that we are misspending it. One of the most fundamental

---

7. Alan I. Leshner, "Addiction Is a Brain Disease—and It Matters," *National Institute of Justice Journal* (October 1998): 2–6; "Genes Linked to the Biological Clock May Play Role in Addiction," *Orange County Register*, August 13, 1999: News 18.

misguided expenses is prisons. Instead of building one new state prison, why not spend that $250 to $300 million on drug treatment, education, and community policing? We would save not only the $250 to $300 million in prison construction costs, but also the tens of millions of dollars per year that we spend just to staff one prison. And, of course, provided we spent that saved money on programs that work, we would need still fewer prisons in the future.

But before we can reap the benefits of programs like these, and pay for them by using the huge amounts of money we will save by abandoning the expensive, unnecessary, and unproductive programs that our current drug policy entail, we must start addressing our drug problems as managers instead of as moralists. As the political philosopher James Q. Wilson put it, "If we are to make the best and sanest use of our laws and liberties, we must first adopt a sober view of man and his institutions that would permit reasonable things to be accomplished, foolish things abandoned, and utopian things forgotten."[8]

I am so convinced of the rightness and the benefits of the course I am proposing that I will end this discussion with a guarantee: If we abandon our failed drug policy and implement the programs I have outlined here, crime in the United States will be reduced by a minimum of 35 percent. I am not talking about straight drug crime, which will also be substantially reduced. The crime reduction will include burglaries, robberies and homicides, purse-snatchings, automobile thefts and check offenses, prostitution, shoplifting, money laundering, and both public and private corruption. And this minimum 35 percent reduction in crime will be realized within as little as one year after the reforms take effect. Public safety and health will increase; taxes will be reduced. And all we have to do to accomplish these positive results is to open our eyes and recognize that these drugs, harmful though they are, are here to stay, but that we can reduce their harm by being truthful and realistic about them and adopting programs that work. This is the best, most logical, and most commonsensical way to regain a country based on strong conservative values.

We are right to be upset about the current situation, but we must not lose heart. People are unnecessarily dying. Lives are unnecessarily being ruined every day. Vast sums of our tax dollars are being squandered, and

---

8. James Q. Wilson, *Thinking about Crime* (New York: Vintage Books, rev. ed., 1985): 250.

people from all walks of life, as well as entire governments around the world, are being injured and corrupted as a direct result of our drug money. The War on Drugs has done as much as anything else to erode the grandeur and integrity of our country. But progress is also being made, and people are beginning to open their eyes to the truth. Arthur Schopenhauer said it best: "All truth passes through three stages. First, it is ridiculed. Second, it is violently opposed. Third, it is accepted as self-evident."

We have unwittingly done some very bad things to ourselves and to the people of the world because we have maintained our drug prohibitionist policy for so long. But we can reduce the bleeding and begin the healing process with a fundamental change of direction. Our drug laws have failed, but we are getting ever closer to the "self-evident" stage. You and I can help our country to get there more quickly by letting everyone know that it is okay to talk about this subject. And that just because we discuss options to our failed drug laws does not mean that we condone drug use or abuse. Let's get this important job done.

The time is now.

Appendix A

Appendix A

Resolution

Whereas, the overall situation regarding the use of drugs in our society and the crime and misery that accompany it has continued to deteriorate for several decades; and

Whereas, our society has continued to attempt, at enormous financial cost and loss of civil liberties, to resolve drug abuse problems through the criminal justice system, with the accompanying increase of prisons and numbers of inmates; and

Whereas, the huge untaxed revenues generated by the illicit drug trade are undermining legitimate governments worldwide; and

Whereas, the present system has spawned a cycle of hostility by the incarceration of disproportionate numbers of African-Americans, Hispanics, and other minority groups; and

Whereas, in our society's zeal to pursue our criminal approach, legitimate medical uses for the relief of pain and suffering of patients have been suppressed;

Therefore be it resolved that our society must recognize drug use and abuse as the medical and social problems that they are, and that they must be treated with medical and social solutions; and

Further be it resolved that an objective commission be immediately empowered by the President and by Congress to recommend revisions of the drug laws of these United States in order to reduce the harm our current policies are causing.

_____

Signature

_____   _____

Name   Address

_____   _____

Title/Org.   City, State, Zip

250

Appendix B

*Government Commission Reports
and Other Public Inquiries*

The evidence against U.S. drug policy is overwhelming and consistent. It can be found in our daily lives, in newspapers and magazines, on radio and television, in scholarly and general-interest books, and in discussions with people who are charged with enforcing that policy. Additional evidence can be found in every major public commission and objective study that has addressed the issue, both in this country and in India, England, Canada, and Australia. Some of these are summarized below. The phrasing may be different, but each study has reached the same conclusions: The War on Drugs is an abject failure. Given that all of these studies are consistent in their findings, why aren't our governments reading and considering their own neutral studies?[1]

Indian Hemp Drugs Commission Report
(India, 1894)

This was an extensive, seven-volume report on the problems with the use of marijuana by the British in India, which concluded, "moderate use of these drugs is the rule, and ... excessive use is comparatively exceptional. The moderate use produces practically no ill effects."

---

1. The author's thanks and appreciation are given to Clifford Schaffer and his Schaffer Library of Drug Policy (see <http://www.druglibrary.org/schaffer>). Some of the summaries below are taken from his library, with permission.

The Rolleston Report
(Departmental Committee on Morphine and Heroin Addiction, England, 1926)

As we have seen, this landmark study by a distinguished group of British doctors appointed by the government codified existing practices of maintenance of addicted people on heroin and morphine by individual doctors, and recommended that the practice be continued without interference. The committee concluded: "The condition must be regarded as a manifestation of disease and not as a mere form of vicious indulgence." These British addiction experts took pains to state that they did not agree with the opinions of "some eminent physicians, especially in the United States," that addicts "could always be cured by sudden withdrawal."

Panama Canal Zone Military Investigations
(U.S. Military, 1916–29)

After an exhaustive study of the smoking of marijuana by American soldiers stationed in the Panama Canal Zone, this panel of civilian and military experts recommended that "no steps be taken by the Canal Zone authorities to prevent the sale or use of Marihuana." The panel also concluded that "there is no evidence that Marihuana as grown and used [in the Canal Zone] is a 'habit-forming' drug."

The LaGuardia Committee Report
(Mayor's Committee on Marihuana, The Marihuana Problem in the City of New York, commissioned by Mayor Fiorello LaGuardia, written by the New York Academy of Medicine, and published by the City of New York, 1944)

This committee reviewed thousands of years of the history of marijuana and provided a detailed examination of the prevailing conditions in New York City. Among its conclusions were that "The practice of smoking marihuana does not lead to addiction in the medical sense of the word" and "The use of marihuana does not lead to morphine or heroin or cocaine addiction, and no effort is made to create a market for those narcotics by stimulating the practice of marihuana smoking." Finally, the committee concluded that "The publicity concerning the catastrophic effects of marihuana smoking in New York City is unfounded."

The First Brain Report
(Interdepartmental Committee, Drug Addiction, England, 1961)

When the Brain Committee first met at the invitation of the minister of health, its mission was to review the advice given by the Rolleston Committee in 1926. That advice had been to continue to allow doctors to treat addicted people with maintenance dosages of powerful drugs when doctors deemed it medically helpful for their patients. Brain I reiterated that advice and, in this first report, recommended that no changes of any significance in the prescribing powers of the doctors be made.

In addition, this report underscored one prior finding of the Rolleston Committee when it authenticated the existence of "stabilized addicts." While many American experts stated doubts about their existence, this report explained that "careful scrutiny of the histories of more than a hundred persons classified as addicts reveals that many of them who have been taking small and regular doses for years show little evidence of tolerance and are often leading reasonably satisfactory lives." Six case histories of "known stabilized addicts" were included in an appendix. They were mature, older patients, functioning normally on what would be huge doses of drugs by American standards.

Interim and Final Reports
(Joint Committee of the American Bar Association and the American Medical Association on Narcotic Drugs, 1961)

This report was the result of the only major combined study of drug policy made by two of the most important professional societies in the country. Chaired by Rufus King, Esq. of Washington, D.C., the committee presented a direct challenge to the tough policies of Federal Bureau of Narcotics Director Harry Anslinger. This blue-ribbon committee included a senior federal judge and was advised by Indiana University's Alfred Lindesmith, one of the most distinguished addiction scholars in history. The report stated, "Drug addiction is primarily a problem for the physician rather than the policeman, and it should not be necessary for anyone to violate the criminal law solely because he is addicted to drugs." The report concluded that drug addiction was a disease, not a crime, that harsh criminal penalties were destructive, that drug prohibition ought to be reexamined, and that experiments should be conducted with British-style maintenance clinics for narcotic-addicted people.

The Second Brain Report
(Interdepartmental Committee, Drug Addiction,
Second Report, England, 1965)

Brain II did not recommend, as many American officials have argued, that the British prescription system be dismantled, nor did it recommend the compulsory registration of addicted people. Instead, Brain II aimed its recommendations toward controlling a few over-prescribing doctors. Accordingly, this Committee recommended that:

1. Doctors who wished to prescribe "restricted drugs" to addicts for the purpose of maintenance be required to obtain a special license from the Home Office;
2. "Treatment centers" be established for treating addicts, who were to be regarded as sick people and not as criminals; and,
3. Doctors and other medical personnel should be mandated to "notify" the Home Office when they encountered an addict in the course of their professional work.

The Wootton Report
(Advisory Committee on Drug Dependence,
Cannabis, England, 1968)

This report on marijuana and hashish was prepared by a group that included some of the leading drug abuse experts in the United Kingdom. These impartial experts worked as a subcommittee under the lead of Baroness Wootton of Abinger. The basic tone and substantive conclusions were similar to all of the other neutral commission reports. The Wootton group specifically endorsed the conclusions of the Indian Hemp Drugs Commission and the LaGuardia Committee. Typical findings were as follows:

1. There is no evidence that in Western society serious physical dangers are directly associated with the smoking of cannabis (i.e., marijuana);
2. Cannabis use does not lead to heroin addiction;
3. The evidence of a link with violent crime is far stronger with alcohol than with the smoking of cannabis; and,
4. There is no evidence that smoking cannabis by otherwise normal people produces conditions of dependence or psychosis that would require medical treatment.

The LeDain Report, Canada, 1970
(Canadian Government Commission of Inquiry
into the Non-Medical Use of Drugs)

The Canadian experts on this governmental commission were led by law school dean and later Supreme Court Justice Gerald LeDain. The report was quite similar to prior commission reports and portrayed casual drug users normally as decent citizens whose views deserved the respect of the government in the process of developing drug-control strategies. The commission recognized that the harm caused by a conviction for simple possession of a drug was "all out of proportion to any good it is likely to achieve," and that "no one should be liable for imprisonment for simple possession of a psychotropic drug for non-medical purposes." It further recommended that serious consideration be given to the legalization of the personal possession of marijuana in the near future.

U.S. National Commission on Marihuana and Drug Abuse
(United States, 1972)

This commission was appointed by President Richard M. Nixon and was chaired by Raymond P. Shafer, a former Republican Governor of Pennsylvania. It had four sitting, elected politicians among its eleven members, as well as leading addiction scholars among its members and staff. The commission issued two lengthy reports. The first one recommended that:

1. Possession of marijuana for personal use should no longer be an offense, but marijuana possessed in public should remain contraband, subject to summary seizure and forfeiture; and,
2. Casual distribution of small amounts of marijuana for no or "insignificant" remuneration not involving profit should no longer be an offense.

The recommendations in this report commissioned by President Nixon were endorsed, among others, by the American Medical Association, the American Bar Association, the American Association for Public Health, the National Education Association, and the National Council of Churches.

U.S. National Commission on Marihuana and Drug Abuse
(United States, 1973)

The second and final report of this commission made many recommendations, including the following:

- All public and private institutions should sponsor research and objective evaluation of drug-related issues, programs and policies;
- Congress should create a single federal drug agency. The accomplishments of this agency should be reexamined four years after its creation, and the agency, by law, should disband within five years; also each state should establish a unified drug agency on the same model as that proposed for the federal government;
- Congress should establish a commission four years hence to determine which measures have justified their costs and which have not, and to propose new policies;
- The Single Convention Treaty should be redrafted to make clear that each nation in the world is free to determine which domestic uses of drugs it will allow;
- Cannabis should be removed from the Single Convention on Narcotic Drugs (1961), since this drug does not pose the same social and public health problems associated with the opiates and coca leaf products;
- Except where the Commission has specifically recommended a change, the present levels of control on availability of psychoactive substances should be maintained;
- With respect to the drug trafficking laws, the trafficking offenses and penalty structures presently in force should be retained;
- The unauthorized possession of any controlled substance, except marihuana for personal use, should remain a prohibited act. The primary purpose of the possession laws should be detection of those persons who would benefit by treatment or prevention services, rather than criminal punishment;
- Federal criminal investigative agencies should concentrate primarily on the top level of the illegal drug distribution network, and state enforcement should concentrate on the lower levels of both licit and illicit distribution networks;
- Local police should receive appropriate training in dealing with the medical needs of drug-dependent persons, including alcoholics;

- The government should continue to prohibit heroin maintenance;
- Each state should establish a comprehensive statewide drug dependence treatment and rehabilitation program, with confidentiality-of-treatment laws;
- Drug use prevention strategy, rather than persuading or "educating" people not to use drugs, should emphasize other means of obtaining what users seek from drugs, which would be better for the user and better for society;
- The role of the federal government should be limited to providing accurate information regarding the likely consequences of the different patterns of drug use;
- A moratorium should be declared on the production and dissemination of new drug information materials, including all drug education programs in the schools; state legislatures should repeal all statutes that now require drug education courses to be included in the public school curriculum;
- Government should not interfere with private efforts to analyze the quality and quantity of drugs anonymously submitted by street users;
- The government should not support programs that compel persons to undergo drug testing, except in limited situations;
- Government should remove legal and bureaucratic obstacles to research into the possible therapeutic uses of currently prohibited substances, such as marijuana and hallucinogens;
- Schools of medicine, pharmacy, nursing, and public health should include the social and medical aspects of drug use in their curriculum; and,
- Drug companies should end the practice of sending doctors unsolicited samples of psychoactive drugs.

Joint Committee on New York Drug Law Evaluation, of the Association of the Bar of the City of New York
(United States, 1977)

This commission was formed to review the Rockefeller drug laws, which were the toughest in the country. The report basically concluded that tougher sentences had provided little, if any, benefit. Instead they had increased the incentive for drug sellers to commit violence and had clogged the criminal justice system. The report also found that tougher penalties had done nothing material to reduce drug use but had instead exacerbated many of the existing problems.

Cannabis Control Policy: A Discussion Paper
(Canadian Government, Health Protection Branch Department of National Health and Welfare, Canada, 1979)

This report discussed eight options for cannabis control, ranging from complete prohibition to complete legalization. The stated conclusion: utilize a form of "semi-prohibition" of cannabis, with no penalties for personal use but criminal penalties for trafficking. The committee stated that its primary concern in reaching its recommendations was to minimize the health and safety risks associated with the use of cannabis, which caused them to weigh the gravity of the harms attributed to cannabis itself with the countervailing costs of any control measures. They concluded that essentially the same measure of public health protection could be attained through a program of semi-prohibition, which would be a less injurious use of the criminal law.

The Facts about Drug Abuse
(The Drug Abuse Council, United States, 1980)

In 1972, a report to the Ford Foundation called "Dealing with Drug Abuse" had concluded that current drug policies were unlikely to eliminate or even greatly affect drug abuse. This conclusion led to the creation and joint funding by four major foundations of the broadly based, independent national Drug Abuse Council. The council was established to review and assess laws, programs, and projects—federal, state, and local, private and governmental—related to the use and misuse of psychoactive drugs. In its final report, the council's board of directors offered a set of observations that were considered central to the process of reaching more consistent, coherent, and responsible approaches to drug use and misuse. The observations included the following:

1. Psychoactive substances have been available throughout recorded history, and will remain so. To try to eliminate them completely is unrealistic.
2. The use of psychoactive drugs is pervasive, but misuse is much less frequent, and the failure to make the distinction between use and

misuse creates the impression that all use is misuse and leads to addiction.

3. There is a clear relationship between drug misuse and pervasive societal ills such as poverty, racial discrimination and unemployment, and we can expect drug misuse to be aggravated by the continued presence of these adverse social conditions.

4. The price of an effective strategy to eliminate drug misuse through the criminal law would be perceived by many Americans as too high in terms of invasions of privacy and abrogations of individual liberties.

5. Drug laws and policies attend insufficiently to the problems of people misusing drugs and too much to the properties of drugs themselves, as though the drugs were somehow inherently to blame.

6. Too many Americans have unrealistic expectations about what drug policies and programs can accomplish.

7. We in the United States have a regrettable tendency to blame our drug problems on others, failing to recognize that our drug problems are products of our own national experience.

The council's directors then offered a set of suggestions, including the following:

1. Treatment for drug dependence should be available chiefly because people need help, rather than as a crime control or behavior control method.

2. There should be a major study of the effects of drug laws and their enforcement on personal decisions to use or not use illicit drugs.

3. Legislative efforts to decriminalize at both state and federal levels for the possession of small amounts of marijuana for personal use should continue.

4. Serious consideration should be given to the use of state and local options as a means of attempting solutions appropriate in one place but not in others. Local options could encourage greater flexibility and ingenuity rather than reliance on an unrealistic, rigid homogeneity in national drug policy. We need to respond to the diversity of people who use and misuse drugs, base all our policies upon a consistent set of principles seeking to discourage misuse, and keep our seemingly innate drug-using behavior within reasonable limits through means which do not themselves produce more harm than they prevent.

Committee on Substance Abuse and Habitual Behavior

(Commission on Behavioral and Social Sciences and Education, National Research Council, National Academy of Science, United States, 1982)

The National Academy of Science Committee on Substance Abuse and Habitual Behavior consisted of some of the leading American experts on medicine, addiction treatment, law, business, and public policy. These experts reviewed all of the available evidence on every aspect of the marijuana question. The committee then recommended that the country experiment with a system that would allow states to set up their own methods of controlling marijuana, as is now done with alcohol. Under this approach, federal criminal penalties would be removed, and each state could decide to pursue any program of rules, regulations, and taxations that it felt was appropriate. In other words, the committee recommended we pursue a policy of "federalism" instead of our present policy of federalization.

Like virtually all other studies, this report stated that excessive marijuana use could cause serious harm but that such use was rare, and that, on balance, the current policy of total prohibition was socially and personally destructive. The report placed great emphasis on the building up of public education and informal social controls, which often have a greater impact on drug abuse than the criminal law. Regarding the possibility of disaster for our youth under any of these regulated programs, the report observed that there is reason to believe that widespread uncontrolled use would not occur under regulation. Indeed, regulation might facilitate patterns of controlled use by diminishing the "forbidden fruit" aspect of the drug, and perhaps increase the likelihood that an adolescent would be introduced to the drug through families and friends, who practice moderate use, rather than by their heaviest-using and most drug-involved peers.

DEA Docket No. 86-22, DEA Chief Administrative Law Judge Ruling on Medical Marijuana

(United States, 1988)

This is the ruling of the DEA's own chief administrative law judge, which resulted from a lawsuit filed against the federal government seeking to reschedule marijuana so that it could be prescribed for medical purposes. Before issuing his ruling, Judge Francis Young heard two years of testimony on both sides of the issue, and accumulated fifteen volumes of research. This was undoubtedly the most comprehensive study of medical marijuana done to date. Some of Judge Young's findings and conclusions were as follows:

> The evidence in this record clearly shows that marijuana has been accepted as capable of relieving the distress of great numbers of very ill people, and doing so with safety under medical supervision. It would be unreasonable, arbitrary, and capricious for DEA to continue to stand between those sufferers and the benefits of this substance. . . .
>
> There is no record in the extensive medical literature describing a proven cannabis-induced fatality. . . . In strict medical terms, marijuana is far safer than many foods we commonly consume. . . .
>
> There are those who, in all sincerity, argue that the transfer of marijuana to "status as a medicine" will "send a signal" that marijuana is "OK" generally for recreational use. This argument is specious. It presents no valid reason for taking an action required by law in light of the evidence.

Advisory Council on the Misuse of Drugs
(England, Part 1 1988, Part 2 1989)

"The spread of HIV is a greater danger to individual and public health than drug misuse," declared the leading drug abuse and health experts of the United Kingdom who sat on this distinguished quasi-governmental advisory group. This concept operated as the guiding principle behind this commission report. The British Advisory Council provided a comprehensive health plan that sought to prevent the use of drugs. However, the plan had realistic goals regarding drug abusers: abstinence as in the American mode, where possible, but above all else, health and life. Thus the Advisory Council accepted the lessons of the "harm reduction" programs of Dr. John Marks's clinic in Liverpool, as well as needle exchanges and drug maintenance programs for addicted people, and recommended that they be spread throughout the entire United Kingdom. This report even went beyond the Liverpool experience when these leading British experts quietly observed, "We believe that there is a place for the expansion of residential facilities where drug misusers may gain better health, skills and self-confidence whilst in receipt of prescribed drugs."

Report of the Research Advisory Panel for the State of California
(United States, 1989)

This panel, which was appointed by the state legislature to regulate all research on controlled substances, reviewed drug policy and recommended that "the legislature act to redirect this state away from the present destructive pathways of drug control." The report noted that the state had followed a path of prohibition over the last fifty years, and concluded that this policy "has been manifestly unsuccessful in that we are now using more and a greater variety of drugs, legal and illegal." In addition, the failure of prohibition has resulted in "societal overreaction [that] has burdened us with ineffectual, inhumane and expensive treatment, education and enforcement efforts." The panel recommended a move toward the formulation of "legislation aiming at regulation and decriminalization" and the winding down of the War on Drugs.

The Research Advisory Panel made three specific recommendations for initial legislative action. They were:

1. Permit the possession of syringes and needles;
2. Permit the cultivation of marijuana for personal use; and,
3. In order to project an attitude of disapproval of all drug use, take a token action in forbidding the sale or consumption of alcohol in state-supported institutions devoted in part or whole to patient care or educational activity.

The panel further recommended immediate and innovative action, and concluded that it is "incontrovertible that whatever policies we have been following over the past generations must not be continued unexamined and unmodified since our actions to date have favored the development of massive individual and societal problems."

The National Commission on AIDS
(United States, 1991)

This commission criticized the federal government's failure to recognize that drug use and AIDS are twin epidemics, and found that the "strategy of interdiction and increased prison sentences has done nothing to change the stark statistics" showing the spread of AIDS by drug users. The commission singled out the Office of National Drug Control Policy for ignoring AIDS and "neglecting the real public health and treatment measures which could and must be taken to halt the spread." Then the commission put forward the following five recommendations:

1. Expand drug treatment so that all who apply for treatment can be accepted into treatment programs;
2. Remove legal barriers to the purchase and possession of injection equipment;
3. The federal government must take the lead in developing and maintaining programs to prevent HIV transmission related to licit and illicit drugs;
4. Research and epidemiological studies on the relationships between licit and illicit drug use and HIV transmission should be greatly expanded, and funding should be increased, not reduced or merely held constant; and,
5. All levels of government and the private sector need to mount a serious and sustained attack on the social problems of poverty, homelessness and lack of medical care that promote licit and illicit drug use in American society.

The National Commission on AIDS echoed the British Advisory Council on the Misuse of Drugs in its report on AIDS and drug misuse in 1988 and 1989, as it made virtually the same policy recommendations. The commission concluded that "the federal government must recognize that HIV and substance use is one of the issues of paramount concern within the 'war on drugs.' Any program which does not deal with the duality of the HIV/drug epidemic is destined to fail." The commission then urged the federal government to move away from a law enforcement approach in controlling drugs and toward a public health approach, which to date has been "seriously neglected."

Legislative Options for Cannabis
(Australian Government, Australia, 1994)

This was the largest study on marijuana laws by the Australian government, and set forth five different options for the control of marijuana.

1. Total prohibition;
2. Prohibition with civil penalties for minor offenses;
3. Partial prohibition;
4. Regulation; and,
5. Free availability.

The report concluded by suggesting that two of the five legislative options—total prohibition and free availability—were not appropriate in contemporary Australian circumstances. The other three options, however, were viable. The report went on to state that even though cannabis usage is commonplace and little evidence exists that cannabis itself causes significant harm when used in small quantities, and even though it was seen as being a viable policy, the cultivation, possession and supply of cannabis remained criminal offenses in all Australian states. Finally, the report stated that Australian society experiences more harm from maintaining the prohibitionist policies than it experiences from the use of the drug.

Special Task Force of the Massachusetts Supreme Judicial Court
(United States, 1995)

This special task force, after finding that alcohol or drug abuse is involved in nearly 80 percent of all criminal cases, recommended to the Massachusetts Supreme Judicial Court that the current "disjointed system" be replaced with a coordinated one that included treatment programs instead of prosecution. Although these recommendations were counter to the "tough on crime" position being taken by the state's governor, the task force stated that there was a strong relationship between substance abuse, domestic violence, and even sexual abuse cases, which put thousands of the state's children at risk, and that the present prosecutorial programs were not protecting children.[2]

---

2. John Ellement and Peter J. Howe of the *Boston Globe*, "Task Force Urges Court Reshaping," *Los Angeles Daily Journal*, March 27, 1995: 5.

Little Hoover Commission for the State of California
(United States, 1998)

In his letter to the government leaders of the state of California, the chairman of this commission summarized the commission's findings as follows:

> In the course of its review, the Little Hoover Commission was presented with compelling evidence that prison overcrowding is not just the product of tougher sentences enacted in recent years. Overcrowding is compounded by inappropriate sanctions for low-level property criminals and a policy of incarceration instead of treatment for drug users, who because of repeated failures end up in state prisons. In addition, two out of three paroled felons in California—far more than in most other states—fail to successfully re-integrate into society. Consequently, they are returned to prison, too often having committed another crime.
>
> But if a multi-faceted correctional strategy were adopted fewer felons would graduate to state prison, fewer paroled felons would return to state prison—and most importantly, fewer crimes would be committed.
>
> That new correctional strategy should incorporate the significant progress in carefully targeting programs and inmates to decrease drug use and violence and increase sobriety and employability—and as a result substantially reduce crimes inflicted on California communities by released felons.

National Academy of Sciences Institute of Medicine
(United States, 1999)

In response to the passage in 1996 of Proposition 215 in California and Proposition 200 in Arizona, which approved marijuana for medical use by people with various diseases on the recommendation of a medical doctor, the Office of National Drug Control Policy commissioned a neutral study into the medicinal effects of marijuana. That study was conducted and released by the National Academy of Sciences Institute of Medicine. It concluded that marijuana was a viable and effective medicine for certain medical problems. Among other things, the Institute of Medicine stated that "Until a non-smoked, rapid-onset . . . delivery system becomes available, we acknowledge that there is no clear alternative for people suffering from chronic conditions that might be relieved by smoking marijuana, such as pain or AIDS wasting."

The institute also stated that there was no scientific basis for the "stepping stone" theory that clinical properties of marijuana lead to the use of other mind-altering drugs. The institute labeled this as a "social theory" and said, "The latter does not suggest that the pharmacological qualities of marijuana make it a risk factor for progression to other drug use. Instead it is the legal status of marijuana that makes it a gateway drug." In other words this study, commissioned by the office of our own Drug Czar, stated very clearly its findings that the very fact that marijuana is *illegal* makes it more potentially dangerous in terms of leading to the use of more dangerous drugs.[3]

---

3. Editorial, "Drug Czar Dodges Medical-Marijuana Facts," *Orange County Register,* July 23, 1999: Local News 8. See also Mary Curtius and Bettina Boxall, "Pot Has Uses As Medicine, U.S. Panel Says," *Los Angeles Times,* March 18,1999, Orange County ed.: A1; and Claudia Kalb, "No Green Light Yet," *Newsweek,* March 29, 1999: 35.

Index